D1562824

Serena Anderlini-D'Onofrio, ̣ ̣ ̣ ̣
Editor

Plural Loves: Designs for Bi and Poly Living

Plural Loves: Designs for Bi and Poly Living has been co-published simultaneously as *Journal of Bisexuality*, Volume 4, Numbers 3/4 2004.

Pre-publication REVIEWS, COMMENTARIES, EVALUATIONS . . .

"HEARTFUL, INSIGHTFUL, PROVOCATIVE, AND STIMULATING. . . . Polyamory is no longer 'the love that dare not speak its name.' . . . It has found a resonance in the hearts and lives of growing numbers of people throughout the world. And with this book, it has finally come to the attention of scholars and conference organizers. In these pages, polyamory provides a context for many kinds of complex relationships that simply refuse to be pigeonholed into neat and exclusive little boxes."

Oberon Zell-Ravenheart, DD, MA
President, TheaGenesis LLC; Founder, Church of All Worlds; Former Publisher, Green Egg *magazine; Author of* Grimoire for the Apprentice Wizard

Harrington Park Press

Plural Loves:
Designs for Bi and Poly Living

Plural Loves: Designs for Bi and Poly Living has been co-published simultaneously as *Journal of Bisexuality*, Volume 4, Numbers 3/4 2004.

The *Journal of Bisexuality* Monographic "Separates"

Below is a list of "separates," which in serials librarianship means a special issue simultaneously published as a special journal issue or double-issue *and* as a "separate" hardbound monograph. (This is a format which we also call a "DocuSerial.")

"Separates" are published because specialized libraries or professionals may wish to purchase a specific thematic issue by itself in a format which can be separately cataloged and shelved, as opposed to purchasing the journal on an on-going basis. Faculty members may also more easily consider a "separate" for classroom adoption.

"Separates" are carefully classified separately with the major book jobbers so that the journal tie-in can be noted on new book order slips to avoid duplicate purchasing.

You may wish to visit Haworth's website at . . .

http://www.HaworthPress.com

. . . to search our online catalog for complete tables of contents of these separates and related publications.

You may also call 1-800-HAWORTH (outside US/Canada: 607-722-5857), or Fax: 1-800-895-0582 (outside US/Canada: 607-771-0012), or e-mail at:

docdelivery@haworthpress.com

Plural Loves: Designs for Bi and Poly Living, edited by Serena Anderlini-D'Onofrio, PhD (Vol. 4, Nos. 3/4, 2004). *"Heartful, insightful, provocative, and stimulating. . . . In these pages, polyamory provides a context for many kinds of complex relationships that simply refuse to be pigeonholed into neat and exclusive little boxes."* (Oberon Zell-Ravenheart, DD, MA, President, TheaGenesis LLC; Founder, Church of All Worlds; Former Publisher, Green Egg *magazine; Author of* Grimoire for the Apprentice Wizard)

Current Research on Bisexuality, edited by Ronald C. Fox, PhD (Vol. 4, Nos. 1/2, 2004). *"Finally, the subdiscipline of bisexual studies has moved forward. This book represents a greater breadth and depth of empirical research on bisexuality than any other work to date. It contributes greater insight into issues ranging from better understanding of the bisexual identity formation process, to friendship patterns, intimate relationships, and mental health. The reader's guide alone is worth the purchase price."* (Michele J. Eliason, PhD, Associate Professor, College of Nursing, University of Iowa)

Bisexuality and Transgenderism: InterSEXions of the Others, edited by Jonathan Alexander, PhD, and Karen Yescavage, PhD (Vol. 3, Nos. 3/4, 2003). *The first book devoted exclusively to exploring the common ground–and the important differences–between bisexuality and transgenderism.*

Women and Bisexuality: A Global Perspective, edited by Serena Anderlini-D'Onofrio, PhD (Vol. 3, No. 1, 2003). *"Nimbly straddles disciplinary and geographical boundaries. . . . The collection's diversity of subject matter and theoretical perspectives offers a useful model for the continued development of interdisciplinary sexuality studies."* (Maria Pramaggiore, PhD, Associate Professor of Film Studies, North Carolina State University)

Bisexual Women in the Twenty-First Century, edited by Dawn Atkins, PhD (cand.) (Vol. 2, Nos. 2/3, 2002). *An eclectic collection of articles that typifies an ongoing feminist process of theory grounded in life experience.*

Bisexual Men in Culture and Society, edited by Brett Beemyn, PhD, and Erich Steinman, PhD (cand.) (Vol. 2, No. 1, 2002). *Incisive examinations of the cultural meanings of bisexuality, including the overlooked bisexual themes in James Baldwin's classic novels* Another Country *and* Giovanni's Room, *the conflicts within sexual-identity politics between gay men and bisexual men, and the recurring figure of the predatory, immoral bisexual man in novels, films, and women's magazines.*

Bisexuality in the Lives of Men: Facts and Fictions, edited by Brett Beemyn, PhD, and Erich Steinman, PhD (cand.) (Vol. 1, Nos. 2/3, 2001). *"At last, a source book which explains bisexual male desires, practices, and identities in a language all of us can understand! This is informative reading for a general audience, and will be especially valuable for discussions in gender studies, sexuality studies, and men's studies courses."* (William L. Leap, PhD, Professor, Department of Anthropology, American University, Washington, DC)

Plural Loves: Designs for Bi and Poly Living

Serena Anderlini-D'Onofrio, PhD
Editor

Plural Loves: Designs for Bi and Poly Living has been co-published simultaneously as *Journal of Bisexuality*, Volume 4, Numbers 3/4 2004.

Harrington Park Press®
An Imprint of The Haworth Press, Inc.

New York • London • Victoria (AU)
www.HaworthPress.com

Published by

Harrington Park Press®, 10 Alice Street, Binghamton, NY 13904-1580 USA

Harrington Park Press is an imprint of The Haworth Press, Inc., 10 Alice Street, Binghamton, NY 13904-1580 USA

Plural Loves: Designs for Bi and Poly Living has been co-published simultaneously as *Journal of Bisexuality*, Volume 4, Numbers 3/4 2004.

The development, preparation, and publication of this work has been undertaken with great care. However, the publisher, employees, editors, and agents of The Haworth Press and all imprints of The Haworth Press, Inc., including The Haworth Medical Press® and Pharmaceutical Products Press®, are not responsible for any errors contained herein or for consequences that may ensue from use of materials or information contained in this work. Opinions expressed by the author(s) are not necessarily those of The Haworth Press, Inc. With regard to case studies, identities and circumstances of individuals discussed herein have been changed to protect confidentiality. Any resemblance to actual persons, living or dead, is entirely coincidental.

Cover design by Lora Wiggins

Library of Congress Cataloging-in-Publication Data

Plural loves : designs for bi and poly living / Serena Anderlini-D'Onofrio, editor.
p. cm.
"Plural loves: Designs for bi and poly living has been co-published simultaneously as Journal of bisexuality, volume 4, numbers 3/4 2004."
Includes bibliographical references and index.
ISBN 1-56023-292-7 (hard cover : alk. paper) – ISBN 1-56023-293-5 (soft cover : alk. paper)
1. Bisexuality. 2. Bisexuals. I. Anderlini-D'Onofrio, Serena, 1954- II. Journal of bisexuality.
HQ74.P58 2004
306.76'5–dc22

2004017659

Indexing, Abstracting & Website/Internet Coverage

This section provides you with a list of major indexing & abstracting services and other tools for bibliographic access. That is to say, each service began covering this periodical during the year noted in the right column. Most Websites which are listed below have indicated that they will either post, disseminate, compile, archive, cite or alert their own Website users with research-based content from this work. (This list is as current as the copyright date of this publication.)

(continued)

Special Bibliographic Notes related to special journal issues (separates) and indexing/abstracting:

- indexing/abstracting services in this list will also cover material in any "separate" that is co-published simultaneously with Haworth's special thematic journal issue or DocuSerial. Indexing/abstracting usually covers material at the article/chapter level.
- monographic co-editions are intended for either non-subscribers or libraries which intend to purchase a second copy for their circulating collections.
- monographic co-editions are reported to all jobbers/wholesalers/approval plans. The source journal is listed as the "series" to assist the prevention of duplicate purchasing in the same manner utilized for books-in-series.
- to facilitate user/access services all indexing/abstracting services are encouraged to utilize the co-indexing entry note indicated at the bottom of the first page of each article/chapter/contribution.
- this is intended to assist a library user of any reference tool (whether print, electronic, online, or CD-ROM) to locate the monographic version if the library has purchased this version but not a subscription to the source journal.
- individual articles/chapters in any Haworth publication are also available through the Haworth Document Delivery Service (HDDS).

Plural Loves:
Designs for Bi and Poly Living

CONTENTS

BI BOOKS

About the Contributors

Hasan Al-Zubi is Professor of English at Mu'tah University/ Jordan. He received his PhD in 1998 from Indiana University, Bloomington. He did several publications on American, English, and Comparative Literature, and taught at Indiana University (the continuing study program) and at Pitzer College, California. He also served as a consultant to the Vice President of the National Center for the Study of Democracy, Los Angeles, California. He can be reached at <halzubi2000@yahoo. com.uk>.

Deborah Taj Anapol attended Barnard College, graduated Phi Beta Kappa from the University of California at Berkeley, and received her PhD in Clinical Psychology from the University of Washington in 1981. Dr. Anapol is the author of *Polyamory: The New Love Without Limits* (1997), co-founder of *Loving More Magazine* and producer of the *Pelvic-Heart Integration* videos (2002). *Compersion: Using Jealousy as a Path to Unconditional Love* is now available in xerox pamphlet form, and she is currently at work on a book about harmonizing feminine and masculine energies. Dr. Anapol has organized and produced several conferences as well as working with couples, families, and individuals who are exploring conscious relating, erotic spirituality and sexual healing. She leads seminars nationwide, and is an inspiring and controversial speaker who has appeared on radio and television programs all across the USA and Canada. She can be reached at <Taj@lovewithoutlimits>.

Wayne M. Bryant is the author of *Bisexual Characters in Film: From Anais to Zee,* available from Harrington Park Press. He is the co-founder of Biversity Boston, president emeritus of the Bisexual Resource Center and film editor for the Bisexual Recource Guide.

Dan Clurman, a communications consultant in the S.F. Bay Area, teaches psychology at Golden Gate University. He is the author of

Floating Upstream, a book of poetry. His forthcoming book of cartoons, *Suppose You Went to Heaven,* will soon be published.

Betty Dodson, PhD, artist, author, and sex educator, is an international authority on women's sexuality. Dodson achieved international recognition in the sixties and seventies as a feminist activist and public advocate for women's sexual liberation through self-sexuality. In 1974, Betty Dodson wrote, illustrated, and self-published her first book, *Liberating Masturbation: A Meditation on Selflove.* Her book was sold to Crown Publishers in 1986. Renamed *Sex for One: The Joy of Selfloving,* it became a best selling trade paperback translated into ten foreign languages. Dodson received a PhD in sexology from the Institute for the Advanced Study of Human Sexuality in 1992. Her bold, innovative teaching methods have been documented in a series of videos that she wrote, directed and produced. Her latest book *Orgasms for Two: The Joy of Partnersex* was published in 2002 and was illustrated by Dodson. She has appeared in the media, has a private practice in New York City and maintains an active Web site: <www.bettydodson.com>.

Eric Francis is an astrologer, journalist and essayist who lives in the northwestern United States. His articles have appeared on Sexualty.org and a variety of other Web sites, as well as in *Loving More, The Village Voice, Sierra, The Mountain Astrologer* and a wide variety of publications in the United States, the UK, Australia and Europe. His writing about masturbation is used as instructional material in the orgasm coach training program of Joseph Kramer, founder of The Body Electric School. His weekly newsletter is available at PlanetWavesWeekly.com. He can be contacted at <eric@ericfrancis.com>.

"Konstanza," MA, has been living with the tantric master Aba Aziz Makaja in a polyamorous "marriage" or *zajedna* for 13 years. With him and their wife, they guide the tantric circle Cherry Blossom, founded in 1985. Cherry Blossom has more than 20 members and the average duration of membership is more than 10 years. Konstanza is the editor of *Eros & Logos: The Book for Saints and Sinners.* She has a master's degree in Slavic Studies and Politics and is responsible for the publications of the international spiritual community Komaja, where she has been active for nearly 20 years. Konstanza is high priestess of Komaja's Church of Love and one of the five masters of the Komaja community. She can be reached at <konstanza@komaja.org>.

Pepper Mint lives near the beach in San Francisco and works at a tech support job. He is 28 and has lived nonmonogamously his entire life. He graduated from MIT with a master's degree in computer science and a concentration in women's studies. He has an avid interest in deconstruction, feminism, queer theory, and polyamory. He can be reached at <inki@atg.com>.

Maria Pallotta-Chiarolli, PhD, is Senior Lecturer in Social Diversity and Health at Deakin University, Melbourne, Australia. Her books include *Someone You Know: An AIDS Farewell*; *Girls' Talk: Young Women Speak Their Hearts and Minds*; *Tapestry: Five Generations in an Italian Family*; *Boys' Stuff: Boys Talking About What Matters;* and *So What's a Boy? Issues of Masculinity and Schooling.* In 1999, Maria received the title of Lifelong Honorary Patron for PFLAG Victoria, Australia. She is a member upon invitation of the Advisors' Committee for the Institute for 21st Century Relationships, and an External Faculty Member of Saybrook Graduate Research Centre, San Francisco. Maria's forthcoming books include *Coming Out with Our Kids: Supporting GLBT Young People in Our Families, Schools and Communities* and *Border Sexualities, Border Families*: *Bisexuality and Polyamory in Our Schools.* With co-researcher Sara Lubowitz, she co-authored an article in the *Journal of Bisexuality* (Vol, 3, 2/3: 2003).

Nathan Patrick Rambukkana is a straight, polyamorous, theory fetishizing SM novice with a penchant for leather. When he isn't talking his long suffering friends' ears off about his latest academic pet project, he cooks, produces student radio, works in a flogger factory, and tries to finish his MA in theory, culture and politics at Trent University in Canada. His research interests include the interaction of communication media and sexuality, the social construction of monogamy, and the politics of sexual subcultures. He can be reached at <beeblefish@hotmail.com>.

Numa Ray, spiritual disciple of Aba Aziz Makaja, has lived since 1990 with her partner in a *zajedna*, which is Komaja's version of a group marriage, together with several other couples from the tantric circle *Kamala*. She is one of the supporting pillars of Komaja's largest European spiritual center and has completed the extensive basic schooling, as well as its multi-year program called The Art of Love. Before moving to Europe, she spent ten years in two different avant-garde communities, including a twenty-member expanded family. During this time she gave birth to her two children, studied spiritual healing and had an apprenticeship with a local Boston healer. In 1979, she graduated from the School of Visual Arts in NYC with a BFA in fine arts. She can be reached at <NumaRay@gmx.de>.

Suzann Robins, MA, has a personal interest in being both bi and poly. She teaches psychology in the New York area, as well as leading a variety of holistic health classes. She is the co-editor of *Body Psychotherapy* newsletter and has worked with Ani Colt to develop the Spiritual/Sexual Union Network (SUN). She can be reached at <chersuz@juno.com>.

Annina Sartorius has an MA in clinical psychology, psychopathology and neuropsychology from the University of Zurich, Switzerland. She works as a psychologist in private practice. She is a member of the German Society for Social-Scientific Sex research (DGSS) and of the Federation of the Swiss Psychologists (FSP), and has given international presentations on alternative love-erotic relationships and group marriage. Since 1985 she has been a member and leader in the international Komaja community, and is now the President of the Komaja Foundation in Switzerland, a member organization of the World Association for Sexology (WAS). She is also a leading member in the tantric group Cherry Blossom and lives together with Makaja, one other man, and four women in a *zajedna*, a form of group marriage founded with Makaja in 1986. She and Makaja have a nine year old son together. She can be reached at <anninasartorius@yahoo.de>.

Sam See is a doctoral student at UCLA and is currently focusing his studies on 20th century British and American literature and queer studies. He has had poetry and short fiction published in small press magazines, and this is his first academic paper to appear in print. He can be reached via e-mail at <samsee79@hotmail.com>.

Taliesin the Bard is a popular pagan pundit, prominent prosex partisan and practicing polyamorist as well as being addicted to atrocious alliteration. An ardent advocate of free speech and personal rights particularly in the areas of erotic expression and alternative lifestyles, Tal is making a mark on the literary world with his unique approach to storytelling, exporing human sexuality in all its marvelous and myriad manifestations. He can be reached at <taliesin@firsttribebooks.com> and <www.firsttribebooks.com>.

ABOUT THE EDITOR

Serena Anderlini-D'Onofrio, PhD, is Associate Professor in the Department of Humanities at the University of Puerto Rico at Mayaguez and a widely published author. She is the editor of *Women and Bisexuality: A Global Perspective*, and the author of *The "Weak" Subject: On Modernity, Eros, and Women's Playwriting* (Associated University Press, 1998), a comparative theory of women's erotic desires and contributions to modern drama. The book is now also available in Italian translation. In 1995-97 she co-coordinated the Bisexual Forum of San Diego. Her recent articles have appeared in *Consciousness, Literature, and the Arts,* and *Women and Language*, while others are forthcoming in *VIA, DisClosure,* and *Traces.* She has finished a memoir about her intellectual, spiritual, and erotic development and is working on numerous other book projects. She can be reached at <serena1@centennialpr.net>.

Introduction

Plural Loves:
Bi and Poly Utopias
for a New Millennium

Serena Anderlini-D'Onofrio

http://www.haworthpress.com/web/JB
© 2004 by The Haworth Press, Inc. All rights reserved.
Digital Object Identifier: 10.1300/J159v04n03_01

[Haworth co-indexing entry note]: "Plural Loves: Bi and Poly Utopias for a New Millennium." Anderlini-D'Onofrio, Serena. Co-published simultaneously in *Journal of Bisexuality* (Harrington Park Press, an imprint of The Haworth Press, Inc.) Vol. 4, No. 3/4, 2004, pp. 1-6; and: *Plural Loves: Designs for Bi and Poly Living* (ed: Serena Anderlini-D'Onofrio) Harrington Park Press, an imprint of The Haworth Press, Inc., 2004, pp. 1-6. Single or multiple copies of this article are available for a fee from The Haworth Document Delivery Service [1-800-HAWORTH, 9:00 a.m. - 5:00 p.m. (EST). E-mail address: docdelivery@haworthpress.com].

"Can bisexuals be monogamous?" The embattled question lingered in the air as I participated in the support meetings and socials of the Bisexual Forum of San Diego, where local bis in a crisis came to heal their wounds and find a community they could call home. A young man felt dejected for his boyfriend and girlfriend had eloped together. A woman's lesbian friends no longer talked to her for she had fallen in love with a man. We were in the early 1990s and bisexuality was emerging as a self-defined identity. The bisexual movement was waiting to happen, as bis felt invisible in conventional gay and lesbian communities and scapegoated by heterosexual society for passing the alleged AIDS virus on. With a positive influence from second-wave feminism, with the space for queer discourse opened by the gay and lesbian liberation movement, bisexuality's claims to a legitimate place in the queer community were being heeded, as that community itself became inclusive of bis and transgendered people. The double pressure from invisibility and scapegoating outed bis who had previously passed as straight or gay, politicizing them into participants and organizers for the movement. It was the beginning of a trajectory during which many other assumptions about the modalities of erotic and romantic love would be questioned. By focusing on intersections of and convergences between bisexuality and polyamory, this collection aspires to indicate the endpoint of this trajectory, showing how the trajectory itself has changed the terms of the debate, providing enthralling answers all along.

Bisexuals can definitely be as monogamous as anybody else, but the good news is that they don't have to in order to be honest with their partners and create responsible love relationships considerate of each participant's feelings. As the Sartorius and Robins articles in this collection indicate, the first modern nonmonogamous communities experimented with polyfidelity, including various forms of group marriage within utopian and/or intentional spaces based on articulate and complex forms of social and family organization. Examples are Oneida, in New York State, which was active in the late 19th century, and Kerista in the San Francisco Bay Area, active throughout the 1970s.

In the 1980s many nonmonogamous groups became more porous and flexible, while female leadership within them brought in more significant reflections on the implications of gender and sexual orientation any nonmonogamous practice involves. Pallotta-Chiarolli's review article in this collection generously honors some of the results of this leadership. Polyamory, or the practice of openly and honestly participating in a variety of simultaneous love relationships, grew parallel to bisexuality, even as, while the latter was more visible as a movement and political identity, the former was more daring in the utopian practices it proposed, disseminated, and created hospitable spaces for.

Polyamorous thinking of the gender and sexual-orientation aware sort shared with bisexuality an interest for pre-modern and "primitive" social organizations where the homo/hetero divide is not enforced. There erotic love is often part of a pantheistic concept of the sacred which calls for a gentler, contemplative, and more "feminine" relationship with nature. With its glimpse at the harmony of today's polyamorous life in Hawaii, and its roots in the islands' premodern culture, Anapol's essay in this collection represents this line of reflection in a significant way.

Compared to 1970s-style polyfidelity, polyamory today is not only more gender and sexual orientation aware, but also more adaptable to a globalizing world, and more effective in rendering this world more harmonious through its workshops and education to love. Loving More and Komaja's workshops are widely accessible oases that welcome participants and initiate them to the art of loving in inclusive, polyamorous ways. They allow frequent and diffused exchanges between utopian spaces and the conventional world, as described in Konstanza's and Numa's contributions to this collection.

Dodson's and Francis's essays carry polyamory's reflection on the emotions and erotic love one step further as they reassess solo sex as a queer practice that participates in bi and poly discourse in several ways. As Francis claims, solo sex often involves fantasies that include same-gender sexual objects, while the object of one's erotic attention is oneself–a person of one's same gender. As a result, Dodson suggests, all self-pleasuring is to some extent queer. Especially when practiced in group situations, Fancis and Dodson further claim, solo sex liberates one's erotic potential and generates harmony and joy in one's inner world. Group solo sex implies a dose of compassion for oneself and those like us who are involved in the erotic play. Compersion is the ability to empathize with a lover's pleasure, to feel it like one's own, even when the pleasure comes from a source other than oneself. This ability to turn jealousy's negative feelings into acceptance of, and vicarious enjoyment for, a lover's joy is a key operative concept in today's polyamorous practices, as Francis' and Taliesin the Bard's contributions indicate. A strong sense of compersion is echoed in the Komaja testimonials by Numa and Konstanza, even as the feeling itself is not named. As members of this polyamorous community based in Croatia, the two women write about their training in the Komaja "virtues" that spiritualize sex, enabling the enjoyment of multiple partner tantric eroticism where the self becomes one with the participating group. The two writers also acknowledge the temporary resurgence of jealous feelings in moments of excessive weakness and self-absorption.

The highly spiritual, slightly utopian, and certainly idealistic principle of compersion, together with its applicability in certain contexts, demonstrates the effectiveness of the new spirituality movements in helping people get away from predefined notions of the sacred. With their insistent questioning of institutionalized religion and monotheism, these movements have prepared for the sacred eroticism that many current bi and poly practices entail. While "monogamy" caused many nineteenth century Westerners to feel superior to "primitives" and non-Westerners for they were capable of "true love," many bis and polys today design lives for themselves in which the sacredness of true love is multiplied for the number of players willing to participate. The nexus between monogamy and monotheism thus becomes transparent. Monotheism can be seen as a self-imposed limitation to love only one deity; monogamy as a similarly self-imposed limitation to love only one partner to the exclusion of everybody else. Polyamory and bisexuality propose a plurality of loves, both in the number of partners and genders thereof. This return to the plurality of polytheism involves a certain primitivism, the feeling of a cosmos pervaded with magic and inhabited by a number of deities, whose plants, animals, and natural sites are sacred. This pre-modern concept of the sacred is especially useful at this time of ecological crisis, for it is conducive of a mode of reasoning that inspires humans with respect for each other and for the biosphere that sustains us. Why restrict the number of partners to one if we can love many as intensely and honestly, as erotically and spiritually, as in a flamboyant romantic tale? Why restrict the experience of erotic love to the shapes, modes, and erotic mechanisms of only one gender? Why not be aware of, own, and interpret all the erotic energies that pass trough and radiate from us?

While a reader's answers to these wider questions will have to be personal, the collection presented herein helps to address them in productive ways. In a historical and critical perspective, the article by Al-Zubi examines the polyamorous and bisexual impulses present in two 19th century novels, showing how they are buried under the materialism of the era, based in the modern Western philosophies that replaced a monotheist god with a racially privileged, allegedly monogamous, and heterosexual "man." The article shows how the characters' pluralistic impulses were seen as aberrant sometimes even by themselves.

In a shorter-range retrospective, Sam See's contribution evaluates how much in the ways of pluralism, experimentation, and vision was lost in the 1980s gay and lesbian attempts to present gay love as mimetic of straight love, except for the partner's gender. His readings of mid-century British queer plays focus on the richness, vastness, and effervescence of their authors' erotic imaginations, and the significant ability to appreciate it a queer-friendly pre-1968 public had.

The two essays by Pepper Mint and Rambukkana present the perspectives of a younger generation that has grown up between the extremes of a sexophobic AIDS era and the aura of bi and poly utopian experiments. The articles' respective foci, the power dynamics of cheating and its function as the obverse of monogamy, and the necessity to create more comfortable bridges between bisexuality and polyamory, intelligently navigate the ocean that separates mainstream and utopian worlds. They also show the benefits of drinking at the fount of alternative thinking in a highly spactacularized, conformist era.

The Sartorius article straddles a similarly intermediate territory, as it proposes *zajedna*, Komaja's form of group marriage, as an alternative to high divorce rates and unstable single-parent and blended families. The two additional contributions of Komaja members place this interesting utopian community in a wider perspective, while they also measure the widespread influence of gender and sexual orientation awareness. Numa's and Konstanza's testimonials offer a direct access to Komaja's utopian world, where, even under male leadership, sex is highly

spiritualized and shared in eminently bi and poly ways. There compersion operates and the self becomes absorbed in the intensity of sacred group love,
while a woman's voice keeps a healthy intellectual autonomy and self-posses-
sion.

The two narratives in the third section echo the collection's themes in a
more literary, creative way. Taliesin's piece and my own are written in a fictional and nonfictional mode, respectively. In an eerie, premonitional way,
Taliesin's story echoes Coward's play *Design for Living* (discussed in See's
article), as it focuses on a perfectly balanced two-men, one-woman triadic relationship. *The Compersion Effect* is both the title of the movie the fictional
triad creates, and the effect such filmmaking could have in helping to reorga-
nize the social world. My own story imagines a world where interracial,
polyamorous, and bisexual relationships with Catholic priests are possible,
while telling the true story of one such relationship which crosses the border
between utopian and conventional worlds, and breaks, ever so briefly, the mo-
nopoly of spirituality the Catholic Church still exercises in many areas of the
world.

With their different foci, modes, and perspectives, the contributions to this
collection point to the effervescence in current bisexuality and polyamory discourse and the benefit of having them resonate with each other, for bis, polys,
and other alternative communities, not to speak of the harmony and peace of
the larger world.

Part One: Perspectives

Sweet Dreams: Sexual Fantasies in J. K. Huysmans's <u>Against the Grain</u> and Leopoldo Alas's <u>La Regenta</u>

Hasan Al-Zubi

http://www.haworthpress.com/web/JB
Digital Object Identifier: 10.1300/J159v04n03_02

[Haworth co-indexing entry note]: "Sweet Dreams: Sexual Fantasies in J. K. Huysmans's *Against the Grain* and Leopoldo Alas's *La Regenta*." Al-Zubi, Hasan. Co-published simultaneously in *Journal of Bisexuality* (Harrington Park Press, an imprint of The Haworth Press, Inc.) Vol. 4, No. 3/4, 2004, pp. 7-27; and: *Plural Loves: Designs for Bi and Poly Living* (ed: Serena Anderlini-D'Onofrio) Harrington Park Press, an imprint of The Haworth Press, Inc., 2004, pp. 7-27. Single or multiple copies of this article are available for a fee from The Haworth Document Delivery Service [1-800-HAWORTH, 9:00 a.m. - 5:00 p.m. (EST). E-mail address: docdelivery@haworthpress.com].

SUMMARY. Stranded in a tradition that was only beginning to acknowledge their existence, writers in the nineteenth century had little but the established forms of heterosexual romance with which to build their works. Sexual practices (homosexuality, bisexuality, fetishism) were commonly understood by nineteenth-century novelists, yet since they were not addressed by the established cultural mechanisms, many European writers came to dramatize these sexual practices implicitly in their narratives. This article examines the ways in which two nineteenth-century novelists, J. K. Huysmans and Leopoldo Alas, employ narrative metaphors and descriptions of homoerotic, bisexual, and fetishistic behavior in order to afford their characters sexual identities opposed to the heteronormative cultural ideal. The article concludes that it is only through immersion in the worlds of artifice and other "deviant" sexual practices that the main characters in Huysmans's *Against the Grain* and Alas's *La Regenta* synthesize the material and philosophical dimensions of their environment and transcend the level of caricature imposed upon them by society. *[Article copies available for a fee from The Haworth Document Delivery Service: 1-800-HAWORTH. E-mail address: <docdelivery@haworthpress.com> Website: <http://www.HaworthPress.com> © 2004 by The Haworth Press, Inc. All rights reserved.]*

KEYWORDS. Fetishism, sexual inversion, *Against the Grain*, *La Regenta*, homosexuality, sodomy, Freud, sexual fantasy, bisexuality

INTRODUCTION

Until the end of the nineteenth century, as several recent studies have pointed out, there existed neither the words nor the established traditions to provide a conceptual framework for bisexuality, fetishism, homosexuality, or lesbian love. "Before the end of the nineteenth-century," writes Catharine R. Stimpson, "homosexuality might have been subsumed under such a term as 'masturbation'" (365); in medical lexicon, George Chauncey explains, "sexual inversion, the term used most commonly in the nineteenth-century, did not denote the same conceptual phenomenon as homosexuality" (116). Henry Havelock Ellis, on the other hand, in *Studies in the Psychology of Sexual Inversion*, volume I, "firmly believed in the biological basis of all forms of sexual behavior, and argued that 'true' sexual inversion was always innate" (qtd. in Storr, 15). Ellis followed the earlier example of the German sexologist Krafft-Ebing in categorizing "cases of women and men who sexually desire both male and female partners . . . as 'psychosexual hermaphroditism'" (qtd.

in Storr 15). By the time Ellis published the third edition of his *Studies in the Psychology of Sex* in 1915 (which discusses cases of women and men who sexually desire male and female partners), he abandoned "the term of 'psychosexual hermaphroditism,'" and extended "the meaning of 'bisexuality' to cover not just sexual dimorphism, but also the sexual desire for both women and men experienced by some of his subjects" (qtd. in Storr 15-6).

In England many scientists considered sex an inappropriate subject of study. In *Dangerous Sexualities: Medico-Moral Politics in England Since 1830*, for instance, Frank Mort discusses the limited attitude to, and representations of, sexuality. He suggests that "sex is not a fit subject for serious study" (5). Most Victorian scientists in England called for direct regulation of sexual conduct in the nineteenth century. The Victorian ideology also opposed the art for its own sake, and believed that art should work for the usefulness of society. As Michael Bronski put it, "the idea that art should–or even could–exist without a utilitarian function was an outright rejection of Victorian ideology which considered usefulness, not pleasure, to be the purpose of life." Many rules of sodomy were enforced in England, and, since sodomy was considered a crime by the Court, many people were convicted. The homosexual critic and playwright Oscar Wilde, for instance, was considered a dangerous threat to the Victorian society not only because he was homosexual, but because of his social, political, and artistic views which opposed the Victorian standards about regulating pleasure and restricting the individual's freedom. Wilde's defense of pleasure and individual freedom and his being gay led the Victorian authorities to imprison him after several trials in 1895 for gross indecency.

Nineteenth-century England also witnessed the emergence of rigid, oppositional, and hierarchical gender identities. Women, Mort argues, were defined in terms of the norm of asexuality and the absence of sexual desire: "the majority of women . . . are not very much troubled with sexual feeling of any kind" (81). Mort adds that women who publicly showed signs of sexual desire were branded as prostitutes, nymphomaniacs, or lunatics (81). Moreover, women were considered inferior to men in a male-powered society. Robert Purks Maccubbin asserts in '*Tis Nature's Fault: Unauthorized Sexuality During the Enlightenment* that gender differences were seen as "founded on an incredible difference of experience" (118).

The legal system of the United States against sodomy and *deviant* sexuality followed the English lead, at least through the nineteenth century. Homosexuality was greatly opposed in the United States. Lawrence Murphy's book *Perverts by Official Order: The Campaign Against Homosexuals by the United States Navy* (1988) is an account of the antigay crusade launched by the United States Navy. The book details the naval operation that led to the court-martial and imprisonment of a number of sailors and civilians accused of homosexuality. French and Spanish cultures were not an exception. The French and Spanish viewed pleasure with suspicion, and tried to make heterosexuality mainstream. Maccubbin reflects that in Paris male homosexuality implied a particular lifestyle. The police, he asserts, kept homosexuals under careful surveillance, and their sexual behaviors were considered a violation of public decency (180-85). In the second half of the eighteenth century, sodomy in France, Maccubbin states, became an entirely new evil, an "unnatural passion" (189). Sodomites (or pédérastes as, significantly, the French police called them) had sexual desire only for other men. Opinions of why this happened, Maccubbin writes, differ: "a stricter moral climate" (176), or "the reorganization of gender identity . . . as part of the emergence of a modern Western culture" (118).

Homoeroticism, bisexuality, and fetishism were commonly understood by novelists in the nineteenth century, and since they were not widely accepted in society, many European writers came to dramatize these sexual practices implicitly in their writings. In his pivotal study *The History of Sexuality,* volume I (1978) Michel Foucault traces the transformation of desire into discursive narratives of disclosure. He explains that transforming desire into discourse evolved into Victorian and later attitudes toward sexuality, cultural construction of sex as at once unspeakable and demanding to be put into words. In the eighteenth and nineteenth centuries, he writes,

> Sex became something to say, and to say exhaustively in accordance with deployments that were varied, but all, in their own way, compelling. Whether in the form of a subtle confession in confidence or an authoritarian interrogation, sex–be it refined or rustic–had to be put in words. (32)

For Foucault, in other words, sex, constructed as the secret and the essence of our inner selves, becomes the truth. Sex is that which we have hidden and must ultimately reveal in different ways, particularly in writing.

In this paper, I explain how sexual fantasies and fetishistic representational images are abundant in nineteenth-century fiction, including two distinguished European novels: *La Regenta (The Judge's Wife* 1884-85) by the Spanish writer Leopoldo Alas, and J. K. Huysmans's *Against the Grain: A Rebours* (1885). Both novels, I argue, provide a reflection of fetishistic images and other *deviant* sexual practices via use of socially accepted narratives. In *Against the Grain,* the hero Des Esseintes is portrayed by Huysmans as a character whose interests and desires are different from those of everyday people. He is deeply interested in *things* rather than people, and chooses to live isolated with artifice. In his *world of things,* Des Esseintes obtains sexual pleasure from objects and undergoes bisexual and homosexual reveries that render his sexual identity fragmented. By the same token, Ana Ozores in Alas's *La Regenta* longs for a mystic identity and a utopian world in which the common herd of people do not fit. As a result, she isolates herself from people and gives up her heterosexual relationships with her husband, Don Víctor Quintanar, and her lover Don Alvaro. In denying her sexual desire for males, Ana undergoes bisexual reveries, and comes even to be a fetishist when she starts releasing her libidinal sexual energy via sexual objects.

SEXUAL FANTASIES: AGAINST THE GRAIN

In *Against the Grain*, Duke Jean Des Esseintes follows different sexual routes, a matter which renders his sexual identity ambiguous. Living with parents who, as a result of a "curious accident of heredity" are "nervous" and "anaemic" (2), Des Esseintes himself, subject to the same laws of genetics as his parents, in turn becomes a nervous product of his ancestry. "The Des Esseintes," explains Huysmans, as a result of "intermarrying among themselves" wasted "the small remains of their original vigor and energy" (1). Des Esseintes's mother, Huysmans explains, died of "general debility," and his father "succumbed to a vague and mysterious malady," and was "worn out with persistent attacks of fever" (2). In the novel, the son leads a distinctive life and proves to be different from the members of his family. Ellis explains in his "Introduction" to the novel that Huysmans abhorred "the society and . . . the average literary man" (vvi). Huysmans believed that a man of genius is a stranger and a "pilgrim on earth" who seeks universal knowledge. Des Esseintes is portrayed in the novel as a genius who is different from the common herd of people. When a student at the Jesuit College, Des Esseintes is recognized as an industrious, independent and restless student, who "devoted himself deeply to certain tasks" (3) in academic life while "his family pretty much washed their hands of him" (3). His mother, Huysmans states, hardly sees him, and neither does his father. Des Esseintes spends most of his time in reading or dreaming, drinking his fill of solitude till nightfall (3). As a consequence of "constantly brooding over the same thoughts," his "mind gained concentration and his still undeveloped ideas ripened towards maturity" (3). His teachers, Huysmans reflects, were "aware of the qualities and limitations of this [Des Esseintes's] alert but indocile intelligence" (4), and fearing the unknown, "they left him to himself to work at such studies [of the decadent ancient]" which "found no place in the curriculum of his classes" (4), but were prominent in the books of his own library.

In the novel, Des Esseintes seeks universal knowledge, and focuses on human nature and the soul. In carefully scanning the books about the ancient people in his own library, Des Esseintes "discovered the apostles of freedom, the wiseacres of the bourgeois, the thinkers who clamored for entire liberty—liberty to strangle the opinions of other people" (6). Comparing his reading of "liberty" to what he supposes it to be, Des Esseintes finds the bourgeois thinkers "to be a set of greedy, shameless hypocrites, whom as men of education he rated below the level of the village cobbler" (6). It is after he absorbs the content of the books that Des Esseintes forms his views of the world, modern and ancient, and his subtly drawn comparisons between the ancient and the modern. Freedom of the modern world, he contemplates, is "false" and the modern people follow a silly conventional way of living in life that makes it very mundane. The triviality of the real world which he finds in opposition to his studious ideals makes him sick and he suffers nervous disorders. Des Esseintes's unhappiness and misery are further expressed when Huysmans asserts, "he [Des Esseintes] was growing to be like the men . . . who are unhappy every where" (6).

Finding himself "stranded," "disappointed," "lonely," "disillusioned" and "utterly and abominably tired" (7), Des Esseintes seeks a "retreat" from the "stupid" world of people, alone and away from the scourge of humanity. His ideal world becomes his house in Fontenay, decorated and formulated in a way that suits his sensual needs and tastes–a house which, as he thinks, will beautify his soul and achieve his dream of the "ancient hope" (206). But by staying alone in that place, by struggling with his past memories, his disillusioned ideals and books, Des Esseintes exhausts his powers. He recalls "the miseries of a wretched and neglected childhood" (10), and longs for "revenge on dreary hours endured in former times" (10) among "humbug" people. Living like a ghost in that "exile," his "laboratory" of the "artifice" and his house, then, Des Esseintes dehumanizes his existence. Bettina Knapp, a critic of French literature, describes this dehumanization as that which "revolve[s] around the acquisition of rave and exotic objects; furnishings, paintings, books, flowers, foods, [and] liqueurs" (203). Never having received love in childhood from his parents or his people, and never having given love; and living alone later on in an unnatural environment in Fontenay, Des Esseintes comes to fulfill his biological needs, particularly the sexual, via sexual objects. His "nervous disturbances," "distress of mind" and "weary fancies" reach an extreme point. Living alone as he does, he comes to suppress his sexual desires–a matter which distresses him further and has a detrimental effect on his nerves. True, living in an artificial world, Des Esseintes seeks his sexual pleasure in the artifice. This point is affirmed by Knapp: "the duke's approach to the world of things . . . had sexual implications; it was a means of sublimating his erotic impulse" (205). Knapp goes further, contending that "like fetishes, objects upon which certain values are projected, Des Esseintes endowed paintings, rugs, plants, or even a bejeweled turtle with dynamic energy, this energy in turn activated his subliminal world" (205).

Des Esseintes becomes, to use Huysmans's phrase, a "collector of things," and his obsession with these things makes him a spiritual owner of them: he comes to adore them for they will be the source of gratification for his sensual and sexual pleasure. That Des Esseintes is a collector of things asserts his fetishistic quality as described by Otto Fenichel, who asserts that for fetishists, "the possessive urge to be the sole owner of the object(s) is particularly stressed, and some fetishists are 'collectors'" (148). Fetishism means the belief that inanimate objects such as plants, furs, sheets, stones, books, jewels, etc., possess human properties. Sigmund Freud in *Three Essays on the Theory of Sexuality* (1905) pathologized the practice of fetishism calling the process whereby a part of the body or some inanimate objects become the sexual object of desire sexual or pathological fetishism (154). The most current types of fetishism are decadent fetishism and matrix fetishism. Decadent fetishism means the taking on of the alien, the foreign, the Other, as a desirable self. The pleasures of decadent fetishism drive from creating, performing and voyeurizing anti-normative and disrupting social norms. Matrix fetishism is abundant in popular culture cyberpunk narratives which revolve around a fantasized computer matrix as a sexualized prosthetic. Matrix fetishism can be identified in many of the cultural surrounding new technologies, where a merging of the self with technology occurs and the subject experiences a non-differentiation of boundaries between: self and Other, subject and object, and the inanimate and animate. In her book *Simians, Cyborgs, and Women,* Donna Haraway talks about the role of objects and technology in the "sexual wishing" and in the construction of one's sexual identity. She explains the relationship between "technology" and "sexuality" in the sense that some people might attach some eroticism to cyborgs which, like all bodies, "are maps of power and identity" (Haraway 222). According to Haraway, cyborg is the materialization of technology into embodiment, and it limits and materializes sensibilities into making sense. The becoming-flesh of technology articulates a desire for socialization between humans and objects (i.e., computers, cars, etc.).

Many psychiatrists explain that sexual fetishism, the type of fetishism Des Esseintes undergoes, is specifically due to unconscious anxieties and to the repression of sexual drives. Des Esseintes's deprivation of love, lack of communication with people, and his depressed nervous state make him satisfy his basic sexual drives via sexual objects. The plants, which he collects, are, in his eyes, intimate active sexual objects. He feels "pleasure" in possessing these "amazing flowers" (95), and treats them as loving beings that arouse his sexual desire. The more bizarre the plants look, Huysmans says, the more Des Esseintes likes them. He sees their petals as "hairy" skin and their leaves as if engraved with furrows ("false veins"):

> The gardeners unloaded from their vans a collection of caladiums whose swollen, hairy stalks carried enormous leaves, shaped like a heart . . . presenting the appearance of a fictitious skin marked by an imitation network of veins. Most of them, as if disfigured by syphilis or leprosy, displayed livid patches of flesh, reddened by measles, roughened by eruptions; others showed the bright pink of a half-closed wounds or the red brown of the crusts that form over a scar; others were as if scorched with cauteries blistered with burns; others again offered hairy surfaces eaten into holes by ulcers and excavated by chancres. (85)

Huysmans presents the plants in the above quotation as animate beings of "fictitious skin" and "hairy stalks" and in a way that confirms Des Esseintes's emphatic though implicit sexual relation to them. The sweet touch, beauty, and monstrous aspect of the plants "moved his [Des Esseintes's] enthusiasm," Huysmans writes, "to a still higher pitch" (86). Des Esseintes envisions them as a fatal and terrifying feminine power that arouses his sexual desire to the extreme. As Knapp argues, "The more macabre, grotesque, and spine-chilling these symbols of destructive feminine forces are, the more he is attracted to them" (216). Indeed, these plants, as Huysmans reveals, are "amazing" beings in which Des Esseintes sees his revenge upon the "folly" world of "humbug" males and females (88). In addition to these plants, Des Esseintes derives an aesthetic and sexual enjoyment from stones, jewels and books. Because of his hyper-responsiveness to the outer stimuli, he sees stones and jewels, shaped according to his own taste, as intimate objects whose shape, luster, texture and color stimulate his desire for artifice. As "suggestive powers," books, indeed, bring him to the "licentious practices" of the ancient world, and inspire him in an amazing way to envision sexual reveries and memories that are buried in his unconscious. Petronius's book *Satyricon* in Des Esseintes's library, for example, arouses his libidinal desire constantly, for it reflects the licentious pleasures and luxuries of Rome and analyzes the mores of the period objectively and with a language of sodomy. Knapp explains that *Satyricon* in particular "opens him up to the bejeweled domain of exciting erotic and masturbational sensations" (208). And commenting on the effect of books in general on Des Esseintes, Knapp writes that the books "encourage him to displace himself via reverie or dream without ever leaving his chair . . . they [the books] have a strong erotic hold and act as a kind of instinctual or vital function" (207).

Other objects that stimulate Des Esseintes's sexual desire are bonbons. When he sucks a "bonbon," letting it "melt in his mouth," he feels a "drop of essence of woman" (97). The taste of the candy evokes a reverie of female image. He sees that this female image is masculinized; he observes an artificial change in the sex of the woman. Being impressed by the masculine power of this woman Des Esseintes becomes castrated by that power within her–a power that, as Huysmans suggests, changes his sex. Merl Storr in *Bisexuality: A Critical Reader* lists different meanings of bisexuality at different times by different authors. One meaning which was advanced by Sigmund Freud is that bisexuality refers to the presence of psychological characteristics of both genders in an individual (3). Another meaning common in medical and sexiological debates during the nineteenth and twentieth centuries is that "bisexuality consists in maleness and femaleness, in a biological or anatomical sense, so that physical features such as male nipples and female facial hair are signs of human 'bisexuality'" (3). The last and most common definition used today is that "bisexuality consists in heterosexuality and homosexuality" (3). Des Esseintes is bisexual for having both feminine and the masculine features. Huysmans writes, "By dint of considering his own qualities and giving the rein to his faculties of comparison, he presently arrived at the conclusion that, on his side, he was himself getting nearer and nearer the female type" (98). The monstrous masculinized power of the female as a force of "castration" that operates a "change of sex" in Des Esseintes brings to his memory other destructive female forces that try to rape and feminize him. First Des Esseintes is obsessed with sexual objects to fulfill the sexual force of his "libido." Then, we notice that he comes to enjoy female figures in his dreams, but finding these females destructive because they feminize him, Des Esseintes recalls reveries that fit his state of castration at that moment. These reveries, in fact, unfold his homoerotic tendencies. In other words, not being able to envision having sex with the destructive females he imagines, he recalls memories in which he is rendered homosexual. Des Esseintes remembers, for example, a lad with whom he enjoyed homoerotic sexual pleasure. He recalls "the face [of the lad] was at once pathetic and strangely attractive; pale and drawn, with regular features shaded by long black looks" (103). Des Esseintes is attracted by the lad's "naiveté" and his "fleshy lips" which are "divided by a line in the middle like a ripe cherry" (104).

Continuous shifts in Des Esseintes's sexual tendencies, both with sexual objects in his house and with females and males that he envisions in his dreams and memories, explain a disequilibrium in his erotic psyche which reveals how undefined his sexual identity is. The hallucinatory dreams, the reveries, the memories, and his delight in *the world of things* and *artifice* are a means of escape from the real for him.

SEXUAL FANTASIES: LA REGENTA

Like Des Esseintes, Leopoldo Alas's Ana Ozores in *La Regenta* experiences a traumatic childhood and suffers deprivation of love, a matter which affects her later development as a woman, and her attitude toward herself and other people. Ozores comes to prefer loneliness and to immerse herself in books, in which she can find her mystic ideals, and in memories of the past, her childhood, to fill the emptiness of her soul. She undergoes a passive mystic experience as a woman that affects her nerves and renders her a contradictory figure. Ana gives up her husband, Don Víctor Quintanar, when she is seduced by Don Alvaro. Feeling repentant later for her heterosexual relationships with several men, Ana decides to enjoy a mystic seclusion which excludes male desire. As a consequence, she comes to enjoy sexual objects as a substitute for male-female sexuality, and this makes her a fetishist, as the paper explains later.

The young Ana is bored in the conventional provincial town of Vetusta (the Spanish adjective of Vetusto–feminine Vetusta–means ancient) and its conservative society. Alas asserts that "Ana hated the Vetustans. . . . Those traditional customs which they observed without any awareness of what they were doing, without any faith or enthusiasm, and to which they returned with a regularity as mechanical as a madman's rhythmical repetition of phrases and gestures; that atmosphere of gloom about which there was no grandeur" (354). For Ana, Alas writes, "Vetusta was her prison" (116), and Don Víctor's house, too, "felt like a prison" (472). Being a wife in a very conventional place, Ana can do nothing except to be alone: "All Vetusta was enjoying itself, with noise, light, music, happiness; and here was she alone, in the cold, dark, sad dinning-room" (205). Ana comes even to suffer from neurotic disorders due to boredom and lack of interest in life. She realizes that her life with Quintanar is insignificant and unbearable. She yields therefore to spiritual contemplations and dreamy abstractions to kill her boredom, and starts seeking sensational life away from the social constraints of Vetusta. Being sensitive and "romantic" by nature (354), Ana becomes polyamorous especially when she lets her love evolve naturally and freely. Deborah A. Anapol reflects in *Polyamory: The New Love Without Limits* (1997) that

> the word polyamory comes from Greek and Latin roots meaning 'many loves.' I use it to describe the whole range of love styles which come from an understanding that love can be forced to flow, or not flow, in any particular direction. ... But to me, polyamory, has more to do with an internal attitude of letting love evolve without expectations and demands than it does with the number of partners involved. (4-5)

Ana lets her love flow blindly to any male that chooses her as a desired object. Ana gravitates, for instance, toward different lovers: the fleshy prospective lover Don Alvaro (who models himself on the Don Juan figure of Spanish literature); a priest and a theologian drawn to her body and soul (Don Fermín De Pas); the Darwinian Frillity, and others. Ana keeps praising and admiring Don Alvaro (361), who keeps seducing her. She enjoys his seduction and finds him "handsome, very handsome" (535). Like Visita, her girlfriend prostitute, Ana is "tormented by temptation" (355). She, Alas explains, treats Don Alvaro very gently and enjoys his gazing at her body: "Ana did not try to stop the seducer from devouring her with his grey eyes, and she returned his looks with a sweet ... unblinkable gaze" (377). Ana enjoys dancing with Alvaro: "She had almost forgotten how to dance. ... Ana was silent, she could not see, she could not hear, all she could do was feel a pleasure which was like fire; this intense irresistible delight terrified her, she let herself be carried on like a dead body" (556). Ana and Don Alvaro, Alas writes, spoke of "covertly love, with good-natured, familiar melancholy and tender, gentle, insinuating passion" (556). She moves then to the love of her religious advisor and soul brother Don Fermín De Pas. Ana hopes to develop the "idealistic passion" she shares with De Pas into a sexual passion. Her sexual desire for De Pas is suppressed and it comes later to be embodied in dreams. John Rutherford writes in his "introduction" to *La Regenta* that Ana's "suppressed desire for a sexual relationship with Canon De Pas is embodied in disguised form in her dreams, and still suppressed as she remembers them afterwards" (9). In chapter XIX, Ana dreams of her early childhood and that all her desires and wishes are fulfilled. She dreams that "life was beginning to stir again in her wasted body . . . life was advancing over the terrain of its uncertain victory" (431). She dreams also that "her doleful ideas had flown away like winter birds, and there . . . she was surrounded by people [Alvaro, Quintanar, De Pas, Frillity], and was the object of all their attention" (431). In chapter XXI, Ana's dream is realized. She has De Pas's confession that he is in love with her, and that he desires not only her soul but also her body. Ana feels now that she is cured from her body illness; her suppressed sexual desire for De Pas can be fulfilled now–the "ideal passion" which Ana and De Pas "declared to each other could well turn into sexual passion" (478). This brings joy to her heart, especially when De Pas "wanted to relish the joy flowing into his soul" (478). De Pas confesses that he "loved all of her [Ana]," and that she is his "woman" (563). Alas describes De Pas's torment of love, anger and jealousy later: "he was dying of love, anger, and jealousy [of Alvaro]. He wasn't her soul brother, he was a man hiding passion–love. . . . she was loved by a Canon" (563). Ana falls in love also with Frillity, the Darwinian scientist. Alvaro tells Frillity: "She is in love with you, I'm sure of that. But, with her, you aren't the man you are with other women" (44).

Earlier in the novel we used to see Ana bored, enjoying mystic speculations, characterized by what Havelock Ellis calls "occultism," "theosophy," and "spiritualism"–"vague forms on the borderland of the unknown" (xxxii). Later, however, we see Ana polyamorous, letting her sexual and loving needs flow freely. The physical attraction of Alvaro overcomes finally her spiritual mysticism. Her body, she feels, is not hers; rather, it belongs to the world: "It [her body] escaped from her, too. . . . It belonged to the world more than it belonged to her" (428). Alas presents Ana's body here as a commodity transacted in the hands of her male lovers. Ana hates herself for having all these heterosexual love affairs, and, being afraid of social judgment and "of what people thought of everything she did" (87), she decides to stop her love from flowing. Turning "her life into a perpetual schooling" and suppressing "all her happy pulses" (87), Ana shies away from people and chooses to enjoy a mystic state of seclusion which excludes the materialistic world. Like Des Esseintes, Ana comes to have dreamy abstractions and fantasies which exclude *the world of people.*

Alas makes a quick reference to Ana's childhood in chapter IV, explaining the kind of suffering and deprivation Ana experienced. Her mother, an Italian dressmaker, dies in "giving birth to Ana" (79). Ana's father, Don Carlos, emigrates, and appoints a heartless governess, Dõna Camila. The governess had tried to seduce Don Carlos but "it was to no avail" (82). Dõna Camila swore then "eternal hatred" for the daughter Ana. The governess brings her new lover Iriarte to the house and the motherless girl Ana remains in the custody of Dõna Camila. Ana hated the governess, and she "would imagine miraculous escapes from these confinements, which were like death to her" (83). Ana, Alas explains, is "put to bed without feeling sleepy, without a story, without caresses, without light"–a matter which stirs in her a strong sensation–a "nostalgia for a mother's lap" and a longing for a father's presence (66). Ana's miserable childhood contributes in shaping her personality the way it is in the novel, and, more specifically, in rendering her sexual identity fragmented. She is not only polyamorous, but also bisexual and fetishist as this paper explains in the ensuing paragraphs.

Alas explains in a childhood flashback that Ana the child finds no one to express her own feelings and desires to. Feeling the absence of her father, Ana, rather than the father's daughter, becomes her father's champion. Heroically, she determines to search for him. She escaped "through the garden gate and ran weeping towards the sea . . . for she wanted to climb into a boat and sail away to the land of the Moors and look for her papa." But the result of this escape is a severe punishment by Dõna Camila (68). Ana's fear of Camila makes her depressed. Ana sees Camila and Camila's lover (who is the only available father image that she may identify with her father at this stage) exchange kisses. This increases Ana's longing and need for her father, the ideal image in her life. But this image of the father, Camila's lover, proves instantly to be false, especially when she receives no sympathy at all from him. Ana's urgent need for her father becomes clear when we know that she escaped a second time to look for him. In Ana's second escape, she secretly follows another path, but she finds Germán–her admirable boyfriend–who represents the second alternative image for her father. Both she and Germán sleep at night in the boat, and the outcome of this is another severe punishment by Camila and her lover. Being deprived of contact with her only heroic lover, Germán, Ana returns back to her loneliness. She succumbs to her imagination to express what she feels and desires.

The feelings of deprivation and loneliness Ana experienced in childhood continue in Ana's life when she is young. She also restores such childhood habits as that of "caressing the sheet with her cheek" (66). Ana does not stop also missing maternal love, and she would succumb to imagination to fulfill her sexual desires and maternal needs. The young Ana comes, for instance, to imagine objects such as the "feather mattress" and the "pillow" as an alternative for the absent tenderness and sympathy of the father and the warmth of the mother's "breast":

> There had never been anything warm and maternal in her life . . . making believe that the pillow was the breast of the mother of her dreams, and that she could really hear the songs which sounded within her brain. Little by little she had become accustomed to having no pure and tender pleasures other than those of imagination. (66-7)

Ana's imaginativeness here foreshadows bisexuality, especially in longing for woman's love–the mother's breast. She escapes the heterosexual relations which she used to have with Quintanar, Alvaro and Germán, and finds a resort in being in love with her own sex. Alas writes that the young Ana "had suffered much trouble and vexation, but now she scorned its memory; a lot of fools had conspired against her, and it was repugnant to remember all this. Her suffering as a young girl . . . aroused her indignation and inspired the sweetest feeling of self-pity" (66). Monique Wittig in her article "'Hispanics,' AIDS, and Sexual Practices" in *The Lesbian and Gay Studies Reader* (1993) conceives lesbians as "runaways" from the heterosexual "totalitarian order." Ana hates herself for having relationships with males, and she starts longing for the innocent child Ana who had never been involved in heterosexual affairs. The young Ana comes even to hate men. Remembering the suffering and innocence of her childhood in chapter IV, Ana comes to like the spiritual suffering of Ana the child, and she comes to admire the child's loneliness:

> As the judge's wife thought about the girl that she had once been, she began to admire her, and to feel that her own life had been divided into two parts, one which belonged to the little Angel [Ana the child] whom she now believed dead. The girl who used to jump out of bed in the dark had been more vigorous than this Anita of the present. (67)

Ana, in fact, begins to imitate unconsciously the behavior of Ana the child; she wants to restore that childhood solitude. She hates all the Vetustans because of the injustice done to her during childhood by the governess Camila and the governess's lover. Indeed, remembering her affair with Germán and the social scandal brought to her by him, she becomes "abashed," "angry," and she determines never to repeat that affair again with any male. She becomes aware of the "uprisings" in her "own spirit": she "loved nobody, pitied nobody" (71). In other words, the young Ana starts working now to restore the innocent suffering of Ana the child but without Germán's episode, following a mystic route. But in doing so, the young Ana's sexual fantasy takes a new direction. In suppressing her sexual desire for males, Ana clings to sexual objects. In playing with these sexualized objects (pillows, sheets, rug, etc.) in the solitude of her soul, Ana fulfills a repressed sexual pleasure, a kind of sexual fetishism:

> Without moving her feet, she let herself fall, face downwards, arms outspread, upon the silky softness of the sheets. She rested her cheek on the bed, keeping her eyes wide open. She took great delight in the tactile pleasure, which ran from her waist to her temples . . . [she] leaped into her bed like a bacchante; yet the pleasurable coldness of the sheets with their hint of dampness only heightened her rage, and she sunk her teeth into the pillow. In order to escape from herself she tried to stop thinking, and half an hour later she fell asleep. (65, 538-39)

Ana's pleasure in these sexual objects renders her a fetishist. In attaching eroticism to these sexualized objects, Ana avoids having a real union of sex with humans. Her attraction to these objects is a means of escape from the *world of people*. But in suppressing her sexual desire for men, she becomes like a fetishistic monster. In addition to the sexual objects mentioned earlier, Ana, like Des Esseintes, finds books a relief to her repressed erotic mysticism. In these books, Ana plays imaginatively the "various roles of saint, mystic, martyr . . . [and] romantic heroine." Despite herself, Alas says, "she derived intense pleasure from the seductive charm of dining at ball," from an "aristocratic lusciousness," from "attending the theater" and from "cheap novels." Commenting on the significance of books in Ana's case, Benigo Sanchez-Eppler, an author of several books on Spanish history and literature, writes, "fetish-like . . . it is widely acknowledged that Ana repeatedly experiences texts as the only outlets available to overcome the limitations imposed on her, first by her guardians, then by her sexless marriage, and throughout, by society in general" (204). Sanchez-Eppler goes further in identifying the books that Ana reads as a way for "wish-fulfillment" of "mystical [erotic] ecstasy" (208).

In *La Regenta* Alas confines his narrative to female sexuality and he reflects an ideological reality about the nineteenth-century Spanish female and the gender codes that existed during that period of time. The novel, John Rutherford asserts, is "about conservative times and conservative society" of a shabby Spanish province town in the 1870s (15). The setting of the novel, Rutherford explains, corresponds to the period where the "conservatives, led by Cánovas del Castillo . . . [were] in a dominant position" (15). Alas pictures Ana in the novel as a female who is entrapped by the social constraints of the Vetusta society. Gender roles played a great role in shaping women's lives and in rendering them as weak and "eroticized" objects for male's pleasure. In his Review "Sex Sells: The Feminine Mystique in 19th Century Spain" David Gies explains that Lou Charnon-Deutsch, a critic of modern Spanish literature, in his book *Fictions of the Feminine in the Nineteenth-Century Spanish Press* (2000) "lays out the many ways the female body was used to construct not only gender difference in 19th-century Spain but also social and political differences" (739). Gies reports that Charnon-Deutsch also discusses images of women in Spanish fiction and media, explaining how men (mostly) managed to associate women with "the natural world, family values, domesticity, powerlessness, exoticism, illness, prostitution, and even death" (739-40). Ana is domestic; her place in the novel is the house, and she is supposed to be an obedient and faithful wife. Her body is commodified and transacted, and it is associated with the natural world; it is owned by everybody. Ana's body, Alas emphasizes, becomes not her own, but of the world: "She looked at her body and it was like earth. 'It was the accomplice of all the others. It escaped from her, too, as soon as it could; it was more like the world than it was like her; and it belonged to the world more than it belonged to her'" (428). Alas shows Ana's body to be possessed not only by her husband, but also by Alvaro, Don Fermín, and others. Her body becomes the "tool" for fulfilling men's "pride" (592). Her body becomes also an object of gaze to the crowd of Vetusta. During the burial procession of the converted atheist Don Pompeyo, Ana dresses in purple and walks barefooted through the streets of Vetusta, "making a spectacle of herself" (589). Ana does this spectacle, Alas writes, as a "sacred vow" (586) and as a "Christian example" (587) to show her "edifying humility" (587) in front of God and people. All the Vetustans gaze at Ana's white flesh and bare feet–her body is transacted and enjoyed by the immense crowd: "the eyes of the whole town [of Vetusta] riveted on Ana's steps, her movements, her clothes, her color, the look on her face! And she was barefoot! Her feet, naked and as white as white, admired and pitied by the immense crowd! . . . All that flesh–white, firm, full, suggestive, serious flesh" (590-91). Ana's flesh arouses the sexual desire of not only the male Vetustans, but also the females. Obdulia Fandino, a servant lady in the church, wishes to be a man when she sees Ana barefoot in the procession. She gazes at Ana's flesh and beauty, "licking her lips, possessed by admiring envy, and conscious of the strange promptings of a kind of crazy, brutal lust, so absurd as to be inexplicable" (591). Obdulia, Alas writes, "felt a vague desire-to-to-to be a man" (591).

Alas associates Ana's body not only with fetishism (i.e., foot-fetishism), but also with sickness and prostitution. Alas explains that Ana is sick, hysterical, and neurotic. Alvaro says of her: "I cannot make any progress at her house. She's a strange woman–a hysterical woman. She has to be studied at depth" (412). Throughout the narrative Alas highlights Ana's "weak flesh" (538), and her "violent nervous attacks" (556). She, Alas writes, is "fallen into . . . prostitution" (594). She enslaves her body to Alvaro and to De Pas: "Ana was his [De Pas's] again: his slave! She had said so on her knees, weeping. And that project, that irrevocable intention to make all Vetusta see on a solemn occasion that the judge's wife was her confessor's slave" (581). Don Fermín enjoys Ana's submission: "Don Fermín was choking with pleasure and pride; his passions were sticking in his throat" (582).

Despite her weakness, Ana has emancipatory aspirations. She dreams to be free of the Vetusta constraints, and to achieve independence. But the male author makes it clear that Ana is too weak to achieve this due to her gender. As a female, Ana is represented merely as flesh, a white flesh to be enjoyed and gazed at by Alvaro, Don Fermín, and other male Vetustans. Ana, in this sense, is a weak subject. Serena Anderllini-D'Onofrio in *The 'Weak' Subject: On Modernity, Eros, and Women's Playwriting* (1998) defines the weak subject as that who "benefits from most privileges enjoyed by the social group, that is central and secure with respect to certain order. Nevertheless, she is disenfranchised by her gender" (52). Ana seems to be deprived of free will and choice in the novel due to her gender. Alvaro and Don Fermín find her a weak woman who yields easily to their sexual desires and needs. Ana, Alas writes, believes that "she had prostituted her self" (605) for rendering her female body as an object for male gaze, choice, and sexual pleasure. Ana's nature, Alas adds, was so "weak" (357) to make a choice and to feel independent in a male-dominated society, and "this did not make her stop feeling annoyed with herself" (357). A typical characteristic of the 'weak' subject, Anderlini-D'Onofrio reflects, is that "sexually, she [the 'weak' subject] is unable to express her preference for she inhabits an order in which only males have the privilege of choosing a sexual partner of the opposite gender. She cannot define her sexual orientation for she cannot express a clear independent will" (52).

CONCLUSION

In *Against the Grain* the male author Huysmans chooses to write about a man–Des Esseintes, following the aesthetic attitude towards art that is commonly called decadent. As Ellis explains, decadence suggests "going down," "individualism," "corruption," and the "breaking up of the whole for the benefits of its parts" (xiv). Des Esseintes is bored of people, and prefers to be alone with *things*. Huysmans flirts with "decadent" mentality to disassociate Des Esseintes from people and to reveal to us the hero's private secrets in Fontenay which are representative also of the author's. As Eve Kosofsky Sedgwick writes in *Between Men: English Literature and Male Homosocial Desire* (1985): "the secrets of class are represented in decadent literature by elements of the bourgeoisie that can disassociate themselves from the productive modes of their class and, by learning to articulate an outdated version of the aristocratic values, can seem to offer some critique of–some ready leverage on–the bourgeoisie official culture" (90). Like Des Esseintes, Huysmans had a "keener sense of the distressing absurdity of human affairs," and led "a retired life . . . abhorring the society and conversation of the average literary man" (vii). Huysmans, like Des Esseintes, loved art and artifice. During the era of writing *Against the Grain* people in Paris showed no great interest in art. Huysmans, in consequence, created a haunting nineteenth-century male, Des Esseintes, whose love for artifice is comparable to that of Huysmans's. Dean de la Motte in "Writing *Against the Grain: A Rebours*: Revolution and Modernist Novel" establishes a strong connection between the protagonist (Des Esseintes) and the author (Huysmans): "the divorce between society and art so typical of *fine-de-siécle* aestheticism allows Huysmans (and, for that matter, Des Esseintes) to believe simultaneously in societal degeneration and artistic generation. . . . Huysmans, in a typically modernist gesture, flees the suffocation of a traditional closure for the hermetic closure of Des Esseintes's expériences (experiments) at Fontenay" (20). Huysmans represents his love for art via the male Des Esseintes, and his representation of women in the novel is decadent. The male Des Esseintes views women in the novel as *femme fatales* that castrate and feminize him. To avoid the love of such dangerous females, Des Esseintes turns to homoerotic reveries. Huysmans's representation of women in the novel is typical of nineteenth-century France where fictional women were depicted as prostitutes or *femmes fatales*, including Emile Zola's *Nana* (1880), Charles Flaubert's *Madame Bovary* (1857), Huysmans's *Marthe* (1876) and *En Route* (1895). *Against the Grain* is no exception. Charles

Bernheimer asserts in his "introduction" to *Figures of Ill Repute: Representing Prostitution in Nineteenth-Century France* (1989) that women in nineteenth-century French fiction were revealed in artists' fantasies as the locus of fears of decay, disease, atavism, and castration. Ranging over a variety of artistic and literary works, in his book Bernheimer explores such images of women and the "strategies [of] control" (2) that artists employed to manage them. Bernheimer makes the statement that "art is the making public of private fantasies" (1)–a definition that turns out to be peculiarly appropriate when discussing works of art (by men) that depicted women as destructive, weak, immoral, or forces of castration. Huysmans's fantasy of women as *femme fatales* is apparent in the novel, and he invites the male viewer to see in these women an inherent degradation whose effects are seen in the social and economic structure of society. His male hero–Des Esseintes–is projected as a victim to the feminine fatal forces that feminize him and determine him therefore as bisexual.

Sigmund Freud did not exist at the time of writing *Against the Grain* (1884) and *La Regenta* (1884-85). Yet, both novels anticipate modern psychology in revealing the sexuality of Des Esseintes and Ana. Huysmans mentions the neurotic disorders that Des Esseintes suffers from, and reveals the repressed sexuality of Des Esseintes which is expressed via sexual objects and fantasies. Huysmans approaches also Des Essentes's fetishism. On the other hand, Ana's dreams (chpt. XIX) in *La Regenta* and their interpretations (chpt. XXI), her traumatic childhood and its effects upon her later development as a young woman, her repressed sexuality, fetishism, and the symptoms of neurosis and hysteria she suffers from are topics which had been approached by Freud and other modern psychologists. Rutherford explains in his "introduction" to *La Regenta*: "I'm sure that only chronology has saved us from a shelf-ful of theses on 'Leopoldo Alas's debt to Freud'" (10). This is not the place to reflect on Huysmans's and Alas's anticipation of modern psychology, and it suffices to say that the way the authors foreclose the multifarious ways by which the sexuality of their characters can be constructed and conceived is psychological.

As this paper has demonstrated, in the course of unraveling the sexuality of Des Esseintes and Ana, Huysmans and Alas invoke sexual fantasies via implicit representational images of bisexuality, fetishism, and homoeroticism. Both authors render characters who are more the exception than the rule in their sexual inclinations. Lacking mechanisms for expressing alternative sexuality in a hegemonic culture coded as heteronormative, Huysmans and Alas utilize accepted sexual metaphors to imply bisexual and fetishistic behavior in order to afford their characters sexual identities. Consumed with infinite ennui of loneliness and deprivation, Des Esseintes comes to seek a compensation for human company which he finds in a distorted artifice of the real in a deserted house, a miniature reflection of his *world of things* that eliminates the *world of people*. But in isolating himself from the people, Des Esseintes dehumanizes himself and his existence, and comes to derive a sexual pleasure from the artifice and several memories and dreams in which he shows homoerotic and bi-sexual inclinations. Accordingly, his sexual identity is distorted. He is not only a fetishist who takes sensual pleasure in sexual objects, but also a bisexual being who imagines himself castrated by monstrous female figures. Ana, on the other hand, represses her sexual desire to the extreme, and in denying her body's biological need, she, like Des Esseintes, shows bisexual and fetishist fantasies. As spectators, we are invited to gaze at Ana's and Des Esseintes's sexuality through Alas's and Des Esseintes's eyes, and this illuminates our understanding of the way male and female sexuality can be represented in writing, and the way it can therefore be encoded in the imagination of nineteenth-century male artists.

WORKS CITED AND CONSULTED

Alas, Leopoldo. *La Regenta.* Translated and with an Introduction by John Rutherford. NY: Penguin,1984.

Allen, Mariette Pathy. *Transformations: Crossdressers and Those Who Love Them.* NY: Dutton, 1989.

Altman, Dennis et al. *Homosexuality, Which Homosexuality? Essays from the International Scientific Conference Lesbian and Gay Studies.* Edited with an "introduction" by Anja Van Kooten Niekerk and Theo Van der Meer. London: GUP, 1989.

Anapol, Deborah A. *Polyamory: The New Love Without Limits.* San Rafael, CA: IntiNet Resource center, 1997.

Anderlini-D'Onofrio, Serena. *The 'Weak' Subject: On Modernity, Eros, and Women's Playwriting.* Madison: Farleigh Dickinson UP, 1998.

Arnup, Katherine, Andrée Lévesque, and Ruth Roach Pierson, eds. *Delivering Motherhood: Maternal Ideologies and Practices in the 19ᵗʰ and 20ᵗʰ Centuries.* London: Routledge, 1990.

Barreca, Regina, ed. *Sex and Death in Victorian Literature.* Bloomington: Indiana UP, 1990.

Bernheimer, Charles. *Figures of Ill Repute: Representing Prostitution in Nineteenth-Century France.* Cambridge, MA: Harvard UP, 1989.

Bérubé, Allan. *Coming Out Under Fire: The History of Gay Men and Women in World War Two.* NY: Free P, 1990.

Bronski, Michael. "Portrayals of Oscar Wilde as a Victim of Homophobia Have Turned the Victorian Social Critic into a Pathetic Caricature." June, 1998. <http://www.bostonphoenix.com/archive/1in10/98/06/BRONSKI.html>.

Charnon-Deutsch, Lou. *Fictions of the Feminine in the Nineteenth-Century Spanish Press.* UP, PA: Pennsylvania State University, 2000.

———. "*La Regenta* and the Sutured Subject." *Revisita De Estudios Hispanicos xxviii* (1994): 65-78.

Chauncey, George, Jr., "From Sexual Inversion to Homosexuality: Medicine and the Changing Conceptualization of Female Deviance." *Salmagundi* 58-59 (Fall 1982-Winter 1983):114-46.

Clark, J. Michael. *A Defiant Celebration: Theological Ethics and Gay Sexuality.* Garland, TX: Tangelwüld, 1990.

Corbin, Alain. *Women for Hire: Prostitution and Sexuality in France after 1850.* Translated by Alan Sheridan. Cambridge, MA: Harvard UP, 1990.

DeJean, Joan. *Fictions of Sappho, 1546-1937. Women in Culture and Society.* Ed. Catharine R. Stimpson. Chicago: University of Chicago P, 1989.

Dilman, Ilham. *Freud and the Mind.* Oxford, England: Basil Blackwell, 1984.

Ellis, Henry Havelock. "Introduction." *Against the Grain (A Rebours).* NY: Dover Publications, Inc., 1969.

_____. *Studies in the Psychology of Sex: Sexual Inversion,* volume I. (1897), excerpted in Merl Storr, ed. *Bisexuality: A Critical Reader.* London, NY: Routledge, 1999.

Epstein, Cynthia Fuchs. *Sex, Gender, and the Social Order.* New Haven, CT: Yale UP, 1988.

Fenichel, Otto. *The Psychoanalytic Theory of Neurosis.* NY: W. W. Norton & Company Inc., 1945.

Flaherty, Gloria. "Sex and Shamism." *Sexual Underworlds of the Enlightenment.* Eds. G. S. Roussea and Roy Porter. Chapel Hill: U of North Carolina P, 1988. 276-80.

Foucault, Michel. *History of Sexuality.* V. I. Trans. Robert Hurley. NY: Vintage, 1978.

Foldy, Michaels. *The Trials of Oscar Wilde: Deviance, Morality, and Late Victorian Society.* Yale: Yale UP, 1997.

Freud, Sigmund. *Fetishism.* Standard edition, vol. 21. London: The Hogarth P., 1927.

_____. *Three Essays on the Theory of Sexuality,* translated and revised by James Strachey, with an "Introduction" by Steven Marcus. NY: Basic Books, Inc. Publishers, 1962.

Gies, David T. Rev. "Sex Sells: The Feminine Mystique in 19th Century Spain." *Virginia Quarterly Review 76.4 (Autumn 2000): 739-44.*

Haraway, Donna J. "A Manifesto for Cyborgs: Science, Technology and Socialist Feminism in the 1980s." *Feminism/Postmodernism,* edited by L. J. Nicholson. NY: Routledge, Chapman and Hall, 1990. 199-233.

_____. *Simians, Cyborgs, and Women: The Reinvention of Nature.* NY: Routledge, 1991.

Hearn, Jeff, Deborah L. Sheppard, and Peta Tancred-Sheriff, eds. *The Sexuality of Organization.* London: Sage Publications, 1989.

Huysmans, J. K. *Against the Grain (A Rebours),* with an "Introduction" by Havelock Ellis. NY: Dover Publishers, Inc., 1969.

Jacobus, Mary, Evelyn Fox Keller, and Sally Shuttleworth. *Body/Politics: Women and the Discourse of Science.* NY: Routledge, 1990.

Jordanova, Ludmilla. *Sexual Visions: Images of Gender in Science and Medicine Between the Enlightenment and Twentieth Centuries.* Madison: University of Wisconsin P, 1989.

Knapp, L. Bettina. "Huysmans' *Against the Grain*: The Willed Exile of the Introverted Decadent." *Nineteenth-Century French Studies* 20 (1992): 203-21.

La Motte, De Dean. "Writing *Against the Grain (A Rebours)*: Revolution and Modernist Novel." *Modernity and Revolution in Late Nineteenth-Century France.* Eds. Barbara T. Cooper and Marray Donaldson-Evans. Newark: U of Delware P, 1992.

Maccubbin, Robert Purks. *'Tis Nature's Fault: Unauthorized Sexuality During the Enlightenment.* NY: Cambridge UP, 1987.

Mohr, Richard D. *Gays/Justice: A Study of Ethics, Society, and Law.* NY: Columbia UP, 1988.

Money, J. *Gay, Straight, and In-Between: The Sexology of Erotic Orientation.* NY: Oxford UP, 1988.

Mort, Frank. *Dangerous Sexualities: Medico-Moral Politics in England since 1830.* London: Routledge & Kegan Paul, 1987.

Murphy, Lawrence R. *Perverts by Official Order: The Campaign Against Homosexuals by the United States Navy.* NY: Haworth P, 1988.

Niekerk, Anja Van Kooten, and Theo Van Der Meer, eds. *Homosexuality, Which Homosexuality? Essays from the International Scientific Conference on Lesbian and Gay Studies.* Essays by Dennis Altman et al. London: GMP, 1989.

Painter, George. The Sensibilities of Our Forefathers: the History of Sodomy Laws in the United States. 1991-2002. <http://www.sodomylaws.org/sensibilities/introduction.htm>.

Pringle, Rosemary. *Secretaries Talk: Sexuality, Power, and Work.* London: Verso, 1988.

Richards, A. K. "Female Fetishes and Female Perversions; Hermine Hug-Hellmuth's 'A Case of Female Foot or More Properly Boot Fetishism' Reconsidered." *Psychoanalytic Review*, 77, No. 1 (Spring 1990): 11-23.

Rousseau, G. S. and Roy Porter. *Sexual Underworlds of the Enlightenment.* Chapel Hill: University of North Carolina P, 1988.

Rose, L. "Freud and Fetishism; Previously Unpublished Minutes of the Vienna Psychoanalytic Society" *Psychoanalytic Quarterly*, 57, No. 2 (1988): 147-65.

Russett, Cynthia Eagle. *Sexual Science: The Victorian Construction of Womanhood.* Cambridge, MA: Harvard UP, 1989.

Rutherford, John. "Introduction." *La Regenta* by Leopoldo Alas. NY: Penguin, 1984.

Sanchez-Eppler, Benigo. "Stakes: The Sexual Vulnerability of the Reader in *La Regenta*." *Romantic Review* 78 (1987): 207-20.

Sedgwick, Eve Kosofsky. *Between Men: English Literature and Male Homosocial Desire.* NY: Columbia UP, 1985.

_____. *Epistemology of the Closet.* Berkeley: University of California P, 1990.

Sinclair, Alison. "Liminal Anxieties: Nausea and Mud in *La Regenta*." *Bulletin of Hispanic Studies* 74.2 (April 1997): 155-77.

Stimpson, R. Catharine. "Zero Degree Deviancy: The Lesbian Novel in English." *Critical Inquiry* 8, No. 2 (1981): 363-79.

Storr, Merl, ed. *Bisexuality: A Critical Reader.* London, NY: Routledge, 1999.

Wagner, Peter. *Eros Revised: Erotica of the Enlightenment in England and America.* London: Seeker & Warburg, 1988.

Wittig, Monique. "'Hispanics,' AIDS, and Sexual Practices." *The Lesbian and Gay Studies Reader.* Ed. Henry Abelove, Michele Aina Barale, and David M. Halperin. NY: Routledge, 1993. 400-33.

Other Kitchen Sinks, Other Drawing Rooms: Radical Designs for Living in Pre-1968 British Drama

Sam See

[Haworth co-indexing entry note]: "Other Kitchen Sinks, Other Drawing Rooms: Radical Designs for Living in Pre-1968 British Drama." See, Sam. Co-published simultaneously in *Journal of Bisexuality* (Harrington Park Press, an imprint of The Haworth Press, Inc.) Vol. 4, No. 3/4, 2004, pp. 29-54; and: *Plural Loves: Designs for Bi and Poly Living* (ed: Serena Anderlini-D'Onofrio) Harrington Park Press, an imprint of The Haworth Press, Inc., 2004, pp. 29-54. Single or multiple copies of this article are available for a fee from The Haworth Document Delivery Service [1-800-HAWORTH, 9:00 a.m. - 5:00 p.m. (EST). E-mail address: docdelivery@haworthpress.com].

SUMMARY. In this article, Sam See argues that contemporary gay/lesbian drama scholars have overlooked bisexual and polyamorous characters and ideas in many 20th-century British plays that were written and produced before the Lord Chamberlain restrictions on theatre were rescinded in Britain in 1968. See contends that these scholars have read Noel Coward's *Design for Living*, Shelagh Delaney's *A Taste of Honey*, and Joe Orton's *Entertaining Mr. Sloane* with homosexist eyes, critical perspectives that regard bisexuality and polyamory only as closeted homosexuality. The author believes such readings issue from the divide between contemporary queer and gay/lesbian scholarship and argues that gay/lesbian scholars seem reluctant (if not explicitly opposed) to regard "queer" as a viable term with which to describe the undeniable variety of non-heterosexual relationships. See hopes to reveal how such "closeted homosexual" readings ironically marginalize the very non-heterosexual lives that contemporary gay/lesbian scholars claim they want to support. *[Article copies available for a fee from The Haworth Document Delivery Service: 1-800-HAWORTH. E-mail address: <docdelivery@haworthpress.com> Website: <http://www.HaworthPress.com> © 2004 by The Haworth Press, Inc. All rights reserved.]*

KEYWORDS. Drama, British, 20th century, polyamory, bisexuality, homosexism, Noel Coward, Shelagh Delaney, Joe Orton, John Clum

> What a funny place to have desire! You might as well
> have it at home as anywhere else, mightn't you?
>
> –Helen, in Shelagh Delaney's
> *A Taste of Honey*

Because of the stigmatizing social and legal prohibitions placed against sexual Others in Britain at the beginning of the 20th century, and because of the currently "visible" and "outed" nature of the gay liberation movement, pre-1968 queer British drama (and much pre-Stonewall queer literature, for that matter) is often read as featuring "closeted" or "inauthentic" representations of queer reality and identity. Exemplified by John Clum's foundational study of gay drama, *Acting Gay: Male Homosexuality in Modern Drama* (1994), in which the chapter devoted to drama from 1930-68 is tellingly titled "Codes and Closets," many contemporary queer theorists and gay/lesbian scholars regard the first half of the 20th century as a period in which inexpressibility, stultification, and at best codification constitute the spirit of queer literature. Much of this sentiment seems tied to the common conflation of sex with identity in queer studies, the essentialist/minoritist[1] notion that queer is queer because of the sex (never mind desire for, never mind affection toward) one has with another person. Thus, in many theorists' eyes, if we see no very visible or vocal representation of this sexuality in literature, we are not reading "real" or "true" representations of queer life.

Certainly, strategies of queer visibility and expression changed substantially throughout the 20th century.[2] While this may be true, I contend that some of the "closeted" and/or "inauthentic" expressions of queer desire and identity in pre-1968 British drama are in fact be anything but stifled, incomplete, or (in Clum's most damning phrase) "heterosexist" (assuming all those heterosexuals are to blame for queer identity suppression). On the contrary, pre-1968 plays like *Design for Living* (1933), *A Taste of Honey* (1958), and *Entertaining Mr. Sloane* (1964) offer voluble, visible, and indeed revolutionary depictions of queer life and identity, particularly of polyamorous and bisexual lives.[3] This is a remarkable achievement considering that these plays were written and produced in a social climate where queerness, acceptable or otherwise, was only in the nascent stages of visibility.

Throughout this paper, I shall address the ways that queer identity is constructed and maintained in these plays through the development of queer communities. I will focus on how the rigid binary definition of heterosexual/ homosexual cannot and does not account for the people these communities include, an exclusion that in turn reinforces the need, strength, and difference (visibility) of those communities. I am particularly interested in surrogate or anti-conventional (read: non-nuclear) family units that, while they may mimic conventional families in interesting ways, resemble communities in a more general sense than they do traditional families. With the aid of sociologist Carol Warren's observations about queer community formations, I will consider how and why these play's characters come together in the relationships that they do and what functions these queer communities/families serve for their members.[4]

Ultimately, then, I am arguing that in some ways *Design For Living (DFL)*, *A Taste of Honey (TH)*, and *Entertaining Mr. Sloane (EMS)* are being misread in the present political climate because of their questionable "queer visibility," as their less than flag-bearing queer characters hardly fit the narrow margins of "positive representation" that queer theorists and gay/lesbian scholars seem to so desire in queer literature. I seek to rectify these misreadings and to suggest that all of these plays in some way overtly challenge social norms through literary and dramatic representation, a process George Haggerty calls challenging the "dominant fictions" (2) and Michel Foucault deems the creation of "reverse discourses," revolutionary ideologies in which

> one is dealing with mobile and transitory points of resistance, producing cleavages in a society that shift about, fracturing unities and effecting

regroupings, furrowing across individuals themselves, cutting them up and remolding them, marking off irreducible regions in them, in their bodies and minds. (96)

These authors' plays are queer plays: they cleave, fracture, and remold conventional identity models; they resist monolithic conceptions of both hetero- and homosexualities. To suggest otherwise, as in the essentialist/minoritizing position that there are right and wrong, good and bad, big and small ways to be queer, is to misunderstand and to do violence to what it means to be queer in this decade and the decades in which these plays were written.

Before assessing the ways that the aforementioned plays challenge social norms and offer revolutionary depictions of queer life in drama, I must address the social and cultural atmospheres in which this literature was written. This will help us to understand why many scholars assume the plays present "coded" or "closeted" representations of queer identity. As Sean O'Connor offers in his informative book *Straight Acting: Popular Gay Drama from Wilde to Rattigan* (1998), the period in Britain between Oscar Wilde's trials in 1895 and the removal of the Lord Chamberlain's restrictions on drama in 1968 was marked by "hostility towards gay men [that] was both legally and socially condoned for the three-quarters of a century after Wilde's conviction, backed by the moral and legal support of church and state" (15). Such moral and legal sanctions included the 1885 Labouchere Amendment, which prohibited all private and public male homosexual behavior, and a number of very public arrest scandals throughout the 19th century, scandals that culminated in Wilde's famous 1895 trial (O'Connor 14).[5] These sanctions were reinforced later in the century by the 1954 Wolfenden Report and the British law reform of 1967, both of which secured the legal boundary between what queers could do in both their public and private lives (Sinfield, "Private," 50).

This prohibitive atmosphere particularly affected representations of queer life in dramatic literature, as the Licensing Act of 1737 essentially restricted all "explicit expression of homosexual relationships and lifestyles on the British stage" (O'Connor 20). While I contend that *DFL, TH,* and *EMS* evaded the Lord Chamberlain's censorship precisely because these plays feature ambiguously "queer" rather than exclusively "homosexual" characters, it is not debatable that many gay-themed plays were banned from public theatre during this period.[6] Coupled with the vitriolic anti-queer legal and social prohibitions of the time, it is unsurprising that contemporary queer scholars believe "such regulations in Britain during the past century inspired a culture of self-censorship and subterfuge by gay writers" (O'Connor 12). Nevertheless, that some plays were subject to the Lord Chamberlain's infamous "kindly blue pencil" (O'Connor 20) of censorship should not lead us to believe that all pre-1968 British plays were stripped of queer content. Such generalizations make for a convenient "repressed/oppressed" foundation for contemporary queer politics, and while such repression and oppression certainly haunted

British queers for centuries, we must be prudent about distinguishing our use of such generalizations between political and literary purposes.

In assessing the ways that *DFL, TH,* and *EMS* defy such categorization, I must also clarify my use of the word "queer" rather than "gay" or "homosexual" to describe the plays' depictions of sexual alterity. "Queer" is a word appropriated by contemporary queer theorists to embrace all forms of sexual otherness, not just the gay/lesbian lives indicated by "homosexual." It is the most apposite term to describe the polyamorous, frequently bisexual characters in these works and the unconventional communities that those characters create.[7] After all, not all queers are gay. Unfortunately, as I have anticipated above, in their search for gay/lesbian literary representations, many contemporary gay/lesbian scholars view these plays' queer relationships as closeted, coded, and ultimately inauthentic representations of *gay* life. For example, as Alan Sinfield notes, many gay/lesbian scholars believe that "'we're all bisexual really' is the commonest evasion" of depicting exclusively homosexual lives and desire ("Orton" 182). John Clum similarly contends that such plays "by homosexual playwrights that deal with homosexuality in an elliptical or coded manner and that also dismiss the possibility of exclusive homosexuality" (xix) are examples of D. A. Miller's "open secret" or Eve Sedgwick's "glass closet" theoretical models.[8] To Clum, they are dramas that involve "the invocation of homosexuality without naming it–or the problematizing of homosexuality without acknowledging its existence" (89).[9]

Clum's use of the open secret and glass closet models is telling, as by presuming that these plays are closeted he assumes there are *homosexuals* in these plays whose secrets are open and whose closets are made of glass. As the foundation of his analysis, Clum "homosexualizes" these plays because in Coward and Orton's cases they are written by homosexuals and in Delaney's case her play features a "problematized" (read: ambiguously bisexual) gay character. To buttress his argument, the critic invokes Eve Sedgwick's concept of heterosexist intentional ignorance[10] and contends that these plays are written with a "closet sensibility" in a "series of performances, maintained by the heterosexist wish for, and sometimes enforcement of, homosexual silence and invisibility" (Clum 88). Clum believes that these plays vacillate between hetero- and homosexual representations because such variability allows the audience to choose what sexual expressions they will and will not see. Allegedly, this ambiguity permitted the plays to be publicly produced in highly homophobic times (Clum 88); hence the utility of Sedgwick's ignorance model.

While I admire his gay liberationist intentions, and while his claim is possibly true of other plays where homosexual lives are sublimated, hinted at, but not explicitly revealed, Clum's argument injuriously ignores the very explicit, very real polyamorous and bisexual lives that *are* represented in these plays. That they are not "homosexual" plays does not mean that they are not queer, and to suggest otherwise marginalizes queer representations in an act of what may be called homosexism.[11] Indeed, while he ironically invokes Sedgwick's concept of heterosexist intentional ignorance to suggest that one can choose what sexual representations one will and will not read in these plays, Clum (among other scholars)[12] commits his own act of *homosexist* intentional ignorance by actively ignoring these plays' very visible polyamorous/bisexual strains.

To avoid this kind of misguided criticism, Andy Medhurst borrows Gayatri Spivak's term "strategic essentialism"[13] to mediate between essentialist and constructionist as well as political and literary perspectives. Medhurst makes an admirable call for balance between politically minded essentialist/minoritist perspectives like Clum's that search for variations of some monolithic version of queer identity and those that see identity as entirely socially constructed, variable, and protean:

> We need to construct our histories through examining the records left by those who went before us, not in a blunderingly literal-minded fashion that sees fictional texts as factual 'evidence,' but by studying how texts mediate the contradictions and challenges faced by those who carried a homosexual identity through a heterosexual world [. . .] To see essentialism and social constructionism as polarized opposites may be useful for rhetorical purposes, but any full-sensitive analysis of culture and sexuality must constantly negotiate between the two. (207)

While Medhurst does not always follow his own advice, I wish to take as axiomatic his and Spivak's support of strategic essentialism to suggest that sexual identity is inherently variable. Instead of forcing sexual representations into a fixed number of identity compartments, we ought simply to multiply the number of compartments we have for identifying those representations.[14]

To buttress this position I also take as axiomatic Eve Sedgwick's necessarily and deceptively obvious observation that *"people are different from each other"* (*Epistemology* 22) to contend that for all the good we do to uncover gay/lesbian lives in literature, we do equal harm to the lives of sexual Others who do not live on either pole of the severe heterosexual/homosexual binary. After all, as Jeffrey Weeks observes,

> We cannot [. . .] simply assume that nothing changes, that gays and lesbians have always existed as we exist today [. . .] that there is a mystical continuity between our desires and their desires across the range of cultures and histories. We do not do it for any other aspect of our social existence. We should not do it for sex. (206)

In assuming that nothing changes, in assuming not only, as Sedgwick has taken to task, "a relatively unified homosexuality that 'we' *do* 'know today,'" but a relatively unified (read: homosexual) experience of sexual alterity, many gay/lesbian scholars "still risk reinforcing a dangerous consensus of knowingness about the genuinely *un*known, more than vestigially contradictory structurings of contemporary experience" (*Epistemology* 45). Because these plays confront those "unknowns," they are, in Sinfield's terms, "faultline" plays, works that "address the awkward, unresolved issues [. . .] they hinge upon a fundamental, unresolved ideological complication that finds its way, willy-nilly, into texts" (*Cultural* 4). It is the central effort of my present endeavor to uncover those unknowns, to address those ideological complications, to expose the variability that has been shrouded beneath so much searching in recent years for same- (homo-) ness.

One of the queerest aspects of these plays' depictions of queer lives is that those depictions come in the form of exclusive, nearly hermetic family structures. In all three plays, the characters establish isolated communities or subcultures where who is kept in the group is just as important as who is kept out. However, as sociologist Carol Warren observes, such queer communities are not and perhaps never have been so terribly uncommon. In regard to the 20th century, Warren argues that dominant moral and social ideologies stigmatized and forced gay[15] folks to establish private lives (and communities) that were markedly different from their public identities: "A community that is secret and stigmatized must quite literally have walls [. . .] Walls imply walling out as well as walling in" (Warren 17). In regard to the plays under discussion, *DFL, TH,* and *EMS* all feature queer communities that actively exorcise a-queer characters in order to preserve the stability and functionality of the queer community; Warren describes this process as protection "from the invasion of outsiders by other kinds of walls [including] the refusal of entry to strangers" (18). I will also consider Julia Kristeva's "Law of the Father" model in this regard, but where Kristeva posits that the Father purges society of sexual transgression and restores patriarchal, heterosexist domination (Clum 48), I wish to reverse her model in the manner of Warren's formation and suggest that these queer communities expel the Father in order to dismantle hegemonic, patriarchal heterosexism and to revolutionize systems of normality.

Furthermore, as I am describing of these plays' queer characters' extreme visibility, Warren notes that "the development of a secret gay world through stigmatization produces an amplification and intensification of the experience of being gay [. . .] the isolation of the gay community makes it more of a haven. The ultimate strategy of secrecy is withdrawal" (98-99). In this sense, these queer characters' private, surrogate family communities serve as proxies for their possibly "inauthentic" (inexplicitly queer) public lives. Literary critic Michelene Wandor concurs with Warren and contends that these proxies are "sustained by private ritual, by ways of speaking and behaving which constitute a private replacement for a real social milieu in which they can be themselves" (67). It is in these queer communities, then, that queers most truly define themselves as such–the alternative family is actually the sexual Other's most highly visible, most highly "othered" locale. After all, the hermetic community unit "enables the development of a homosexual identity. After this identity is assumed, the continuing division of inner and external time deepens the division between worlds and reinforces the sense of 'being different'" (Warren 43).

With these observations in mind, then, because they are isolated, because they establish hermetic family units in which to operate, the characters of *DFL*, *TH*, and *EMS* make themselves all the more visibly queer-identified, creating distinctly queer representations that defy the ambiguously straight, heterosexist formations suggested by Clum (104), Medhurst (198), and other contemporary critics. Rather than providing inaccurate representations of queer life, Coward, Orton, and Delaney quite accurately represent the secretive/stigmatized/isolated nature of many queers' pre-Stonewall lives, but they do so publicly (and, so, revolutionarily) through the theatrical forum. No glass closets these communities: rather, they explicitly show queer life as many queers really do live and have lived.

If, then, queer communities are all the more "queer" for their consolidation, their hermeticism, their isolation, how much more revolutionary, how much more markedly queer could these plays be than to present such communities in the public forum of the theatre? Noel Coward's *Design for Living* (1933) offers a strikingly early case of this kind of enclosed yet highly visible queer community. Exemplifying the early 20th century British drawing-room comedies later challenged by kitchen-sink and "Angry Young Man" plays like John Osborne's 1956 *Look Back in Anger* (Medhurst 201; O'Connor 175), *DFL* is a revolutionary depiction of a Bohemian *ménage à trios*, a polyamorous triad, in a historical era when all forms of queerness, including polyamory and bisexuality, were still publicly condemned if even tacitly acknowledged.

The play's three central characters, Otto, Leo, and Gilda, form a hermetically sealed family unit that resembles the "triangulated desire" model originally formulated by Rene Girard and reconfigured by Eve Sedgwick in *Between Men*. While Sedgwick's version focuses on how homosocial desire between two men is accentuated by the presence of a female in the triangle (*Between* 23), Girard's original version treats "the erotic triangle as symmetrical–in the sense that its structure would be relatively unaffected by the power difference that would be introduced by a change in the gender of one of the participants" (Sedgwick, *Between*, 23). Girard's triangle consists simply of a subject, an object, and a mediator of the subject and object's desire; the role of each person in the triangle can shift depending upon how the participants' affections flow (Girard 225). Thus, for my present examination I prefer Girard's model, as it better accounts for the fluidity of desire so evident in *DFL*'s erotic triangle. Sedgwick's version, while helpful for understanding homosocial desire, risks reducing our reading of this triangular relationship to a homosexual bond that is merely mediated by a token female.[16] Such an interpretation is the very type of reading I am challenging with this study.

Using Girard's model of triangular desire, then, we can see how the shifting bonds between Otto, Leo, and Gilda alternate in strength depending upon who is subject, who is object, and who is the mediator of the relationship at any given moment, a dynamic Leo calls "life [. . .] a process of readjustments" (*DFL* 40). Leo delineates the possible manifestations of these readjustments when he tells Gilda, "The actual facts are so simple. I love you. You love me. You love Otto. I love Otto. Otto loves you. Otto loves me. There now! Start to unravel from there" (*DFL* 19). Except for Gilda's anomalous relationship with Ernest, the trio's desires are contained within the erotic triangle (what I am calling their queer community), but the fluidity (read: queerness) of their desires permits for shifts in who plays which role when and between whom the "primary" (subject/object) bond exists.

In this sense, regardless of the modifications, there is always a subject/object bond and always a mediator of that bond in the three characters' relationships. In fact, this queer family *depends* upon the presence of a mediator between the subject/object bond, even though that mediator may be physically absent from the relationship and even though the subject/object bond is ostensibly the "strongest" of that present moment. For this reason, the polyamorous term "hinge" may be the most apposite term to describe the mediator, as "without the hinge [in a vee relationship], the other people often go their separate ways" (Polyamory). In *DFL*, when found without one of the triangle's "sides," the members of that bond inevitably realize that their relationship is incomplete without the hinge partner–that, as when Gilda and Leo are together without Otto, "something's missing" (DFL 37) without the full triangle in its ever-revolving formations of desire.

As examples of these shifting configurations, at the beginning of the play Gilda and Otto share the subject/object pairing, and Leo exists on the outskirts as hinge. Then Ernest reveals that, before they met Gilda, Leo and Otto enjoyed a relationship that Leo describes as "something very deep" (*DFL* 71); here Gilda acts as hinge in the present for Leo and Otto's past relationship. Gilda and Leo then become subject and object when they move to London, but they think and speak constantly of Otto, who acts as hinge (*DFL* 47). Leo and Otto then resume the subject/object pairing when they travel the globe and Gilda marries Ernest, but they return to fetch Gilda (hinge), realizing that they cannot live without her.

This triangulation continues throughout the play and climaxes with Gilda's realization that, "We're all of a piece, the three of us. The early years made us so. From now on we shall have to live and die our own way. No one else's way is any good, we don't fit" (*DFL* 109). Reinforcing the notion that this is a hermetic community, a cohesive "piece" apart from the mainstream population, Gilda suggests that the normalizing standards of the outside world do not suit these queer characters' lives. And while we are given no reason to expect that the variability of roles (subject, object, and hinge) will cease after play's end (indeed, the three's squabbling seems to preclude the possibility of this community's stability), Gilda's renunciatory proclamation and her split from Ernest indicate that the triad will maintain its private queer community, will revolt privately against the standards of the dominant public world beyond play's end.

Intensifying this public/private divide, Ernest, although temporarily breaking the triangle's cohesion, strengthens *DFL*'s queer community by reminding Otto, Leo, and Gilda of their deep and sustaining need for one another. By disrupting the hermetic unit just as a foreign organism disrupts the animal body, Ernest forces the broken family to reunite *en masse* in order to purge its "invader." As Warren has suggested of queer communities in general, such unified resistance emphasizes the triad's solidarity and, as such, amplifies its visible queerness.

Ernest's expulsion is anticipated early in the play when Gilda doubts whether he, a representative of the prevailing "normalizing" ideology, can understand the queer love she shares with Otto and Leo: "Do you? Do you really? I doubt it. I don't see how anyone outside could" (*DFL* 12). Consistent with Warren's postulation that queer communities delineate between private and public, inside and outside worlds, Gilda builds a wall between herself and Ernest that, despite their temporary marriage, is reinstated by play's end when Ernest is almost forcibly exorcised from the triangle (*DFL* 111). Here Ernest makes real Gilda's earlier predictions when he denounces the group as a "disgusting three-sided erotic hotch-potch," "unscrupulous, worthless degenerates," "shifty and irresponsible and abominable" (*DFL* 110-1). Leo is quick to identify these epithets as silly, "pompous moral pretensions" (*DFL* 111) that, to use modern terms, seem to represent the governing heterosexist ideology of this early 20th century British society.[17]

In this manner, Ernest's expulsion from the group reinforces the bonds that fasten the triad within their queer triangle. *Sans* intruder, the group reforms all the tighter and mocks Ernest with weeping laughter through curtain's fall. Such solidarity makes this queer community even more revolutionarily *visible* on the theatrical stage. In fact, the audience's last image of the trio is of Otto, Leo, and Gilda physically entangled with one another, a remarkable theatrical display considering that the play was written and performed in the early 20th century amid the prohibitive social and legal circumstances that I have elsewhere delineated. With Ernest's ejection from the queer triangle, Coward sends the Father out of the home, and His abrupt departure could not be more strikingly conspicuous or more poignantly felt. By challenging social norms through the creation of a hermetic queer subculture, with *Design for Living* Noel Coward offers revolutionary ways of thinking about sexual identities and sexual lives.

Nevertheless, in contrast to my reading of this queer community, some gay/lesbian scholars regard Otto, Leo, and Gilda's queer relationship as a sophisticated cover for Otto and Leo's exclusively homosexual relationship. John Clum, for example, suggests that "Coward has kept Otto and Leo's sexual relationship hidden in the exposition, and they use terms of endearment that could be read as terms of friendship. The only hint we get of the physical aspect of their relationship is the recounting of a violent argument, in which Leo pushed Otto into a bathtub and doused him with cold water" (101). Notwithstanding the fact that elsewhere Leo and Otto display their physical affection for one another (such as the moment in which the men sob on each other's shoulders after discussing their loneliness (*DFL* 83)), Clum makes the troubling assumption that Otto and Leo are somehow obligated as queer characters to physically demonstrate their affection for one another in order to be recognized as queer.

Echoing Clum's sentiment, Andy Medhurst argues in his study of Coward that, "Even when Coward seems to be advocating sexual experimentation, he stops far short of specific details. As Alan Sinfield has put it, he 'validates deviant sexuality when it is part of a general bohemianism'[18] but nothing more concretely radical is put forward" (202). Are we to assume from this argument that the sexual act itself is the only "real" or "radical" (in the face of heterosexism) expression of queer affection? For Clum, Medhurst, and Sinfield, it would seem that saying "I love you" is not a sufficient expression of queer love.

However, as George Haggerty contends, "Love as *eros* and love as *philia* cannot be readily distinguished in any culture, or indeed in many social situations, as well today as in the eighteenth century; [. . .] it is too easy to eliminate the erotic when dealing with relations between men" (14). With this observation in mind, why should we automatically exclude the possibility of erotic love between Otto and Leo simply because we *do* see signs of *philia*? After all, Leo's "everyone loves everyone" speech is stylistically paratactic: each love relationship is placed on equal ground with the next; love for Gilda is not seen as "superior" or "more real" than the men's love for each other. As Leo tells Gilda, "It doesn't matter who loves who the most; you can't line up things like that mathematically. We all love each other a lot, far too much" (*DFL* 19). And since we know that "love" for Gilda is both erotic and friendly (both men at one point sleep with Gilda), why should we not assume that "love" between Otto and Leo is equally composed of both *eros* and *philia*? And more to the point, since they have already proclaimed that they "love" one other, what do we really care what these men choose to do in bed? Is the sexual act the only way we can define or identify queer love? Indeed, the queer *philia* Otto and Leo share is the very sort of non-overtly sexual demonstration that needs to be acknowledged and embraced by gay/lesbian and queer scholars. Sex is an important part of what defines us as queers, but it is not all.

Furthermore, in regard to Otto and Leo's "friendship," as Haggerty has posited of eighteenth-century queer literature,

> It would be a mistake to dismiss [male-male friendship expressions of] love as 'simple friendship,' not only because in certain cases [. . .] it is definitely more, but also because there is no such thing as the 'simple friendship' the phrase implies. Friendship can be animated by many things, including rivalry, jealousy, desire, and love. (5)

Remembering too Eve Sedgwick's foundational study of homosocial desire and the erotic manifestations of friendship forged therein (*Between* 25), I wish to extend Haggerty's important and admirable observations about male love to my present discussion of Otto and Leo to suggest that this male couple's "friend"ship is a relationship, a friendship, a partnership, a branch of a polyamorous triad–in sum, a queer love that takes many forms where deep friendship (*philia*) is indeed one if not the only one of those forms.

Put another way, contrary to Clum's assertion that the men's use of the term "friend" (*DFL* 71) is a coded hint "in gay parlance [. . . to] continue to read the scene as a presentation of a homosexual relationship; straight audience members could hear that line as a disclaimer of hints of homosexuality" (101), might we not assume that these characters really mean what they say, just as they might really mean what they say when they express their love for one another *and* their female counterpart (*DFL* 19, 71)? Can sexual partners not also be *friends*? As Haggerty contends, "The constant insistence that we look for the 'genital' in erotic relations is like searching for keyhole testimony in a sodomy trial. What does it prove or disprove?" (18). Why should we in our search for the genital deny these characters the affection (let us call it love, let us call it friendship) that they so clearly express for one another?

Queers' relative perspectives on their own sexual identities underscore the need for a strategic essentialist perspective in critical theory that allows for variability in identification and that, above all, *denormalizes* sexual practices and sexual identities. Otto and Leo are queer characters in an intimate relationship despite the fact that they do not fuck onstage (*pace* Louis and the Man in Tony Kushner's *Angels in America*). Unfortunately, to Clum, Sinfield, and Medhurst, Otto and Leo's friendship cannot be anything other than Coward's coy (perhaps cowardly?) veiling (read: closeting) of their sexual relationship. Based upon the precedent established throughout the rest of the play, however, it seems clear that Otto and Leo are lovers who are also friends who are also bath buddies who are also sob sisters who are also fabulous world travelers; they are, for all their variability and indefinability, *queer*. We should not be shocked to realize that, without jumping into bed with one another, queers really can be all of these things and more.

Additionally, while Clum at one point grants that *DFL* is not focused on homosexuality but, rather, "on the freedom not to be defined by codes of sexual behavior–not to have to be heterosexual or homosexual," the critic discredits his own argument that the play is "revolutionary" by claiming that "the triangle–and the focus on Gilda's anguish and confusion–[. . .] hides Otto and Leo's relationship for some, defuses its danger for others" and by observing with no small disappointment that homosexual desire is neither "eroticized nor connected to the possibility of an exclusive homosexual relationship [. . .] Coward does not in his plays deny homosexual desire or love, but he does deny exclusive homosexuality as a social identity" (103).

Here Clum's minoritist leanings are at their most evident, as it would seem for this play to be an "authentic" or "uncloseted" or "un-diffused" representation of queer identity Otto and Leo must be exclusively homosexual. Sinfield makes a similar postulation when he argues that Coward's "word encodes a subordinate, negotiated discourse within a dominant discourse [. . .] traces of homosexuality in the plays were heard and appreciated distinctively by different sectors in his audiences" ("Private" 49). Again, while acknowledging a revolutionary strain in Coward's work, Sinfield allows the monolithic *homo*sexual to overshadow his ability to see the otherwise highly visible polyamorous *bi*sexuals in this play.

Considering these critics' fine insights into *DFL*'s depiction of sexual variability, it is unfortunate and puzzling that they minimize the play's revolutionary portrayal of queer life in the face of "closeted homosexuality." After all, the play's characters' defiance of social norms is everywhere spoken, as when Otto proclaims, "Our lives are diametrically opposed to ordinary social convention. We've jilted them and eliminated them and we've got to find our own solutions for our own peculiar moral problems" (*DFL* 58). Leo echoes this statement when he tells Ernest, "Our lives are a different shape from yours" (*DFL* 110). In *Vice Versa* (1997), her foundational study of bisexuality, Marjorie Garber argues that such defiance of sexual norms is integral to the very nature of bisexuality:

> The question of whether someone was 'really' straight or 'really' gay misrecognizes the nature of sexuality, which is fluid, not fixed, a narrative that changes over time rather than a fixed identity, however complex. The erotic discovery of bisexuality is the fact that it reveals sexuality to be a process of growth, transformation, and surprise, not a stable and knowable state of being. (65-6)[19]

With their explicit rejection of social norms and conventions, Otto, Leo, and Gilda shift the paradigm of relationality in desire, a shift that Brad Wishon suggests is *required* of queer love: "In queer relationship [. . .] the old structures, by and large, do not work. Therefore a change in the way we create relationship is mandated by the very nature of queer relationship" (109). Evidenced by their queer triangle, perhaps these characters are not closeted homosexuals at all; perhaps they are really just queer.

In this sense, if we assume, in Sinfield's cultural materialist perspective, that different camps in early 20th century audiences "heard and appreciated" different sexualities in the plays, why would we deny the possibility of another camp who sees polyamority and bisexuality, arguably the most clearly heard and acknowledged sexualities in *DFL*? Since Sinfield believes that "we make sense of ourselves and our situations within an ongoing contest of representations" and that "when your subculture is not acknowledged–'there exists a moment of psychic disequilibrium, as if you looked into a mirror and saw nothing,' [as] Adrienne Rich says" (*Cultural* viii-ix), why would we deny some queers the opportunity of making sense of themselves with these dramatic representations? Why would we want to disregard their subculture and, as such, disregard them? Why should we continue to hunt for homosexuality (elusive game in these plays) when polyamority and bisexuality are already everywhere found in abundance? The answer lies in gay/lesbian criticism's new Law of the Father, a law that might well be called the Law of the Homosexual: here the monolithic hetero/homo binary reigns supreme, and it must be revised in our present day as surely as Coward attempted to revise it with *DFL* some 70 years ago.

Two decades after Coward challenged models of sexual normativity with *Design for Living*, Shelagh Delaney published *A Taste of Honey* (1958), regarded as a truly revolutionary play in the history of British drama for its landmark depiction of an openly gay character named Geof.[20] While I shall argue that Geof, like Otto and Leo, is not necessarily homosexual but ambiguously queer, various productions like Joan Littlewood's in 1958 defied the Lord Chamberlain and quite clearly depicted Geof as homosexual at a time when overt homosexuality was forbidden from the stage (O'Connor 21). Notwithstanding this important development, however, the queer community in which Geof lives is even more revolutionary in that the character himself and the play's queer family overtly challenge the heterosexist standards of "kitchen sink" drama, a style of drama typically associated with *TH*.

In the play, Jo (the frustrated product of a frigid mother, Helen, as well as perpetual uprooting) and Geof room together after discovering that Jo is pregnant. With Jo's child, the two form a queer family unit, also called a "PolyFamily" (Polyamory): Geof, a possibly gay man and not the father of Jo's child, stands as mother (*TH* 196) for Jo, a heterosexual mother who loathes motherhood and quite queerly proclaims, "I don't want to be a mother. I don't want to be a woman" (*TH* 213). Before their coupling, both Geof and Jo are resistant to the limited conventions of their predetermined social roles: Geof, perhaps thinking himself "exclusively" homosexual, has "never kissed a girl" before meeting Jo (*TH* 198), yet he also never consummates a relationship with another man. Jo, on the other hand, finds herself doomed by domesticity and the "symbolic" institution of heterosexual marriage (*TH* 166). In addition, as becomes a theme throughout the play, Jo is damaged by Helen's inadequacy as a mother and believes that conventional family structures impair personal growth and success (*TH* 180, 195). In this sense, Geof, as a queer (atypical) gay man, and Jo, as a queer heterosexual woman, are outsiders, "a couple of degenerates" (*TH* 193) in a world where gender roles are absolute, a world where gays are supposed to be one thing and straights another, a world where (as today) the hetero/homo binary dictates sexual identity politics.

To alleviate their dissatisfaction, consistent with Wandor's observations above, Geof and Jo establish an alternative community where traditional roles and identities have proven unsatisfying. While both Geof and Jo were unhappy in their previous lives, lives defined and confined by prevailing homo-sexual and heterosexual ideologies, the couple's new *queer* life together proves fulfilling. Geof, for example, who Jo calls a "cure" (*TH* 212), reveals to Jo, "Before I met you I didn't care one way or the other–I didn't care whether I lived or died. But now . . ." (*TH* 199). Similarly, reflecting upon her difficult past in the face of her vitalizing present life with Geof, Jo proclaims to her mother, "I've been performing a perfectly normal, healthy function. We're wonderful! Do you know, for the first time in my life I feel really important. I feel as though I could take care of the whole world. I even feel as though I could take care of you!" (*TH* 218). Replacing their previously despairing lives with nights of dancing and friendly banter, Geof and Jo are happiest, liveliest, and most satisfied in their PolyFamily.

Amplifying this celebration of the queer community, Jo's choice of the words "normal" and "healthy" in her speech to Helen are deliberately radical, as her life is, by the standards of the Law of the Father, anything but normal and healthy. Jo reveals that her mother is a failure of the patriarchy's standards of motherhood and that Geof, in fact, is a better "mother" to her baby than ei-ther Jo or Helen ever could be. But Delaney's revolutionary ideas do not stop there. In the play's most radical challenge to readers and audiences, Helen (the play's Father), after complaining to Jo about her new life ("I don't know what's to be done with you, I don't really") addresses the audience directly and demands, "I ask you, what would you do?" (*TH* 223), overtly questioning heterosexual standards of domesticity and sexuality. By exposing the hypoc-risy of harmful, conventional family units and lauding the salutary effects of the PolyFamily, with *A Taste of Honey* Shelagh Delaney defiantly queers the kitchen sink.

However, because the play was written for staging during the Lord Cham-berlain policy's sovereign regulations, many contemporary critics read *TH* as the product of closeted and stereotypical ideologies. John Clum, for instance, contends that

> Geoff [sic] is the kindly Nellie who is the heroine's best friend, another common stereotype. After Jo, the heroine, has been left by her promiscu-ous mother and made pregnant by a sailor, Geoff moves in to be Jo's companion. He is derided by Jo's mother and her mother's boyfriend. He is a "pansy," a "lily," and a "fruitcake." [. . .] Geoff is supposedly homo-sexual, but he doesn't have any relationships with men, reinforcing the shibboleth that the only acceptable homosexual is celibate. (106-7)

Clum's analysis of Geof as a stereotype is heavily reinforced by the epithets Helen and her boyfriend Peter pitch about throughout the play. Like Ernest in *DFL*, Helen and Peter speak for the Law of the Father, the hegemonic, heterosexist ideology of this pre-Stonewall British society, and Clum is quick to note their presence and their slanders against Geof as stigmatizing forces that reduce "the possibility of an affirming homosexual friendship, much less a homo*sexual* relationship. One way or the other, the homosexual is isolated by either his sensitivity or his effeminacy" (107).[21]

Were this strictly a play about homosexuals, and were we to believe that Helen and Peter have more insight about Geof's sexual identity than Geof has insight about himself, Clum's contention might prove more buoyant and illuminating. However, judging by the play alone, Clum searches (as he does in *DFL*) for the homosexual where the bisexual or ambiguously queer is always-already present.[22] After all, despite his apparent affection for men, Geof never has a relationship (physical or otherwise) with a man, but he is more than ready to have both a physical and emotional relationship with Jo. In fact, he at one point proposes to and kisses her (*TH* 198). Why not read this affection for Jo for what it is rather than try to pinion Geof as a repressed homosexual who pitiably opts for girls where boys seem to be prohibited? Why must Geof be "really" gay underneath and only "passing" as straight with Jo? Why can he not be bisexual and quite content with his variable desires?

As I have argued about *DFL*, Clum's insights into Delaney's "stereotypical" presentation of Geof more illuminate the critic's political opinions about gay stereotypes than elucidate who this queer character really is. Furthermore, by ignoring Geof's queer status, Clum also ignores the fact that as a queer character Geof actually defies gay stereotypes by recognizing the possibility of desire and affection for members of both sexes. For Geof, the hetero/homo binary through which stereotypes are constructed has no meaning. In this sense, and central to my disagreement with much of the criticism I have been contesting, though *in the play* Geof is queer, *in much of the criticism about the play* Geof is a stereotypical homosexual. The transformation between the two is telling, and, as "social movements do not simply organize people with pre-given identities; they also play a role in constructing, deconstructing, and reconstructing identities" (Lehr 79), it underscores my concerns about the sometimes-conflicting political and literary aims of gay/lesbian and queer scholarship.

Concurring with Clum's contention that the queer family is finally marginalized in *TH*, Michelene Wandor observes that while Geof and Jo's family is nurturing and vitalizing, "It cannot be validated [because] the 'natural' rights intervene, and the mother/daughter relationship, however fraught, overrides any other kind of chosen relationship" (42). Like Clum's, Wandor's argument would hold better if the strength of *TH*'s PolyFamily were not so clearly the play's dominant and sustaining force. Through Helen's abominable career as a mother as well as Jo's resistance to traditional gender roles and motherhood, Delaney revolutionizes familial normativity and depicts a world where conventional family units are destructive and queer families/communities are life-sustaining.

Furthermore, while Geof is indeed "expelled" by the Father (Helen) from the community by play's end, so too is Helen driven out of Jo's home, if only momentarily for yet another evening of debauchery. More importantly, despite his physical absence, Geof's presence is acutely felt at the end of the play, as Jo sings "Geof's song" and smiles wistfully at his memory (*TH* 223-4). The implication is that *that* design for living worked and *this* one doesn't. Despite Helen's disruption of Geof and Jo's queer family, then, it is Geof's presence we feel at play's end; it is Geof who gets the final word; it is the queer community for which Jo ultimately longs. Kathy Rudy sees such "positive, communal aspects of gay culture [as revolutionary] because these communities are one of the few remaining places where the hegemony of heterosexist, capitalist, patriarchal, nuclear family is challenged" (209). By being the model of successful, "authentic" living, *TH*'s PolyFamily prevails in the face of its Fathers, among them Helen, proponents of 20th-century heterosexist ideologies, and gay/lesbian scholars like Clum, Sinfield, and Medhurst.

In contrast to Coward and Delaney's more positive depictions of relatively "happy" or "well-adjusted" queer families, in his 1964 *Entertaining Mr. Sloane*, Joe Orton perverts both conventional morality and conventional family structures by creating a queer community where violence, duplicity, and betrayal rule the day. Written only a few years before the Lord Chamberlain policies were lifted, *EMS* affords perhaps the most radical challenge to sexual normativity of the three plays I am examining, and its proximity to the LC's dissolution is not coincidental. As Alan Sinfield notes, "The 1960s intensified both libertarian and reactionary attitudes and their conflict was staged in the theatre. These were the circumstances that permitted Orton's notoriety. Earlier, he would not have been tolerated" ("Orton 178). *EMS* anticipates the unambiguous vocality and physicality of post-1968 queer plays, and it paves the way for an era in which "the trend toward sexual permissiveness accelerated" (D'Emilio 23), an era Michelene Wandor describes as important "both because it heralded the end of theatre censorship [. . .] and also because it made possible an assimilation into theatre of all the exciting political and cultural ideas which had been building up throughout the 1960s" (156-7).

In the play, Sloane, a young bisexual man, enters and disrupts the brother/sister/father family community comprised of Ed, Kath, and Kemp, respectively. Wandor provides an excellent analysis of how Sloane, Kath, Ed, and Kath's near-term baby restructure the conventional family unit to form a queer community that bridges the triangle and PolyFamily models we have seen in *DFL* and *TH*:

> In an inverted Persephone myth [where Sloane is alternately kept by Ed and Kath for six-month periods] Sloane becomes the child (property) in this unholy semi-incestuous brother-and-sister-parent relationship, as if the presence of tabooed sexualities, mother/son, brother/sister, man/man, have themselves totally overthrown all standard familial and sexual values, but can still only be justified if they ape the semblance of a conventional family structure. (56)

As in *DFL*, desire in *EMS* is triangulated, but as in *TH* the queer community in some ways resembles a family unit. Orton here confronts what Jonathan Dollimore cites as the two greatest "anxieties of the post-war period": the family, "vulnerable to deviant sexual desire, especially from within," and homosexuality (Dollimore 54-5), which for reasons that I have earlier explained I shall expand to be sexual otherness. However, Wandor's final observation disrupts the flow of her otherwise insightful description of this queer community, as she assumes that because they are queer (Sloane bisexual, Ed homosexual, Kath an incestuous mother/sister) these characters must "justify" their existences by "aping" conventional structures. She assumes that they can only define themselves in oppositional terms, can only half-mimic (and so live incompletely within?) the heterosexist systems to which they will never belong.

Based upon *EMS*'s farcical elements, however, Orton does anything but try to "justify" his characters' lives through obedience to social norms. On the contrary, the playwright perverts those social norms to raise "questions about the stability of hetero- and homosexuality, terms that imply their opposites but that also imply a stability of desire counter to the language of farce" (Clum 114). Again, as with *DFL* and *TH*, neither hetero- *nor* homosexuality is seen as the only acceptable or wholly satisfying category for naming sexual identity. Rather than try to bind this group into a relationship with normative structures, we would more profitably recognize that, in terms of sexuality, Sloane likes boys and girls, Ed likes boys (particularly athletic boys), and Kath likes sons and brothers. Instead of forcing their sexual desires into conventional models, these characters scorn those models and create a community of their own, using whatever terms and models they see fit.

For example, in his attempt to woo Sloane away from Kath, Ed mocks the public stigma to which Carol Warren attributes the queer community's identification:

> I can't have my sister keeping a common kip. Some of my associates are men of distinction [. . .] You don't want them talking about you. An' I can't guarantee my influence will keep them quiet. Nosy neighbours and scandal. Oh, my word, the looks you'll get. (82)

Here Ed simultaneously recognizes and mocks the social standards to which queer lives are held. He acknowledges, as Warren would, that the queer community is isolated by stigma and is "walled off" from the outside world, but he also recognizes the arbitrariness and hypocrisy of such standards, as indicated by his sarcastic tone and mock disapproval ("Oh, my word, the looks you'll get"). Moreover, as a component of Orton's dark comic style, rather than simply defy those standards like the characters in *DFL* and *TH*, Ed uses the stigma in question to his advantage to catch Sloane for himself. Ed knows how social stigma works, and he works it to one-up Kath in the game of winning Sloane's affection.

With these observations in mind, we may see Wandor's use of the verb "ape" as an astute word choice insofar as aping means not so much just imitating (though this is the sense in which Wandor uses it) but mocking, scorning, and deriding through imitation. In fact, contrary to Wandor's doubts otherwise, queer theorist Leo Bersani would characterize *EMS*'s sardonic, radically separatist "aping" as the most liberating and socially challenging form of queer community identification, as for him "resignification cannot destroy; it merely presents to the dominant culture spectacles of politically impotent disrespect [. . .] It is, in any case, doubtful that resignification, or redeployment, or hyperbolic miming, will ever overthrow anything. These mimetic activities are too closely imbricated in the norms they continue" (51).[23] Sloane, Ed, Kath, and Kath's baby do not create a queer version of a heterosexual family; they quite simply create a queer family, a group in which all standards are overthrown. They do not try to justify their lives, but in challenging systems of normality they quite radically ask the dominant ideology to justify itself.

Compounding the trio's status as a queer community, upon Sloane's entry into the home, Kemp (this play's Father) suspects the young man of being an unsavory character (*EMS* 73), a common reaction of Fathers in the plays I am discussing. Unlike in *DFL* and *TH*, however, in *EMS* the Father's derision turns physical when Kemp attacks Sloane with a fork (*EMS* 75), a moment that Orton plays for laughs rather than uses to highlight the Injustice of the Queer Being Attacked by His/Her Oppressor. Again, Bersani's observation that "resignification [creates] little more than a consolatory community of victims" (52) elucidates the idea that this queer family does not resignify the patriarchy but, rather, challenges, indeed in some ways *victimizes* the dominant group. After all, Sloane himself is no victim, and Kemp's attack does not go unpunished. In another characteristically excessive Ortonian modification, rather than simply expel his Father from the queer community as Coward and Delaney do in their plays, Orton has Sloane kill the Father, enhancing this family's queerness and making Orton's depiction all the more radical.

Considering this violent expulsion of the Father along with Ed and Kath's blackmailing each other to win Sloane (*EMS* 145), Kath's incestuous impulses (*EMS* 95, 102), and Ed's kinky preference for leather trade (*EMS* 86-8), Bersani would say that the play's emphasis on the forbidden and on the "outlaw" nature of this play's sexual Others makes those characters all the more distinct from the majority and, hence, all the more conspicuously queer. Unlike the genteel queers of *DFL*'s drawing-room comedy, and unlike the somewhat more conventionally "familial" queers of *TH*, the rough and tumble queers of *EMS* are kitchen sink with a vengeance (perhaps Angry Young Queers?). With all its emphasis on betrayal, crime, and duplicity, *EMS* portrays sexual alterity as "truly disruptive–as a *force* not limited to the modest goals of tolerance for diverse lifestyles, but in fact mandating the politically unacceptable and politically indispensable choice of an outlaw existence" (Bersani 76). They are "*anti*communitarian" (Bersani 53) queers who reject all standard notions of relationality and community to create a truly radical space in which to live, a space in which they can, as Orton himself says, "reject all the values of society and enjoy sex" (quoted in Lahr, *Diaries*, 251).

Based upon these observations, it should be easier to recognize the interpretive missteps made by some critics of *EMS*. As noted above, for instance, Alan Sinfield's contention that the play is less revolutionarily "queer" because Orton "had difficulty conceiving a positive view of the homosexual" and "sidelined" homosexuality through "bisexual evasion" is fundamentally disproven by the text ("Orton" 182). While by the standards of conventional morality *EMS*'s characters are certainly not "positive" queer representations, Bersani's revised notions of positive and negative representations suggest that traditional moral standards are in the first place reductive ways by which to think about queer identity. This queer family is in Bersani's view the most "positive" representation of queer identity because it actively repudiates all standards of normality and manifestly defies all prescribed and prepackaged ways of living. As with Clum, Sinfield's complaint that the sexual fluidity of Orton's characters' desires "keeps a distance from very many actual homosexuals; it was not how Orton lived, or others that he knew" ("Orton" 182) presumes much about the playwright's desire to "write gay" and more importantly ignores the fact that this sexual fluidity is in close proximity to very many actual queers. It is surely how many lived then, and it is surely how many live today.

Similarly troubling is Clum's assertion that, particularly in the scene in which Ed "breathlessly" inquires about Sloane's physique (EMS 86-7), "Orton's plays are exercises in phallic power" and misogyny and that this emphasis "aligns him with the prejudices behind traditional gay stereotypes even as he was exploding those stereotypes" (133). The critic concludes that "Orton, then, is not the great gay comic writer some heterosexual critics would make him [. . .] He rejected the queen stereotype of traditional farce but had no positive vision with which to replace it; he dramatized guiltless homosexual desire but never portrayed homosexual love" (133). Here again Clum reveals his universal disdain for homosexual stereotypes, but more tellingly the critic shows his frustration with the play's lack of a "positive vision" of "homosexual love." Notwithstanding my observations above about *EMS*'s revolutionary (and so "positive"?) depiction of queer life, Clum's argument is most troubling for its assumption that Orton somehow has a responsibility as a gay writer to represent homosexual love in a positive light, an ironic assertion considering that Orton was brutally murdered by his homosexual lover, Kenneth Halliwell.

While I do not suggest that Orton could not have written of gay love if he had wanted to, I am more concerned by the onus that gay/lesbian critics like Clum place on gay writers from this or any other generation to present only "positive" depictions of gay/queer life. Certainly queers are as variably moral/amoral, law-abiding/law-breaking, honest/deceitful as any other sexual persons. Why then do we assume as queer scholars and writers that in order to "liberate" ourselves from oppressive circumstances we must *mis*represent the queer community as only a place where love blooms bright and happy gays grow? As Bersani suggests in his anticommunitarian theories, perhaps Orton's play is all the more liberationist (and, as such, all the more "positive") for its defiance of such standards, standards that seem to normalize what it means to be queer (read: homosexual) just as oppressively and as surely as heterosexist standards seek to normalize and oppress sexual Others.

In light of these three revolutionary pre-1968 depictions of queer communities in the theatre, portrayals that defied and reconceptualized accepted social standards of normality as well as accepted literary standards of dramatic representation, *Design for Living*, *A Taste of Honey*, and *Entertaining Mr. Sloane* stand as representative examples of the strategic essentialist notion that queers have always existed, if always in fluid, variable, and ever-fluctuating forms. By confusing and redefining conventional representations of both hetero- and homosexual communities, Coward, Delaney, and Orton expose the constructionist nature of sexual identity and thumb their noses at those who would attempt to pinion sexuality in easily delineated categories. In these authors' plays, *nothing* is normal; queer is the order of the day. They are plays in which, in Harold Beaver's terms, "By disqualifying the autonomy of what was deemed spontaneously immanent, the whole sexual system is fundamentally decentered and exposed" (115-16). *People are indeed different from each other*: by denying or ignoring the reality of these plays' queer community representations, as queer scholars we risk *un*exposing, *re*centering, and *rei*fying that oppressive sexual system, an effort that poses deleterious consequences for sexual liberation politics and queer literature alike.

NOTES

1. As used by Eve Kosofsky Sedgwick, "minoritist/minoritizing" are synonyms for "essentialist/essentializing." For Sedgwick's antihomophobic goals, the former terms avoid the latter's potentially dangerous question of "the origin of sexuality." Because I have no allegiance to one term over the other, and because both are frequently used in queer and gay/lesbian scholars' writing, I will use these expressions interchangeably throughout this paper. For additional information on Sedgwick's terms see *Epistemology*, p. 40.

2. However, one might well question whether full frontal nudity like in Martin Sherman's *Bent* (1979) or onstage male-male fucking like in Tony Kushner's *Angels in America Part 1: Millennium Approaches* (1993) constitute more "realistic" or "accurate" portrayals of queer life simply for their explicit representations of queer *eros*.

3. For more information on the definitions of terms used in polyamorous studies, see http://www.lovemore.com/terms.html and http://www.polyamorysociety.org/language.html.

4. Of course, the focus of this study is not sociology as such as it is on the far-reaching literary and sociological implications these three plays might have on our

understanding of queer lives past and present. As Zoltan Simon notes in his study of the family in contemporary gay and lesbian drama, little scholarly work has been completed in this area to date: "A more systematic examination of the dramatic treatment of this newly emerging family model seems to be an important task of future scholarship" (213). It is my hope that by exposing the queer family/community units in these plays I will contribute to our understanding of both the literature at hand and of what it means to be queer in a contemporary context. In regard to Simon's study, my "queer" focus is important here, as I will look more broadly at anormal family systems rather than at pseudo-heterosexual families that just happen to be populated by displaced homosexuals.

5. For extended discussions of these very public and thus highly scandalous arrests (particularly the 1870 arrests of Fanny Boulton and Stella Park, two male transvestites), see O'Connor (*Straight* 15) and Sinfield ("Private" 44).

6. One of the more visible examples of such restrictions is John Osborne's *A Patriot for Me* (1965), a play steeped in gay themes that was banned by the Lord Chamberlain and produced in a private theatre after Osborne refused to capitulate to the Chamberlain's revisions. For more information on *Patriot* see O'Connor, p. 20 and Clum, pp. 210-214.

7. Although my use of the word "queer" to describe these relationships is undoubtedly anachronistic, I maintain the strategic essentialist position that desire is desire, both constructed and essential, and that even though Coward, Delaney, and Orton did not have the word "queer" in their lexicons as it is used today, the desire depicted in their plays *is* queer (i.e., defiant of normativity). It is all the more fortunate, then, that we now have a word to describe this desire where previous efforts to describe it as gay or homosexual (the very efforts I am contesting in this paper) have proven inaccurate and misleading. For more information on the etymology of the word "queer" and its use in present-day queer politics, see William Turner's *Genealogy of Queer Theory* (Philadelphia: Temple UP, 2000), pp. 8-9.

8. For more extensive discussions of these terms, see D. A. Miller's *The Novel and the Police* (Berkeley: UC Press, 1988), p. 207 and Sedgwick's *Epistemology of the Closet*, p. 164.

9. These readings evoke memories of Havelock Ellis, who in 1897 argued that homosexuality is actually heterosexuality *inverted*, that sexual variation is actually sexual *mistake*, that queerness is *misplaced* normality (Garber 40-1). By reading closeted homosexuality in these plays, the cohort of critics I have isolated essentially read bisexuality as misplaced sexual desire and suggest that object choices are of one and only one gender. Bisexuality is obviated so that homosexuality (and, in turn, heterosexuality) might be accommodated.

10. See Sedgwick, *Epistemology*: "There exists instead a plethora of *ignorances*, and we may begin to ask questions about the labor, erotics, and economics of their human production and distribution. Insofar as ignorance is ignorance *of* a knowledge [. . .] these ignorances [. . .] are produced by and correspond to particular knowledges and circulate as part of particular regimes of truth" (8). It is my contention that by claiming ignorance of the range of queer desire, gay/lesbian scholars reify a homosexual, but hardly queer, regime of truth.

11. Just as heterosexism marginalizes homosexuality in its normalization of heterosexuality, so too does homosexism marginalize queerness in the effort to defend homosexuality from heterosexism. Such potentially well-intentioned goals run the risk of negating queer liberationist strategies. It is my belief that as queer scholars we must reas-

sess our evaluations of homosexual/queer literary representation if we are (1) to make illuminating, accurate observations about queer literature and (2) to not risk sabotaging the attempts of queer liberation strategies to acknowledge/emancipate *all* sexual Others.

12. While I have chosen to focus on Clum's formation in depth here, Andy Medhurst ("Thrill" 198), Sean O'Connor (*Straight* 12), and Alan Sinfield ("Private" 47) make very similar and similarly contestable arguments.

13. For more information on Spivak's formation, see Judith Butler, "Gender Trouble, Feminist Theory, and Psychoanalytic Discourse" in Linda J. Nicholson (ed.), *Feminism/Postmodernism* (London: Routledge, 1990), p. 325.

14. To be fair, as I shall note during my examinations of each play, the critics I am considering (Clum, Sinfield, O'Connor, and Medhurst in particular) typically acknowledge strains of queerness/bisexuality in their analyses, but those admissions are almost universally minimized in favor of the critics' larger arguments for homosexual suppression, oppression, and misrepresentation. Alan Sinfield, for example, just before his "bisexuality is the commonest evasion" quotation cited above, makes the argument that Orton's *EMS* "seems radical; it is against stereotypes and appropriates nature." Nevertheless, his argument that Orton's queer, not homosexual, play "also keeps a distance from very many actual homosexuals; it was not how Orton lived, or others that he knew" ultimately wins out in Sinfield's analysis ("Orton" 182). Despite the otherwise fine contributions many gay/lesbian scholars have made with their examinations of this literature, then, critics often misrepresent the plays by assuming they are incomplete representations of *gay* life instead of possibly complete (or, at least, not incomplete) representations of *queer* life.

15. Warren appears to use the word "gay" throughout her study for two central reasons: first, she studies an almost exclusively gay male community; second, she writes before Teresa De Lauretis's appropriation of the term "queer" to describe sexual alterity. (See Lauretis's "Queer Theory, Lesbian and Gay Studies: An Introduction" in *differences: A Journal of Feminist Cultural Studies* 3/2 (Summer 1991; special issue), pp. iii-xviii.) Nevertheless, I consider Warren's observations here because they concretely describe the social dynamics that constructed sexually "other" identities in this particular historical period. As Eve Sedgwick notes of the relationship between history and sexuality, "Modern 'sexuality' and hence modern homosexuality are so intimately entangled with the historically distinctive contexts and structures that now count as *knowledge* that such 'knowledge' can scarcely be a transparent window onto a separate realm of sexuality but, rather, itself constitutes that sexuality" (*Epistemology* 44). Thus, Warren's historical/sociological insights into gay identity formation can help us better understand the specifics of queer identity formation in these plays.

16. Such is Sinfield's reading of the play: "The emotion of Otto and Leo is homosocial, effecting a male bonding via their desire for Gilda. The relationship between the two men may be the main pressure, but its focus upon the woman depends on and effects an apparent exclusion of homosexuality" ("Private" 47).

17. Recalling the contemporary use of such similar epithets ("abominable" being the age-old favorite, stemming from Biblical use), we would also likely (and appropriately) today deem Ernest a queer-basher.

18. See Sinfield, "Orton," p. 270.

19. Garber further argues that ignoring bisexuality is an intensely political move. In her mind, for gays and lesbians to achieve stable or acceptable identities on the broad scale of identity politics, bisexuality must be simultaneously "identified" and occluded to stabilize the straight/gay binary (Garber 87). Such an equivocal move, I am arguing,

is evident in the readings made by Clum, Sinfield, and Medhurst, among others. Garber deems such argumentation the product of "'coulda-shoulda-woulda'" thinking (118): these poor gays coulda, shoulda, and woulda come out if only they'd had the gumption and resources to do so. As is, they have to resign themselves to the only partially satisfying realm of bisexuality.

20. While her observations are beyond the present scope of this paper, Michelene Wandor notes that the play was also revolutionary for breaking two other taboos: one, Jo has a relationship with a black sailor; and two, "The appearance of motherhood as subject matter (an 'outsider' subject?) breaks an unspoken taboo on theatrical content, which in the vast majority of plays is defined by issues of direct concern to men" (40). For more of Wandor's insights into *TH*, see *Look Back in Gender*, pp. 39-43.

21. Although she believes Geof is a positively represented gay character, Wandor concurs with Clum's belief that Geof's expulsion "problematizes" the homosexual (42).

22. With gratitude, I here borrow George Haggerty's phrase the "always-already queer," an expression he adapts from Jean Baudrillard to describe ostensibly ambiguous sexual identity that is at its very core queer. The assumption here is that it takes more effort *not* to see queerness than it does to see it (*pace* Sedgwick's ignorance model).

23. While Bersani's observations are made in reference to homosexuality, I wish to appropriate and expand his insights to include all forms of sexual alterity, as it has been my goal throughout this paper to expand our understanding of queerness and its presence in pre-1968 dramatic literature.

WORKS CITED

Beaver, Harold. "Homosexual Signs." *Critical Inquiry* 8 (Autumn 1981): 99-119.

Bersani, Leo. *Homos.* Cambridge: Harvard UP, 1995.

Clum, John. *Acting Gay: Male Homosexuality in Modern Drama.* New York: Columbia UP, 1994.

Coward, Noel. *Design for Living. Play Parade.* New York: Doubleday, 1933. 1-111.

D'Emilio, John. *Sexual Politics, Sexual Communities: The Making of a Homosexual Minority in the United States 1940-1970.* Chicago: U of Chicago Press, 1983.

Delaney, Shelagh. *A Taste of Honey. Seven Plays of the Modern Theatre.* New York: Grove Press, 1962. 153-224.

Dollimore, Jonathan. "The Challenge of Sexuality." *Society and Literature, 1945-1970.* Ed. Alan Sinfield. New York: Holmes & Meier, 1983. 51-85.

Foucault, Michel. *The History of Sexuality. Volume 1: An Introduction.* Trans. Robert Hurley. New York: Vintage, 1978.

Garber, Marjorie. *Vice Versa: Bisexuality and the Eroticism of Everyday Life.* New York: Simon & Schuster, 1997.

Girard, Rene. "Triangular Desire." *Literary Theory: An Introduction.* Ed. Julie Rivkin and Michael Ryan. New York: Blackwell, 1998. 225-27.

Haggerty, George. *Men in Love: Masculinity and Sexuality in the Eighteenth Century.* New York: Columbia UP, 1999.

Kushner, Tony. *Angels in America Part One: Millennium Approaches. Stages of Drama: Classical to Contemporary Theater.* 4th ed. Ed. Carl. H. Klaus, Miriam Gilbert, and Bradford S. Field, Jr. New York: Bedford/St. Martin's, 1999. 1340-73.

Lahr, John, ed. *The Orton Diaries.* New York: Harper & Row, 1986.

Lehr, Valerie. *Queer Family Values: Debunking the Myth of the Nuclear Family.* Philadelphia: Temple UP, 1999.

Medhurst, Andy. "That Special Thrill: *Brief Encounter*, Homosexuality, and Authorship." *Screen* 32:2 (Summer 1991): 197-208.

O'Connor, Sean. *Straight Acting: Popular Gay Drama from Wilde to Rattigan.* London: Cassell, 1998.

Orton, Joe. *Entertaining Mr. Sloane. Joe Orton: The Complete Plays.* New York, Grove Press, 1976. 63-150.

Polyamory Language Page. Home page. 2 March 2003. <http://www.polyamorysociety.org/language.html>.

Rudy, Kathy. "'Where Two or More Are Gathered: Using Gay Communities as a Model for Christian Sexual Ethics." *Our Families, Our Values: Snapshots of Queer Kinship.* Eds. Robert E. Goss and Amy Adams Squire Strongheart. New York: Haworth, 1997. 197-216.

Sedgwick, Eve Kosofsky. *Between Men.* New York: Columbia UP, 1985.

_____. *Epistemology of the Closet.* Berkeley: UC Press, 1990.

Simon, Zoltan. "Homosexuality and the Family: Redefining Notions of Marriage, Parenthood, and Family in Contemporary Gay and Lesbian Drama." *Journal of Evolutionary Psychology* 3-4 (1998): 208-14.

Sinfield, Alan. *Cultural Politics–Queer Reading.* Philadelphia: U of Pennsylvania Press, 1994.

_____. "Private Lives/Public Theater: Noel Coward and the Politics of Homosexual Representation." *Representations* 36 (Fall 1991): 43-63.

_____. "Who Was Afraid of Joe Orton?" *Sexual Sameness: Textual Differences in Lesbian and Gay Writing.* Ed. Joseph Bristow. London: Routledge, 1992.

Turner, William B. *Genealogy of Queer Theory.* Philadelphia: Temple UP, 2000.

Wandor, Michelene. *Look Back in Gender: Sexuality and the Family in Post-War British Drama.* London: Methuen, 1987.

Warren, Carol A. B. *Identity and Community in the Gay World.* New York: John Wiley & Sons, 1974.

Weeks, Jeffrey. "Against Nature." In *Homosexuality: Which Homosexuality?* Ed. Dennis Altman et al. Amsterdam: Free University/Schorer Foundation, 1987. 206.

Wishon, Brad. "The Transforming Power of Queer Love." *Our Families, Our Values: Snapshots of Queer Kinship.* Eds. Robert E. Goss and Amy Adams Squire Strongheart. New York: Haworth, 1997. 107-13.

The Power Dynamics of Cheating:
Effects on Polyamory and Bisexuality

Pepper Mint

http://www.haworthpress.com/web/JB
© 2004 by The Haworth Press, Inc. All rights reserved.
Digital Object Identifier: 10.1300/J159v04n03_04

[Haworth co-indexing entry note]: "The Power Dynamics of Cheating: Effects on Polyamory and Bisexuality." Mint, Pepper. Co-published simultaneously in *Journal of Bisexuality* (Harrington Park Press, an imprint of The Haworth Press, Inc.) Vol. 4, No. 3/4, 2004, pp. 55-76; and: *Plural Loves: Designs for Bi and Poly Living* (ed: Serena Anderlini-D'Onofrio) Harrington Park Press, an imprint of The Haworth Press, Inc., 2004, pp. 55-76. Single or multiple copies of this article are available for a fee from The Haworth Document Delivery Service [1-800-HAWORTH, 9:00 a.m. - 5:00 p.m. (EST). E-mail address: docdelivery@haworthpress.com].

SUMMARY. Rampant scorn of cheating is used to reinforce monogamy in our culture. The author argues that cheating and monogamy are interdependent, and should be addressed together, since each position in a cheating situation provides scripted opportunities for personal power. He also observes that the tools of cultural conformity that are used against cheaters will also be deployed against both polyamory and bisexuality. Simply denying the conceptual link between cheating and polyamory or between cheating and bisexuality will not prevent this. Polyamorous people need to emphasize the relationship between monogamy and cheating. Finally, he suggests that bisexuals need to use new forms of visible nonmonogamy to create visible bisexuality. Polyamory and bisexuality are conceptually connected through a common oppression, so activism that aids one community will inadvertently aid the other. *[Article copies available for a fee from The Haworth Document Delivery Service: 1-800-HAWORTH. E-mail address: <docdelivery@haworthpress.com> Website: <http://www.HaworthPress.com>* © 2004 by The Haworth Press, Inc. All rights reserved.]

KEYWORDS. Monogamy, cheating, polyamory, bisexuality, monosexuality, duality, adultery

INTRODUCTION

My purpose in this article is to unearth the relationship between cheating and power. In the first section, I describe the cultural treatment of cheating in the United States. The following section argues that the construction of cheating forms part of a monogamous system of enforcement. Following that, I lay out the power dynamics of cheating on a personal level, establishing the cheating dynamic as a tool of interpersonal power. The "Cheating and Polyamory" section delineates the ways that the cheating construction and the cheating dynamic are used to hamper polyamory. The "Cheating and Bisexuality" section does the same for bisexuality, drawing connections from the cheating construction to the invisibility of bisexuality. The final section notes that bisexuality and polyamory share a common opposition in the cheating dynamic, and concludes that joining conceptual forces is critical for the political success of both communities.

THE CULTURAL RESPONSE TO CHEATING

Cheating and cheaters are almost universally disdained in our culture. Self-help books, talk shows, tabloids, and big Hollywood productions all agree: cheating is bad. Cheaters and adulterers are dishonest, sick individuals who need to be dumped, divorced, or at the minimum castigated. Cheaters need to change the error of their ways.

I generally agree that cheating is dishonest. However, I think that there is a lot more to cheating than bad behavior and its consequences. Specifically, the cultural response to cheating is more self-serving than it is righteous.

Cheating Is Commonplace and Expected

Cheating in the U.S. is like smoking weed in California: it's definitely against the rules, and it could land you in serious trouble, but nobody is surprised when they find out you've been doing it. This is because a significant portion of the population cheats. Everyone knows someone who has cheated or has been cheated on, or both. At various points, surveys have confirmed that cheating is a culture-wide occurrence.[1]

The act of cheating is what I call an "expected failure." It is well-scripted by the media and the culture at large: people know how to cheat, what happens when you cheat, and how other folks are supposed to react. People who cheats are not doing anything particularly revolutionary (in an ideological sense), but rather following an over-determined plan fed to them by movies, television, and their acquaintances.

In other words, our culture condemns cheating while providing people with enough information and role models to make the act of cheating conceptually and emotionally easy. Seen this way, cheating is at its base a normal act and the people who do it are normal people, even though they are not behaving as the cultural norms say they should.

Cheating as a Spectacle

Our culture and media create a circus spectacle of cheating. For example, think of Clinton's Oval Office and the stains on the dress. Tabloids do the same thing on a weekly basis. Movies unceasingly address cheating and adultery as a major plot device. However, none of these compare with the assault of infidelity brought to us by talk shows and reality shows like *Temptation Island*.

The same spectacularization is carried out on an interpersonal level. When people discuss relationships, their assessment of the likelihood of cheating is often included. Knowledge of actual cheating spreads through a social group like wildfire. People in relationships consult with outside experts such as counselors and private detectives when they are suspicious of cheating or after a cheating drama has unfolded. The constant discussion around cheating keeps it fresh in everyone's mind, creating a sustained level of fear and vigilance.

The reason we raise a common sin to high theatre is to provide an example of what not to do. The visible reenactment of the cheating drama names a common temptation, draws a supposedly typical person into that temptation, and then lays out the terrible results of their fall from grace. The spectacle of the discovered cheater or adulterer is a modern morality play, with a fairly fixed script that is endlessly reused. In this spectacle, the cheater plays the common cultural part of the demonized other, a yardstick that normal people can measure their morals against. Like other systems of demonization, this one operates by naming the outsider ("cheater") and leaving the normative behavior unnamed and unexamined. In order to describe people who are not cheaters, we have to make up nouns like "cheatee" or "monogamist."

It is the ubiquity of this spectacle that makes it into an effective morality tool. People watch repetitive cheating plots on television not because they are entertained, but because they are moralizing. The cheating script is so well established that when the Clinton/Lewinsky scandal broke, everyone knew what to do. Bill Clinton knew that he should apologize tearfully, Hillary knew that she should forgive him equally tearfully, and the Congressmen knew that they should descend like zealous missionaries on a moral quest. With everyone behaving as they should, the public was satisfied, even though we have no idea what really happened in the Clintons' relationship.

Talk shows and other forms of public spectacle can therefore praise and reinforce monogamy without even mentioning it. They do this by endlessly condemning its opposite. This is the common cultural trick of validating a cultural norm by interrogating and demeaning violations of the norm, and it has been used throughout the last century to implicitly praise heterosexuality (by condemning homosexuality), sex for procreation only (by pathologizing all other sexual acts), and white people (by maintaining focus on the problems of non-white people), to name a few examples.

Cheaters Are Marked and Punished

A discovered adulterer faces very real social and economic consequences. Divorce law in many states punishes adultery, through financial settlements and the removal of children. Unmarried cheaters do not have as many legal repercussions, but often face social disapproval and the economic problems associated with breaking up.

Worse, cheating is often understood to signify an essential moral weakness. Once a person has cheated, we expect them to do it again, or we expect them to have to fight the temptation from that point onward. In this manner a cheater is marked for life. This marking is not as strong as others used in our culture (like "homosexual" or "drug addict"), but the act of cheating is attached to the person and their body (through imagined uncontrollable lust) in a very similar manner.

THE MONOGAMY/CHEATING SYSTEM

The Conceptual Apparatus of Cheating Enforces Monogamous Standards

Monogamy needs cheating in a fundamental way. In addition to serving as the demonized opposite of monogamy, the mark of the cheater is used as a threat to push individuals to conform to monogamous behavior and monogamous appearances.

Actual sexual behavior is just the beginning of this enforcement. The appearance of monogamy is very important in our culture, and we generally feel the need to maintain a certain monogamous decorum in view of friends and acquaintances (in addition to the actual partner). The purpose of this decorum is to avoid gossip, scorn, scandal, and possibly exposure to the partner. (In my experience, the social group is often more critical than the monogamous partner.) The actual level and manner of imposed self-restriction varies greatly depending on the social circle and situation, but our culture attaches sexual or romantic meaning to a whole host of actions that are not explicitly sexual or romantic. Some of these actions are: traveling with a person, spending a lot of time with one person at a party, helping someone financially, talking about someone when they are not present, spending time alone with someone, meeting their parents, holding hands, and of course flirting, touching, or smiling too much. All of these actions are signifiers of a possible sexual relationship in our culture, and this is what makes them socially dangerous. In order to avoid a sexual subtext, a person in a monogamous relationship must act carefully if they are with someone of an attractive gender who is not their partner. Through this mechanism, the social control of monogamy escapes the bedroom and inserts itself into everyday situations, by policing not just sexual activity but any activity that symbolizes the possibility of sex.

Monogamy is thus a locus through which social power is exercised, one of a number of such loci which are ostensibly based in the body but really act almost entirely through social discourse. The cultural ideas of cheating and adultery do one portion the work of enforcing monogamy; the other portion is accomplished through jealousy.

Cheating and Monogamy: A False Duality

Our culture sets us up with a false choice: we are faithful or we are cheating. Both options are highly scripted and allow the operation of power through restrictions. However, this false choice hides the fact that monogamy and cheating form a single ideological system, and it is possible to step outside of the system. In fact, ideological resistance to monogamy often takes the form of a repudiation of the entire system, by denying both the monogamist and cheater roles. Lesbian communes in the seventies, gay male subcultures, sex radicals, bisexual communities, and polyamorous people have all accomplished a certain distancing from both monogamy and cheating.

Western (specifically U.S.) culture is laden with false identity dualities of this nature: man/woman, heterosexual/homosexual, black/white, virgin/whore, etc. The monogamist/cheater duality is not as strongly based in identity as some of these, but the false duality forms a single power-infused system in a manner similar to other systems (the system of race, the sex/gender system, the system of sexuality, the madonna/whore complex). Each one of these systems has a false unexamined assumption at its core. The monogamy/infidelity system is based on the assumption that sexual fidelity is natural and always desirable.

Because monogamy and cheating are oppositional choices, they are conceptually interdependent and cannot be successfully addressed independently. They represent two sides of the same coin, one shiny and one tarnished.

Resistance to dualistic systems of power can take the form of addressing the power inequality (feminism, the civil rights movement, slut pride) or it can try to expose and jettison the entire system (the transgender movement, bisexuality, lesbian separatism). We have seen both forms make up the resistance to the monogamist/cheater system. Polyamory seeks to rewrite the rules inherent to the system. The emergent "down low" identity seeks to put a positive and sexy spin on unsanctioned sex.[2] Websites such as the Ashley Madison Agency[3] do the same for women. Certain sexual identities, such as bisexuality, carry inherent resistance to monogamy as part of their very definition. By acknowledging more than one desire, bisexuality makes a lie of the monogamous myth of a single object of sexual desire.

INTERPERSONAL POWER DYNAMICS IN THE MONOGAMY/CHEATING SYSTEM

It Takes Two to Cheat

The second person is the "cheatee," the person who is cheated on.

At a personal level, the drama of cheating requires that the cheatee is hurt or offended in some way. If the original partner does not care what their lover does, then it is hard to create blame in a situation where no one is hurt, though the social circle surrounding the couple may consider the arrangement weird, scandalous, or just a bad idea. (Note that the culture at large still considers such arrangements to be cheating, even when everyone is knowledgeable and happy with the situation.) While social scorn is definitely powerful stuff, it can be ignored. The full pain of the cheating experience requires that the cheatee feel dismayed, betrayed, jealous, and so on. In this manner the monogamy/cheating system relies on the role of monogamist (or cheatee) to ensure that the actual cheating experience matches its depiction in the media as painful and damaging.

The role of monogamist or cheatee is largely unexamined in our society, in order to protect it from criticism. Once we make monogamous people visible, it becomes possible to address monogamy directly. Any assault on the monogamist/cheater power system requires a critique of this invisible yet empowered role.

Cheating as a Way to Take Power and Create Personal Happiness

So far I have discussed cultural and personal responses to cheating, but I have left the cheater unexamined. I believe that every action a person takes is for a good reason involving personal gain, and cheating is no exception.

Cheaters get their cake and get to eat it too. In addition to the physical and emotional fun of an outside affair, cheaters retain the privileges and trappings of monogamy. (I believe that this win/win situation is the "cheating" that cheating actually refers to. The cheater is actually cheating the rules of monogamy itself.) The retained benefits include the monogamous intensity of the primary relationship, the social privileges of the relationship, and the social privileges and validation accorded to the appearance of monogamy. Though most people would like to think that cheating always takes the form of a short-term affair, cheating situations can actually last years, decades, or a lifetime, so the cheater may actually reap their benefits for quite some time. The actual experience of cheating can be very different from its media portrayal as a dead-end disaster.

The idea that cheating is always temporary and unstable helps cheaters maintain a monogamous identity even in the face of their own nonmonogamy. Presenting cheating as part of a choosing process allows the cheater to be read as essentially monogamous even when they are not acting monogamous. Using cheating as a mechanism for reading monogamy into nonmonogamous situations conveniently returns cheaters to monogamy. So if a cheater simply refutes one of their relationships or claims to be in the process of choosing, they can avoid being marked as morally suspect, even when exposed.

In addition, the act of being exposed as a cheater (or more often, self-exposing) actually carries its own power benefits. It can be used as an emotional bludgeon or a reminder that leaving the relationship is possible. Possible future cheating is often used as a threat to coerce behavior.

If a cheater is unmarried and childless, they can usually avoid the worst legal consequences of cheating. Often cheatees are just as scared to expose the affair as cheaters, due to the social pity and scandal that will be heaped upon them, and because the other benefits they receive from the relationship outweigh the power gain from exposure. While the outside affair typically ends at exposure, the cheater can pick up a new one or revive the old one and start the cycle over again.

So we should not be surprised at the culture-wide prevalence of cheating: while it is officially condemned, it constitutes an available and well-scripted grab for personal power and pleasure. Media depictions of cheaters assume that most or all cheaters are men, but women and men actually have outside affairs at a similar rate.[4]

A political move against the monogamist/cheater system should address the failings of cheating as well as the inherent weaknesses of monogamy. However, criticizing cheaters as dishonest or bad people is not an effective way to do this, because it serves to reinforce the system itself. Rather, cheaters should be located within the system that makes cheating advantageous, in order to expose the underlying problems of monogamy.

It Takes Three to Cheat

The third person is the "other woman" or "other man." (I will just refer to the "other lover.") The very name of this position implies both an outsider quality and a competitive aspect. The other lover is generally frowned upon by our culture, in a manner somewhat similar to cheaters. (For example, the term "adulterer" can be applied to either a cheater or the other lover.) The suspense and horror sections of the video store are full of movies whose plots revolve around an encroachment by a lover, usually a woman. The other lover typically ends up dead or confined in these movies. In short, the other lover is generally stigmatized on a culture-wide level.

In a system of monogamy, any three-person situation is assumed to be unstable and short-term. Therefore, our culture considers a cheating situation to embody a competition between the faithful partner and the other lover. To the extent that the affair is successful or continues, the outside lover is seen as "winning," and the primary relationship is losing. If the affair is halted, the primary relationship wins, and the other lover loses. The end goal of the affair (and of the other lover) is supposedly to end the primary relationship and establish the affair as the new primary relationship. In other words, affairs are seen as an attempt to steal the cheating person.

In this manner, the outside lover has a certain prestige linked to their ability to attract the cheater and maintain the affair. The outside lover gains personal power as the cheater turns towards them, and loses it as they turn away. It is this power to steal or compete that makes the other lover a somewhat attractive position in the cultural imagination.

In conjunction with this accorded power, the stigma of the other lover is much more forgiving than that of cheater. In our culture, the other lover is not necessarily marked as morally weak or corrupt, as the cheater is. They are seen as taking actions that are reasonable or understandable, though still bad. The affair is not so much their fault as it is the fault of the cheater. The culture recognizes the other lover role as a legitimate power grab. Aside from the occasional "loss of companionship" lawsuit, there are no legal repercussions to being the other lover.[5]

The role of the other lover is well-scripted by our culture (and not entirely negatively) and therefore forms a real alternative relationship position, albeit one that is simultaneously demonized by the culture that acknowledges it.

The Monogamy/Cheating System and the False Duality Between Couples and Three-Person Cheating Situations

The other lover role, along with the cheater and monogamist roles, forms a lopsided V-structure relationship format. The monogamy/cheating ideological system simultaneously acknowledges the possibility of this three-person situation and (often falsely) characterizes it as unstable, short-term, competitive, and painful for everyone involved. The stigmatized V-structure is cast as the only alternative to the normative couple, and it is used as an example of what couples should not do.

The monogamy/cheating system is therefore setting these two relationship models in opposition (as a second false duality). Monogamy gives us only one model for a three-person situation, and it is not a pretty one.

It should be noted that four-person relationships (often called quads in poly terminology) and larger group arrangements fall prey to the same stereotyping. Any larger arrangement (or a fully connected triad) can be broken down into multiple V-structures, each of which can be separately cast as a problematic (cheating) V-structure. In other words, mainstream culture does not really address large and complex relationship structures directly, but instead breaks them into smaller components for consideration. These smaller pieces are then compared directly to the cheating dynamic.

Any three-person or larger situation is viewed as having unbearable and destabilizing internal tensions, even if no such tensions actually exist. In this manner the monogamy/cheating duality is used to stigmatize any nonmonogamous arrangement, even structures that do not resemble the cheating V-structure.

Polyamory and Bisexuality Provide Three-Person Structures Not Modeled on Cheating

Polyamory gives us other positive models for three-person relationships, and these models break this false duality. The V-structure, the simple fact of one person loving two (or more) other people, can be seen as the basis from which all polyamorous arrangements spring. Much of the difficulty and the reward of polyamory is that it seeks to reclaim the stigmatized V-structure as cooperative, long-term, and positive for everyone involved.

Bisexuality provides another alternative V-structure, but this one is based in desire. By definition, a bisexual has the ability to desire more than one gender. Because desire is heavily based in gender object choice, this implies that bisexuals have the ability to desire more than one sort of person. These multiple desire possibilities can be conceptualized as a V of desire, with the two points of the V representing desire for men and women. In his book *The Bisexual Option*, Fritz Klein refers to this as "dual sexuality."[6] Of course, the desires of actual bisexuals are much more complex and interesting than this simple representation, and this simple V does not address the possibility of transgendered object choices. However, mainstream culture almost always imagines bisexual desire as forked because it the easiest way to compare bisexuality to heterosexual monogamy. Because monogamous heterosexuality is one gender/one desire/one partner, monogamous heterosexual people will conceptualize bisexuality as two genders/two desires/two partners.

The ability to desire more than one gender therefore implies that it is done simultaneously. Mainstream culture always imagines bisexuality as involving simultaneous relationships with at least one man and one woman, forming a relationship V. While this is very different from the way bisexuals actually live their lives, this mainstream assumption means that bisexuality always carries connotations of nonmonogamy.

When bisexuality and nonmonogamy are actually combined, another alternative structure emerges: the erotic triangle. The erotic triangle is not just a collection of other V-structures, but is also a basic relationship structure in its own right, somewhat divorced from the mainstream culture's couple-based models. Bisexual and homosexual polyamorists have been taking advantage of this, forming triads and larger interconnected relationships. These triangles always stand in opposition to cheating dynamics, as they can be seen as healing the rivalry between the cheatee and the other lover.[7]

CHEATING AND POLYAMORY

Polyamory and the Monogamy/Cheating System

The maintenance of false dualities depends on their ability to relegate any ambiguous behavior (or appearance) to the negative category. The monogamy/cheating duality is no exception; any behavior that is not clearly monogamy can be considered cheating, even if it does not fit the formal definition of cheating.

This is the conceptual trap that polyamory falls into. While it is fairly rare for someone to outright claim that polyamory is always cheating, mainstream culture will deal with polyamory as if it were cheating at any particular level: in the media, in the legal system, in social interactions, and even within personal relationships. For example, surveys on adultery or cheating rarely differentiate between approved extra-relationship sex and illicit extra-relationship sex, considering any such sex to constitute cheating.[8] In a similar vein, divorce laws generally do not distinguish between sanctioned and unsanctioned extra-marital sex in their definitions of adultery.

At the social (or media) level, people who know polyamorists will typically assume that there exists some level of tension between the various relationships. This assumption is an implicit comparison to the cheater's V-structure relationship. If there is no preexisting tension between relationships in a polyamorous situation, then this assumption by outsiders constitutes a social pressure to create tension. The social pressure shows itself when a monogamous person discovers that their friend's relationship includes a third partner, and immediately asks, "Well how does [the partner they know about] feel about this?" Other assumptions, like the assumption of a hierarchy of relationships, occur when observers equate polyamory with cheating. Each one of these assumptions creates pressure for its own ratification. In this way, the implicit social comparison of polyamory to cheating attempts to recreate the power dynamics of cheating (and therefore monogamy) within polyamorous relationships.

The pressure to imitate cheating power dynamics can come from inside a polyamorous relationship as well as from outside. Polyamorists, as members of the culture, have access to all of the conceptual power mechanisms available in the cheating V-structure, and often use them. While polyamorists usually do not identify with the monogamy/cheating system, they can easily internalize the dynamics of the cheating situation. The practice of polyamory requires that poly people constantly resist this internalization.

Polyamorous culture and publications are not necessarily immune to this internalization, either. I consider the heavy focus on primary/secondary arrangements in poly discussions to reflect an inherent comparison with the cheating V-structure.[9] Also, the common assumption that polyamory is somehow essentially more difficult than monogamy seems to be based in the assumption of power dynamics similar to those found in cheating situations. [10]

Legal and Financial Penalties of Cheating and Polyamory

Child custody laws and fault-based divorce are two legal avenues through which nonmonogamy of any sort can be punished. In the case of divorce, it is possible to lose child custody or monetary awards through sleeping around. Even outside of divorce, unfit parent laws can be used to remove a child from the home of a polyamorist. This has already happened, to someone who agreed to be interviewed for a television documentary.[11] Any form of poly visibility will generally be followed by similar legal attacks.

A lack of discrimination laws is another concern. Right now it is legal to discriminate based on sexual or relationship behavior in most states. Coming out as poly can result in the loss of a job or housing, with no recourse.

Changing this legal situation should be a priority of the polyamorous movement. However, the current laws are based on the assumptions of the monogamy/cheating system, and those assumptions must be altered before the laws can be changed.

The Success of the Polyamory Movement and Its Escape of the Cheating Label

So long as polyamorists are placed within the monogamous/cheating duality, they will be forced to reenact the cultural scripts of cheating. Polyamory itself is an attempt to create a valid third option, in the ideological space between the two existing options. To leave the negative side of the duality, poly people either need to expand the definition of monogamy or restrict the definition of cheating. Both routes have been attempted, but because monogamy is overly restricted and cheating is so vague, they have had more luck redefining cheating.

The poly movement is taking advantage of a conceptual disparity between one particular definition of cheating (rule breaking or dishonesty) and its general usage (any nonmonogamous act). In other words, polyamorists are saying, "If no one lies, it isn't cheating." Even though most people will agree, this is still a radical step, because it forces the culture to consider the feelings of the relationship members in addition to the actual physical acts.

Polyamorists often push the redefinition project on a personal level by disparaging cheating or cheaters. A polyamorist who puts down cheating is implicitly saying, "I am not a cheater" and therefore "polyamory is not cheating." A monogamist who says "cheating is bad" is usually implicitly including polyamorists, and is therefore using a different definition than a polyamorist who says the same thing. The focus on extreme forms of honesty in polyamorous literature and culture can be seen as an attempt to distance polyamory from cheating and (by extension) to roll back the usage of cheating so that it does not include polyamory. [12]

CHEATING AND BISEXUALITY

In her book *Bisexuality and the Eroticism of Everyday Life*, Marjorie Garber states that visibility is a central problem of modern bisexuality. [13] This begs the question, what is it that keeps bisexuality invisible? It is not just assumptions of heterosexuality. There is a certain conceptual difficulty to performing bisexuality, which we can trace to monogamy/cheating.

The monogamy/cheating system makes bisexuality invisible in a two-stage process. First, the assumptions of monogamy hide the fact that there are monogamous bisexuals. Second, bisexuals are assumed to be cheaters in the same way that poly people are assumed to be cheaters.

The Myth of the One True Love and Bisexual Invisibility

Monogamy is not just the idea that you have sex with only one person at a time. It also includes the myth of the one true love, the idea that a particular person is really only attracted to one other person during the course of their entire lives. Most people recognize this as an entirely unrealistic proposition, but it shapes our understanding of relationships nonetheless. Modern relationships go to great lengths to create and maintain the illusion of the one true love. Because of the need to maintain this façade, it is common for people to repudiate their earlier attractions as somehow hollow or false. Even if there is no such repudiation, the social circle will act as if there had been, conveniently forgetting old attractions. In other words, the only desire given social validity is a person's current relationship.

This social myopia prevents the culture from recognizing the possibility of monogamous bisexuals. If a person is seeing only one other person, then they are unable to claim attraction to more than one gender in a manner that is believable. Specifically, the culture at large will refuse to recognize their earlier attractions as legitimate. The Anne Heche/Ellen DeGeneres Hollywood romance is a great example of this in action. When Anne and Ellen started dating, the tabloids all assumed that Anne was a lesbian, and that she had been a lesbian all along. (Apparently the string of men she had relationships with earlier did not count.) When they broke up and Anne went on to date some new man, she was suddenly straight and her affair with Ellen was recast as a passing fancy. Using this sexual identity sleight-of-hand, the media managed to avoid any serious consideration of bisexuality, even though most people would consider Anne's overall behavior to be bisexual.

Because of the myth of the one true love (or desire), the mainstream imagines bisexuality to be inherently nonmonogamous. Mainstream depictions of bisexuality (such as the movies *Basic Instinct* and *Y Tu Mama Tambien*, as well as the spate of "bisexual chic" magazine articles in the mid-90s) universally depict the bisexual as having simultaneous relationships with both men and women, preferably in the same bed at the same time.[14] Garber calls this concurrent bisexuality, and differentiates it from sequential bisexuality, where a bisexual person dates only one gender at a time.[15] Our culture's persistent refusal to acknowledge a person's erotic history makes it difficult or impossible to present as a sequential or monogamous bisexual.

Of course, most real bisexuals do not spend all their social time with a gender on each arm. Bisexuals move in and out of relationships, and life often catches them dating only one gender. There are plenty of self-identified monogamous bisexuals, though they seem to be a minority within bisexuality (possibly due to this failure of the cultural imagination). Monogamous bisexuals often have difficulty claiming both monogamy and bisexuality, above and beyond the normal bisexual identity issues. People assume that monogamous bisexuals are actually monosexual (based on the gender of their current attraction) even when they actively claim a bisexual identity. Bisexuality becomes invisible in monogamous situations.

Concurrent Bisexuality Compared to Cheating

This begs the question, why are concurrent bisexuals also invisible, even though they fulfill the mainstream image of the bisexual? Concurrent bisexuals fall into the same conceptual trap as polyamory: because they are not monogamous, they are treated as cheaters. Note that this happens as a direct comparison instead of a logical two-stage process. Because our culture conceptualizes bisexuality as inherently nonmonogamous, a single set of associations are drawn directly from bisexuality to cheating, instead of being drawn from bisexuality to nonmonogamy to cheating. In this view, bisexuality is just another form of nonmonogamy, and is therefore cheating. Because bisexuality is read as cheating, all of the social, legal, emotional, and interpersonal repercussions of cheating can be used to repress bisexuality.

Media representations of bisexuality mirror this association, frequently presenting bisexuality in the context of cheating. A recent article in the *New York Times Magazine* on the emerging down low identity follows this pattern.[16] The "down low" is both an identity and a descriptive term for black and Latino men who sleep with other men but keep their liaisons hidden from relatives, friends, and partners. The men on the down low interviewed in the article did not consider themselves bisexual, and actually denied it during the interviews. However, the article relentlessly brings up comparisons to closeted gay and bisexual men, creating a connection even in the face of this denial. The article focuses on black and Latino men who cheat on their wives and girlfriends by sleeping with other men, supposedly providing a route of AIDS infection. (Other articles in the down low moral panic follow the same pattern.) In this article, bisexuality is presented as leading directly to cheating, even requiring it, even though some of the men in the article are not actually cheating.

The down low moral panic is a mirror image of the (white) bisexual male AIDS panic of the 1980s, with the added bonus of racist stigma. In both cases, the men involved did not actually identify as bisexual, but the media imposed the bisexual label on them. In both cases, male bisexuality was presented as being synonymous with cheating and infection.

It is not just bisexual men that suffer from the association of bisexuality with cheating. The central bisexual character in *Basic Instinct* sets up a rivalry between her long-term woman lover and her recent male lover. The rivalry ends when the man drives the woman off the road, killing her. This is the classic cheating scenario of a stolen lover, even though there is little or no secrecy involved. Other suspense movies (*Poison Ivy*, for example) ritually present bisexual women in cheating situations.

The persistent cultural association of bisexuality and cheating imbues bisexuality with some of the qualities of cheating. In particular, cheating is incorrectly seen as a temporary arrangement, a process of choosing between two stable (monogamous) possibilities. Seeing bisexuality through the lens of cheating allows the mainstream to view it as a temporary arrangement, even in the face of long-term concurrent bisexual behavior. Bisexuality is therefore rationalized as a short-lived situation, the process of moving between two stable (monosexual) desires.

The casting of bisexuality as temporary state of choosing ("just a phase") is actually an attempt to erase bisexuality itself, by reducing it to a summation of two monosexual possibilities. We can pretend that a cheater is a monogamous person in transition, and we can use the same logic to pretend that a bisexual is a monosexual in transition. Attempts to recast bisexuality as cheating are therefore attempts to invalidate bisexuality altogether, making it into an invisible stepping stone between two visible sexuality choices.

This explains why the media brought bisexuality into articles describing the down low lifestyle, even though everyone interviewed refused the bisexual label. It was simultaneously an attempt to discredit the men involved (as being closeted) and an attempt to discredit bisexuality (as being hidden, ephemeral, and transitory). The down low articles managed the neat trick of contributing to the invisibility of bisexuality by bringing up the possibility of bisexuality.[17]

THE BI/POLY ALLIANCE

Polyamory and Bisexuality Aid Each Other

In a chapter on literary erotic triangles, Garber suggests an innovative strategy based on the connection between cheating and bisexuality. Instead of reading bisexuality as cheating, she reverses the relationship, and reads heterosexual cheating as bisexuality. Heterosexual cheating becomes bisexuality because the rivalry between the two men (in her examples) is itself a homosocial relationship.[18] Garber's bisexual reading suggests a political strategy: cheating and other forms of nonmonogamy are potential sites for bisexual visibility.

This is already happening in the poly movement. There is a strange connection between bisexual and poly identities. Informal online surveys show that about half of online poly people identify as bisexual.[19] In my personal experience, bisexuals tend to be nonmonogamous, and most of the bi folk I know are poly.

On the surface, the connection between bisexuality and polyamory appears as a number of happy coincidences. Bi people and poly people appear in the same subcultures and social groups. Both polyamory and bisexuality borrow concepts and ideology from the gay and lesbian movements, and align themselves with those movements. Both bi and poly ideologies speak of freedom, openness, and possibility. Bi people tend to develop polyamorous identities and poly people tend to develop bisexual identities.

These surface correlations are really a reflection of deeper conceptual connections. Both bisexuality and polyamory seem to reflect a certain "greedy" attitude towards sex and relationships, one that refuses to accept limitations on intimacy. Note that cheaters are "greedy" in a similar way, because they gain the advantages of both monogamy and nonmonogamy. In fact, both bisexuals and poly people qualify as "cheaters" in that they are cheating the system: they purposefully break the rules of attraction and try to get away with it. Bisexuals cheat the rules of a single gender attraction. Poly people cheat the rules of sexual and emotional exclusivity. Both sets of rules are instrumental for the maintenance of the monogamy/cheating system.

In other words, polyamory and bisexuality are facing off against the same conceptual opposition, specifically the monogamy/cheating duality and the myth of the one true love. It is this shared opposition that makes them convenient bedfellows. If a person can take the steps necessary to claim one of the two identities, they will have done most of the work to claim the other identity. This conceptual linkage is evidenced in the way the two identities enable each other. Poly people are typically given the relationship space to experiment with their own desire, making the move towards bisexuality much easier. Bisexuals are used to dealing with a multiplicity of desire, which eases the transition to polyamory.

Polyamory and the Production of Bisexual Visibility

Visibility is currently a central problem in bisexual liberation. While the possibility of bisexuality seems to be everywhere, it is rare to see the actual ratification of that possibility in the form of visible bisexuals. Bisexuality is difficult to perform. Part of this is invisibility of sequential bisexuality, caused by the myth of the one true love. The other part is the invisibility of concurrent bisexuality produced by the monogamy/cheating duality. The former invisibility can be addressed by creating new forms of sexuality that incorporate understanding of a person's erotic history, but this unfortunately requires reconstructing love and sexuality. However, the latter invisibility can be addressed through bisexual-friendly forms of nonmonogamy.

Unfortunately most nonmonogamous movements have been distinctly unfriendly to bisexuality. Historically, this includes movements as diverse as swinging, gay bathhouse culture, and lesbian-feminist communes. There is a certain desperate quality to this opposition: any form of nonmonogamy carries connotations of bisexuality, because it also opposes the monogamy/cheating system. In other words, these groups are unfriendly to bisexuality partly because their nonmonogamy exposes them to allegations of bisexual deviance.

Polyamory seems to be an exception. This is largely for historical and cultural reasons: both movements have grown from the same ideology, and they have shared a significant overlap of members and subcultures. In fact, the large number of bi people in the poly movement provides evidence that bisexuality is one of the major driving forces behind polyamory. In other words, polyamory was created and spread partly to satisfy the need for bisexual relationship structures. Bisexuality has been heavily represented within polyamory at least through the 1990s, and it shows up in every major poly publication. Furthermore, poly people have pursued a strategy of coming out based on LBGT tactics.

This production of visible polyamory enables visible bisexuality. To the extent that polyamory is believable, bisexual polyamory will be believable, because it is simply polyamory with partners of different genders. The monogamy/cheating duality is a trap for bisexuality, but the conceptual victories of polyamory can provide bisexuality with a way out. To the extent that polyamory can escape the monogamy/cheating duality, it will create a hole that bisexuality can also escape through.

It therefore comes as no surprise that poly activism is one of the most dynamic areas of contemporary bisexual activism. Poly forums routinely address and validate bisexuality. Poly outreach will bring up bisexuality, because the majority of poly activists are also bisexual. In our current cultural moment, there is a certain inevitability about this connection: anywhere polyamory goes, bisexuality will travel with it. Poly activism is bi activism.

The corollary is that polyphobia will often also qualify as biphobia. For example, some LBGT speaking organizations discourage poly people from joining or speaking about their poly experiences, in order to make the group more palatable to the mainstream. Unfortunately, this practice makes it hard to perform bisexuality, reducing the visibility or believability of the bisexuals in the group.

Bisexual and poly activists should keep this connection in mind, because it makes activism that much easier. This is not to say that bi activists necessarily need to push polyamory or vice versa, but rather that the two communities allied will grow much faster than they would grow individually.

There are a number of ways that this cross-enabling can inform bi and poly activism. Bi activists should address polyphobia and poly activists should address biphobia: either prejudice hurts both causes. They should recognize that "bi and poly" is becoming its own identity category, with numbers comparable to monogamous bisexuals and poly monosexuals. This overlap group can form a conceptual and social cement between the two communities. More importantly, the two forms of activism should be sharing ideology. Bi activists can use poly arguments to address problems of feasibility and comparisons to cheating. Poly activists can use bisexual discourse to describe a multiplicity of desire and to enable certain relationship structures, like triads and intimate groups. The two communities can learn a lot from each other.

CONCLUSIONS

Mainstream culture does not address monogamy in everyday discourse, either in personal discussions or in the media. This is convenient: monogamy does not have to be named, claimed, debated, or defended. Instead, monogamy functions as a hidden assumption, ever-present and unexamined. When the culture actually needs to discuss monogamy, in order to delineate its borders, uphold its ideals, or enforce its conformity, the discussion is carried on indirectly, through a discourse on cheating.

Whereas discussions of monogamy are rare, references to cheating are everywhere, from personal fears to so-called women's magazines to daytime television to the plots of movies. These constant reminders push the possibility of cheating into everyday life, and the invisible assumptions of monogamy are pulled in with it. The endless discourse on cheating is a culture-wide project, a constant reaffirmation and reconstruction of monogamy itself.

The omnipresence of cheating is not only talk, of course. Plenty of people actually cheat. Cheating provides a convenient escape from the restrictions of monogamy, while not actually challenging monogamous assumptions. Through a discourse on cheating, actual nonmonogamy is rationalized as transient, immoral, or pathological.

Nonmonogamous movements of any sort fall into this rationalization trap. Bisexuality is also caught here because the close relationship between monogamy and monosexuality renders bisexuality as a form of nonmonogamy. Through explicit or implicit comparisons to cheating, these movements are demonized or rendered invisible. In order to be successful, these movements must find ways to escape or defuse the discourse on cheating. They therefore share a common conceptual and political opponent. This common opposition creates a certain unity of purpose and ideology among otherwise disparate communities. When this unification is not actively opposed, communities can share victories, strategies, and members.

Bisexuality and polyamory are currently undergoing this conceptual collaboration. Lessons on sexuality and desire flow in one direction. Anti-monogamous strategies travel in the other direction. The collaboration seems to be increasing the numbers in both communities. It is the duty of activists to acknowledge and strengthen this bond, and to move this collaboration into the cultural and political realms. The bi/poly dynamic has the potential to move both communities towards a point of culture-wide visibility, which is a necessary step on the road to acceptance.

NOTES

1. Numerous surveys have confirmed that cheating rates run at a third to a quarter of the population. Specifically, in *The Janus Report on Sexual Behavior*, 35% of married men and 26% of married women surveyed admitted to having had extramarital sex. The numbers were much higher for divorced men and women, 56% and 59% respectively. (Samuel Janus and Cynthia Janus, 1993. pp. 195-198). Even though these numbers have been widely reported as representing cheating, we have no way of knowing how much of this extramarital sex was covert and how much was by agreement or arrangement with the spouse. However, other sources have confirmed that the significant majority of extra-relationship sex is illicit. For example, *The Day America Told the Truth* specifically asked about affairs, and got back an overall rate of 31% among

married men and women. In the context of this paper, it is interesting to note that among those in affairs, only 17% of men and 10% of women planned to leave their spouse (James Patterson and Peter Kim, 1991. pp. 92-99).

2. "Double Lives on the Down Low" by Benoit Denizet-Lewis, New York Times Magazine, August 3rd, 2003. This article did a fairly good job of letting the men involved speak for themselves, compared with a number of alarmist and moralizing articles that came out around the same time. One such was "Down Low" by Jabari Asim, Washington Post, August 11th, 2003.

3. <www.ashleymadison.com> is a dating service Website that ostensibly caters to married women. Its presentation is a mix of messages explicitly relating to cheating, open marriages, and polyamory. There are actually more registered (for money) men than women on the site, but not by much.

4. In Janus and Janus (note i) more married men than married women (35% versus 26%) admitted to extramarital sex. However, slightly more divorced women than men reported extramarital sex (59% versus 56%).

5. However, it should be noted that these lawsuits take a very real toll. A Mississippi jury recently awarded a divorced husband $50,000 in damages from the man his wife had slept with while they were married (*Richard J. Gorman v. Charles Harry McMahon*, Mississippi Court of Appeals No. 1999-CA-01761-COA, decided 4/10/2001. http://www.mslawyer.com/mssc/ctapp/20010410/9901761.html). Also in Mississippi, a man was awarded $175,000 this year in a similar situation ("Man Ordered to Pay for Marriage Breakup," Associated Press, printed in the The Clarion-Ledger. Jackson Mississippi, August 8th, 2003. http://www.clarionledger.com/news/ 0308/08/m10.html).

6. Fritz Klein, *The Bisexual Option* (New York: Harrington Park Press, 1993). p. 11.

7. Marjorie Garber, *Bisexuality and the Eroticism of Everyday Life* (New York: Routledge, 2000). pp. 423-428. Garber points out that bisexuality can form triangles out of cheating models.

8. Janus and Janus (note 1) only survey extramarital sex, with no regard to whether or not it was illicit. Another major survey that did not make an illicit/sanctioned distinction is *The Social Organization of Sexuality: Sexual Practices in the United States* (Edward Laumann, John Gagnon, Robert Michael, and Stuart Michaels, University of Chicago Press, 1994). pp. 208-216.

9. Both older and newer poly publications maintain a focus on primary/secondary arrangements, including *The Ethical Slut* (Dossie Easton and Catherine Liszt, Greenery Press, 1997) and *Redefining Our Relationships* (Wendy-O Matik, Defiant Times Press, 2002).

10. Poly people in online forums usually take a "difficult but rewarding" attitude towards polyamory. One good place to see this happening is livejournal: <www.livejournal.com/community/polyamory>.

11. In November 1998 in Memphis, Tennesee, April Divilbiss's infant daughter was removed to the daughter's paternal grandparents by court order, because April was polyamorous and pagan. The case ended without April regaining custody. "Pagan Mother Battles for Custody" by Woody Baird, Associated Press, January 11th, 1999. This article can be found online at <http://www.polyamorysociety.org/Yahoo-Divilbliss_Article.html>.

12. *The Ethical Slut* (see note 9) has two chapters on communication, conflict resolution, and agreement strategies. *Redefining Our Relationships* (see note 9) says, "I strongly recommend the importance of honest communication at the onset of a new

connection" and makes other remarks about honesty, and has a section on conflict strategies.

13. Marjorie Garber, *Bisexuality and the Eroticism of Everyday Life* (New York: Routledge, 2000). On page 24 Garber states "Visibility is, indeed, what bi's have said they lacked, for years." The quest for bisexual visibility is a central theme of the book.

14. "Bisexuality is the wild card of our erotic life. Now it's coming out in the open—in pop culture, in cyberspace and on campus. But can you really have it both ways?" by John Leland, Steve Rhodes, Peter Katel, and Claudia Kalb. Newsweek, July 17, 1995.

15. Marjorie Garber, *Bisexuality and the Eroticism of Everyday Life* (New York: Routledge, 2000). p. 147.

16. "Double Lives on the Down Low" by Benoit Denizet-Lewis, New York Times Magazine, August 3rd, 2003.

17. Both the NYT Magazine article and the Washington Post article (see note 2) brought up bisexuality in this manner.

18. Marjorie Garber, *Bisexuality and the Eroticism of Everyday Life* (New York: Routledge, 2000). pp. 423-428.

19. One great place to find such surveys is the polyamory community on the livejournal system, <www.livejournal.com/community/polyamory>. Dr. Geri Weitzman is currently working on a more formal Internet survey of bisexual and polyamorous identities.

WORKS CITED

The Ashley Madison Agency <http://www.ashleymadison.com/>.

Asim, Jabari. "Down Low." *Washington Post* 11 August 2003.

Baird, Woody. "Pagan Mother Battles for Custody." *Associated Press* 11 January 1999. <http://www.polyamorysociety.org/Yahoo-Divilbliss_Article.html>.

Denizet-Lewis, Benoit. "Double Lives on the Down Low." *New York Times Magazine* 3 August 2003.

Easton, Dossie, and Catherine Liszt. *The Ethical Slut.* San Francisco: Greenery Press, 1997.

Garber, Marjorie. *Bisexuality and the Eroticism of Everyday Life.* New York: Routledge, 2000.

Janus, Samuel, and Cynthia Janus. *The Janus Report on Sexual Behavior.* New York: Wiley & Sons, 1993.

Klein, Fritz. *The Bisexual Option.* New York: Harrington Park Press, 1993.

Laumann, Edward, John Gagnon, Robert Michael, and Stuart Michaels. *The Social Organization of Sexuality: Sexual Practices in the United States.* Chicago: University of Chicago Press, 1994.

Leland, John, Steve Rhodes, Peter Katel, and Claudia Kalb. "Bisexuality is the wild card of our erotic life. Now it's coming out in the open—in pop culture, in cyberspace and on campus. But can you really have it both ways?" *Newsweek* 17 July 1995.

"Man Ordered to Pay for Marriage Breakup." *The Clarion-Ledger* 8 August 2003. <http://www.clarionledger.com/news/0308/08/m10.html>.

Matik, Wendy-O. *Redefining Our Relationships.* Oakland: Defiant Times Press, 2002.

Patterson, James, and Peter Kim. *The Day America Told the Truth*. New York: Prentice Hall Press, 1991.

Polyamorous Community's Journal. <http://www.livejournal.com/community/polyamory>.

Richard J. Gorman v. Charles Harry McMahon. 1999-CA-01761-COA Mississippi Court of Appeals. <http://www.mslawyer.com/mssc/ctapp/20010410/9901761. html>.

[Haworth co-indexing entry note]: "Is Bisexuality Becoming Extinct?" Clurman, Dan. Co-published simultaneously in *Journal of Bisexuality* (Harrington Park Press, an imprint of The Haworth Press, Inc.) Vol. 4,
No. 3/4, 2004, p. 77; and: *Plural Loves: Designs for Bi and Poly Living* (ed: Serena Anderlini-D'Onofrio)
Harrington Park Press, an imprint of The Haworth Press, Inc., 2004, p. 77. Single or multiple copies of this article are available for a fee from The Haworth Document Delivery Service [1-800-HAWORTH, 9:00 a.m. -
5:00 p.m. (EST). E-mail address: docdelivery@haworthpress.com].

Three and More in Love:
Group Marriage
or Integrating Commitment
and Sexual Freedom

Annina Sartorius

http://www.haworthpress.com/web/JB
Digital Object Identifier: 10.1300/J159v04n03_06

[Haworth co-indexing entry note]: "Three and More in Love: Group Marriage or Integrating Commit-
ment and Sexual Freedom." Sartorius, Annina. Co-published simultaneously in *Journal of Bisexuality* (Harrington Park Press, an imprint of The Haworth Press, Inc.) Vol. 4, No. 3/4, 2004, pp. 79-98; and: *Plural Loves:
Designs for Bi and Poly Living* (ed: Serena Anderlini-D'Onofrio) Harrington Park Press, an imprint of The
Haworth Press, Inc., 2004, pp. 79-98. Single or multiple copies of this article are available for a fee from The
Haworth Document Delivery Service [1-800-HAWORTH, 9:00 a.m. - 5:00 p.m. (EST). E-mail address:
docdelivery@haworthpress.com].

SUMMARY. This article discusses and reflects upon the topic of polyamory, an insufficiently researched subject whose popularity is growing. Group marriage, a relationship structure with lasting and intense exchange of energy including three or more partners, is a possible answer to the desire to satisfy one's need for sexual freedom and variety on the one hand, and for commitment on the other. Various examples of polyamory and group marriage in the last two hundred years are presented and discussed. Komaja, the international spiritual community founded in 1978, is presented here in detail as an example of a successful utopian community with a spiritual background and focus. The article presents Komaja's culture of love, its life, master, art of tantra, group marriage, and attitude towards bisexuality. The article explains the concept of *zajedna*, Komaja's form of group marriage, presented at the 2001 World Congress of Sexology. It also summarizes the results of an analysis of the sexual and mental health of approximately 70 people who have regularly attended Komaja's tantra courses for years, as presented at the World Congress of Sexology in 2003. *[Article copies available for a fee from The Haworth Document Delivery Service: 1-800-HAWORTH. E-mail address: <docdelivery@haworthpress.com> Website: <http://www.HaworthPress.com> © 2004 by The Haworth Press, Inc. All rights reserved.]*

KEYWORDS. Polyamory, bisexuality, spirituality, *zajedna*, tantra, love, Komaja, community

For me sex is the celebration, worshipping of life and celebration of the Divine with our *lingams* and *yonis*. Love for life, love for the strength and the magnificence of life, for the divinity of life and for God in general, who is the root of all life and all phenomena and also of all love-erotic phenomena. This is what I celebrate. Constantly. Only this.

–Aba Aziz Makaja

MONOGAMY OR NONMONOGAMY?

A reflection on adult sexuality includes among other things the examination of the different modes in which sexualities are practiced. It is a well-known fact that in Western Europe nearly one in two marriages ends in divorce. So-called "patchwork families," families consisting of two or more adults with children from different parents (Rauchfleisch, 1997), and one parent families have become common.

In newspapers and magazines we find a growing number of articles on topics such as "Instructions for an Extramarital Affair," "The Lover–A Third Member of the Marriage," and so on. The fact that a huge gap exists between public morality and actual intimate behaviour is common knowledge, thanks to studies by Bornemann, Hite and others. Studies show that in fact, from a statistical viewpoint, sexual infidelity is much more usual and widespread than sexual faithfulness. The Spring and Spring (1998) report, for instance, states that 90% of the men and 75% of the women interviewed had had at least one extramarital affair.

So, does this mean that the human species is just one more species for whom nonmonogamy is nothing but a natural phenomenon? There is increasing evidence from animal research that far fewer animal species are truly monogamous than was first thought: in the animal kingdom, less than 5% of all animal species are now thought to be monogamous (McCullough & Hall, 2003). Approximately 85% of the 1270 human societies listed in Murdoch's *Ethnographic Atlas* display some form of multi-spouse relationship. It is a well-known fact that our Western societies have trouble enforcing their so-called monogamy; this can be seen through their actions and is reflected in divorce rates, rates of infidelity, number of teen pregnancies, and other similar statistics.

> Eros is the moving power of life, the hunger for connection, the passion for reunion.
>
> –Paul Tillich

THE SEARCH FOR SEXUAL FREEDOM: FROM CHURCH TO PARLIAMENT

If we take a look at the intimate lives of well-known people and leaders of Western societies who live in responsible nonmonogamous relationships, we can see the full range from those who live "closet" nonmonogamy to those who live their nonmonogamy publicly. In *The Poisoning of Eros; Sexual Values in Conflict* (1989), theologian Raymond Lawrence explains how the Church Fathers and other religious leaders dealt with sexuality and religion. The book revealed the shocking love life of Paul Tillich and Karl Barth to many theological experts. By the most highly regarded theologians, these two men are considered to be "the most influential shapers of religious thought and ethical practice in the Western world of the 20th Century" (Lawrence 1989, 24). Paul Tillich led a well-documented love life, in which love erotic abundance was present every day. He led a diverse sexual life and had sexual relationships with more than one woman at the same time. After his death his wife wrote the biography *From Time to Time* where she revealed and reported in detail about his lovemaking with other women, about their sexual experiences together with people outside of their relationship as well as her experimentation with bisexuality. As Lawrence comments, "Frivolous or not, the Tillich's sexual lives now stand as a serious critique of conventional religious sexual morality." Karl Barth, who Pope Pius XII considered to be "the greatest theologian since Thomas Aquinas," lived for four decades with two women and had sexual relationships with both of them.

Also the famous psychiatrist Carl Gustav Jung, the founder of Analytic Psychology, lived for decades with two women, Emma Jung and Toni Wolff (Dorst, 1995). At the official funeral of the former President of France, Francois Mitterand, his wife, their sons, his long-term mistress and their daughter walked together beside his coffin to his grave. Through this, the carefully guarded secret of his ménage à trois was revealed (Foster, Foster & Hadady, 1997). These examples stand as representatives for many others who are trying to find a responsible form of living beyond monogamy.

> In order to survive, Western man (sic) must take the long step away from primitive emotions of hate and jealousy and learn the meaning of love and loving as a dynamic process.

> –Robert Rimmer

PROMOTING NEW WAYS OF LIVING TOGETHER

What Sociologists Say

When looking at relationship structures, sociologists recognize a developmental shift from the old morality regarding behaviour, as in "you have to behave in accordance with the traditional conservative code" (Horx, 1999). The shift is from conventional marriage to a new morality of negotiation in which everything is allowed if based on mutual consent. I would rather say here: if it is based on love and mutual consent! The future belongs to diversity in family structure: Horx sees "combination families" with complex networks of relationships beyond (mere) genealogic lines. A long term study by Richter, in *Psychologie heute*, confirms that "families of choice" are becoming more important than biological relationships (Saum-Aldehoff, 2000). A turning point in the German attitude toward a new social oneness can now be seen.

Group marriage is a relationship structure with lasting and intense emotional, mental and sexual exchanges and which includes three and more partners. It is a possible answer to the desire to satisfy the need for sexual freedom and variety, as well as the need for commitment. This style of loving and living is a phenomenon that has been poorly researched to date, although it is becoming increasingly established at this current time of family diversity.

"Do it!": The Communities Movement

Only a few of the communities that over the years have looked for a new way of living together and found workable solutions are documented. This does not mean that more such communities do not and have not existed; rather, it could indicate that many such communities prefer to live privately and do not wish to expose themselves to the criticism of society. I will hereby provide descriptions of some of the most significant communities that practice responsible non-monogamy. A more in-depth presentation of Komaja will follow. Komaja has existed for more than 25 years, and its members successfully practice various forms of relationship, including 'zajedna,' their form of group marriage.

Oneida

The most significant example of well known group marriages in the past is the Oneida community. Oneida was founded in 1848 in Putney, Vermont, and then moved to Oneida, New York. It was said to be the most radical religious and social experiment of nineteenth-century America. It existed for more than thirty years and, at its peak, it included over 200 members (Klaw, 1993 and Fogarty, 2000). The community was established by a young student of theology, John Humphrey Noyes, and its people followed a deeply religiously based philosophy according to which perfection is what has to be reached and realized in every aspect of life. In order to accomplish this goal, they also practiced a form of group marriage called "complex marriage." All adults were considered married to each other. "Special love," that is, romantic attachment, was a subject for criticism and judged as selfish love, since it was believed that this "spirit of monogamy" threatened the communal order (Sill, 1990).

The end of Oneida community came about as a result of different factors, mainly due to power struggles related to the question who would be the successor to the charismatic leader Noyes.

The Harrad Communities

During the late 1960s and mid-1970s, millions of people were fascinated by the *Harrad Experiment*, a fictional bestselling novel by Robert Rimmer (1966) describing a social experiment where 400 students lived and loved together and attempted to achieve what the author described as a world where men and women can and must relate their sexual drives and needs for another into a unified whole so that the act of sex is a perfectly wonderful consummation of a much larger ecstasy and pride and joy and respect for the amazing fact that each of us, men and women, are human beings, and we loved because we liked each other. (Rimmer, 1990, 58)

Rimmer postulated that "in order to survive, Western man must take the long step away from primitive emotions of hate and jealousy and learn the meaning of love and loving as a dynamic process" (1990, 9). He further specified that "It would be a wonderful world if what the male and female could learn in this interaction could be extended to embrace every human interrelationship" (1990, 119).

Following the possibilities highlighted by the *Harrad Experiment*, by *Proposition 31*, another novel by Rimmer, and by *Stranger in a Strange Land* by Heinlein (1961), a number of other novels followed with a shared vision of living a communal life in sexual freedom. From this several communities and networks were born which aimed to bring this Utopia into reality. In Rimmer's words, all of these people were "individuals embarking on a voyage into an unexplored land where the premise is that man is innately good and can lift himself by his bootstraps into an infinitely better world" (1990, 13).

Sandstone Retreat

There is little information on the Sandstone Retreat, originally intended to be a sexually open community and a place to create alternative living, founded in the 1970s by John and Barbara Williamson near Los Angeles (Anapol, 1997). It was about much more than sex, since people could socialize, learn and enjoy. People became friends and stayed friends, coming to the Sandstone Retreat and studying sexuality (Talese, 1993). Sandstone lasted just four years under the Williamsons but many of the former members had an impact on the swinger and polyamory movement in general.

Kerista

In 1991 the Kerista commune had been active for twenty years in the San Francisco Bay Area, with approximately 30 members (Steward Sill, 1990 and Slomiak, 1997). It was founded in 1971 by Brother Jud, an acronym for Justice Under Democracy, and became well known for its members' sexual freedom and its liberalism with respect to the use of marijuana, and its successful computer business. Its slogan was "Do It."

Kerista's form of group marriage required fidelity among the members, namely polyfidelity. They called their group marriage B-FIC, an acronym for

Best Friend Identity Cluster. They cleared all their conflicts and difficulties in the "Gestalt-O-Rama," their form of group therapy. When the issue of AIDS came up, Kerista decided to introduce strict hygienic rules with an initial phase of sexual abstinence, followed by extensive medical testing, before one could enter a B-FIC. As a result, Kerista had no problems with AIDS or other sexually transmitted diseases.

By working on themselves, Kerista members caused jealousy to disappear, and replaced it with "compersion," their term for the emotion opposite to jealousy, namely a partner's happiness for his/her loved ones when they have love erotic enjoyment with another person. Kerista's peak was in the 1970s and 1980s and they never had more than about 30 members. Tensions within the community finally led to the exclusion of Brother Jud from his B-FIC and eventually to the community's demise.

Twin Oaks

There are numerous communities where sexual diversity including practising polyamory is tolerated, even encouraged, but kept private. Twin Oaks is today one of the most famous intentional communities in the U.S. It was founded in 1967 and currently consists of approximately 100 people. It is an ecovillage in Louisa, Virginia, where people live and work together, with their lifestyle reflecting their main values of egalitarianism, ecology and nonviolence. After five years of experience Kat Kinkade, one of the founders, reflected upon the community in the following terms:

> Twin Oaks has taken a firm stand in favor of sexual freedom and nonpossessiveness, and that brings problems with it. Problems notwithstanding, we did not have any real choice about taking this stand. Any group that settles on monogamy as a norm has to figure out how to defend it. Without a heavy Puritan religious bias this is very difficult. Philosophy isn't the only problem with monogamy, either. Sexual rules are hard to enforce in any society, and more so among free-thinking communitarians. The closer people live together, the higher will be the opportunity for attraction. A commune has to take the choice between dealing with jealousy in an open way or dealing with complicated questions of sin, dalliance, adultery. I conjecture that a group norm of free choice in sexual matters is not only philosophically consistent but literally easier to manage than any compromises would be. (Kinkade, 1994)

Twin Oaks is an interesting example of an intentional community with a lifestyle which reflects not only the values of equality and nonviolence, but also the value of tolerance concerning the different forms of relationships, which are present in this community.

Komaja is the radiant love. It is our ideal, our main objective and the foundation of our method. We practice to be powerful in love simply because we have understood that love makes us most happy in life.

–Aba Aziz Makaja

KOMAJA: THE COMMUNITY OF THE FUTURE

"Komaja" means "Radiant Love." It describes a spiritual-philosophical system as well as an international spiritual community which celebrated its twenty-fifth anniversary in 2003. Knowledge is Komaja's connecting spiritual thread, radiant love its principal virtue. The primary reason that Komaja's members, or Komajas, have come together is to develop spiritually and it is easier, in many ways, to study and practise in community than alone. This means that the Komaja community is the vehicle but not the aim itself; the community, as well as the love-erotic partnership, are considered to be a path, a method by which the spiritual aspirant attempts to bring spirituality into every corner of his or her life, namely to spiritualize soul *and* body. Spiritualizing sexuality, via asceticism or by being sexually active, is considered to be an important task on the path of self-realization. Methods of realization are given for both paths (Makaja 2003), and these were presented at the 16th World Congress of Sexology in Cuba, 2003.

Community and partnership are viewed as sources of inspiration and support for the aspirant and as mirrors for individual and group strengths, and weaknesses. Community and partnership are considered to be fields for self-realization, ways to enhance spiritual transformation, as happens in the monasteries, convents, and ashrams of other cultures.

THE PHILOSOPHY

The ideal and main goal to achieve in Komaja is the development of love. Makaja teaches and shows through his own example, which is reflected in the activities of the community, that expressing love through deeds of love is an absolute imperative. Radiant Love is the most succinct definition of Komaja. And, according to Makaja, only the love which radiates has a healing and spiritualizing effect on the individual as well as on the community. Expressed in common spiritual-philosophical terminology, Komaja is a specific form of tantric kundalini yoga, developed by Makaja. To be able to radiate love, one has to systematically open one's higher energy centres or chakras, first of all the heart-center, and then, step by step, one has to awake one's life force or kundalini.

Love is set free and radiates when "the alchemy of transforming the unconscious and limited human 'I' into a conscious and unlimited Divine 'I'" takes place (Makaja, 2003). God, or the Essence as omnipresent and eternal source of Life is also present at the innermost core of every being. This is why infinite development is possible.

Komaja claims that the Supreme God or the Source of Life or Essence can be reached via Christ, Krishna or Personal Gods, or in many other ways. There are many ways leading to the top of the mountain.

THE COMMUNITY

Komaja was founded in 1978 by the well-known tantric master Aba Aziz Makaja, and offers a deep and non-dogmatic access to spirituality. Makaja is not only the founder but also the spiritual father of the community, he is at the core of Komaja's life and its development. Today Komaja has more than 350 members and, as a community open to the world, has many friends who draw inspiration from its model of living. Komaja members live all over Europe, with small groups of members and friends in Australia and North America. A large number of members choose to live in Komaja ashrams as they feel this significantly supports their spiritual growth.

The only "must" to be a member of Komaja is the duty to follow the seven conditions described as (1) nonviolence; (2) honesty in sexual relationships; (3) abstinence from alcohol, drugs and meat/fish; (4) believing in good; (5) to talk about Komaja and spirituality as much as and in such a way that the listeners are open to it; (6) to work on becoming aware, controlling, refining and transforming sexual energy; and (7) the effort to bring one's own goals into accordance with the needs of mankind. Everything else is open for members to choose, including the methods members would like to follow for their spiritual growth (although Komaja itself offers a complete and highly appreciated system of spiritual schooling); the spiritual master they wish to follow (if one wishes to have any); and the way they wish to live, including their favorite forms of intimate relationships.

With many being members of Komaja for a long time, the commitment to the community is high, but there is also a strong emphasis on individual autonomy.

Most of the members earn their living outside the community, through various types of jobs, mostly academic. Most of those who live together in Komaja ashrams do not share their personal income but many invest a lot in the community, because this way of life seems to satisfy them to a high degree both personally and financially. Members are expected to be active in the shaping of communal life and its activities. Long-term members can become members of the Council. The Council makes democratic decisions about the life and development of the community. Without a doubt, Makaja as founder and spiritual leader of Komaja is the one who gives most suggestions for Komaja and its development.

Questions are often asked about the way in which conflicts are resolved in the community and about how people living together in these alternative forms of relationships deal with problems. To begin with, one important prerequisite for a Komaja member to criticize something is that he or she must have a concrete suggestion to improve the issue in question. In addition the work of dealing with conflicts is considered to be within the work towards self-realization, since conflicts in the outer world are seen as mere reflections of inner conflicts. In this context, working on conflicts can be done using the same methods as the ones of self-realization. The methods created by Makaja include Love Meditation, Komaja Meditation, Polytherapy, and Theatre of Truth (Makaja, 1998 and 2003). They can be, and are, applied to individuals as well as in group settings, especially in Komaja's Spiritual Schooling and in the Art of Love. In the context of the community, conflicts are resolved in the framework of Council meetings, which are held regularly and extraordinarily.

Komaja was born in Makaja's home country Croatia during the time of Communism, in secret, and suffering discrimination and persecution by the government of that time. In spite of all these hindrances, the Komaja community grew quickly and spread to all republics of the former Yugoslavia. In 1986, the first Komaja organization was founded in Switzerland, with other Komaja organizations in Western Europe following.

Later, Makaja became the most widely read author of spiritual literature in Croatia. He promotes, teaches and lives new, revolutionary ideas shaped both personally and culturally. Makaja and his community are socially involved in many countries and influence them in numerous ways. For example during the war in former Yugoslavia, under Makaja's guidance, the Komajas founded two humanitarian organizations and brought medical and financial help to war zones for a total of about 1,250 million Euros. In Macedonia, Komaja has become well known for the form of therapy Makaja devised to overcome drug addiction (Makaja 2001 and Holjac, 2001); and for its ecological activities, the most significant in Macedonia so far. Komaja is also involved in scientific activities in the field of Sexology, with one of Komaja's organizations a member of the World Association for Sexology (WAS). Makaja has also been lobbying for the introduction of love-erotic education into secondary schools of (Catholic!) Croatia.

Of course, Komaja's personal and cultural models also invite criticism, especially from the Catholic churches of Croatia and Bosnia Hercegovina. Makaja is currently in court proceedings for slander against the Catholic church, with this being only the third time the Catholic church has been taken to court in Croatia in the last forty years. The trial started in early 1994 and is still going on, bringing much public appreciation to this small yet but courageous community.

POLYAMORY AND BISEXUALITY
FROM THE VIEWPOINT OF KOMAJA

We are creatures without gender–gender is an illusion of the material level of the universe. A self-realised human being is a human being who has completely developed his female as well as his male nature, not only in the physical but also in the psychic sense, who has transcended the illusion of the physical, emotional and mental body and all illusions of the gender related to it.

–Aba Aziz Makaja

After a wonderful night of celebrating life with her male and female lovers in the way of Komaja's tantra, the author of this article, herself a member of Cherry Blossom (one of Komaja's zajednas, or group marriages), summarizes her experience which at the same time reflects the essence of Komaja's attitude concerning polyamory and bisexuality:

I love you and you and you and you . . . I love you all . . . these are men and women. This is a celebration of love. Together we are touching the Holy and carrying this experience in everyday life. And again and again touching the Holy, we start to live the Holy more and more. We become the Holy. In the eyes of all these men and women I meet the One Life, I meet the most deep, the most valuable of Life. And this is what makes a relationship, for me, it is not important whether someone is hetero, bi or homosexual. (from the author's diary, summer 2001, Dubrovnik, Croatia)

The Komaja community includes heterosexual, bisexual and homosexual people. There has been no conflict over sexual identities. There are numerous members living in a bisexual way and few in a homosexual way. Many of them speak openly about their other way of living, for instance at Komaja's courses and schools. Another example is one homosexual member from the southslavic countries, who went to live with his partner in England and who received permission to live there precisely because he outed himself as a homosexual who wanted to live together with his partner. (Two testimonials from women in Komaja are included in this collection.)

Most of the people living bisexually are members of Komaja's tantric groups. Since in Komaja partnership is considered a spiritual method and because most of the people are living together in groups, it is natural that these topics are discussed. On the other hand we are just loving and living together without talking so much about it. In Komaja one's sexual orientation is not of primary importance and neither is one's form of relationship. The most important thing to strive for is love: the passion of the heart. What counts is the culture of love, as the foundation for a new society. Makaja asks: "In what way, with what vibration do you approach sex in your head, in your heart and in your will? This is a sacrament, this is the most sacred thing there is!" (Makaja, 2003,11). As he further explains,

> On the material level, of all the activities, it is only sex that gives us everything, that satisfies all our needs, releases us from our fears and frustrations etc. Consequently, of all our bodily activities sex is most from God. Through complete surrender, by means of sex you will bring to your consciousness your Divine part. And once you have brought this Divine part of you into stable consciousness, in other words when you make it conscious enough in this way, in the end you will begin to live this Divine part even if there is no sex. For by frequent contact with your own Divine foundation, you become conscious in other situations as well. And it is the easiest to contact your Divine foundation through sex, for sex is the most divine of all our bodily activities. (Makaja, 2003, 12)

And concludes,

> In the temples of different religions there is always a fire burning, a sacrifice to God. Days and nights, for centuries, it never stops burning. Our sex is like this, it is the temple fire in our individual temple. It must always burn, you must take care of it! This is God through you! (Makaja, 2003, 13)

Makaja calls for integrating into wholeness all aspects of one's being and points out the central importance of recognizing that sex is holy. As the theologian and psychologist William Stayton confirms, "In splitting sex and spirit, we cut ourselves off from both our animal and our spiritual nature. We deny ourselves the experience of finding our wholeness, our true identity, our core self. . . ." And, echoing Makaja's principles, he concludes: "Our bliss is rooted in our wholeness, not in schizophrenia" (Francoeur, 1999, xii).

In this adventure of acquiring knowledge about life, of self- realization, in this "struggle for wholeness," as Stayton calls it, gender and sexual orientation lose their importance; life is enriched when one has known that what counts the most is the essence of life and that the central thing in life is to strive to come near to this essence, to touch it, to live it as often as possible.

According to Komaja's philosophy, the human being carries everything within itself. This means that we are not "halves" searching for the other half in order to be completed. We are the whole, but we are only on the path to become aware of it. In this sense sexual orientation, gender and partnership themselves are but concepts on the path to wholeness.

NEW FORMS OF RELATIONSHIPS FOR A NEW SOCIETY

Aside from its spiritual schooling, Komaja also developed a social concept for living together. It is an avant-garde community, a utopia being lived in the present, unique sociologically in many ways. Komaja is not a polyamorous spiritual community; Makaja doesn't push people to live in polyamory, nor does he force members to live their sexual lives in any particular way, but teaches the freedom of the spirit and body and postulates that this inner freedom, which is the real aim, can be achieved only by devotion to the Highest and discipline with regard to one's self-realization.

However, although the form in which love is lived is not essential, in Komaja, the percentage of people living in polyamory is much higher than among the average population. There are numerous people practising *zajedna*, Komaja's form of polyamory.

Zajedna is a word created by Makaja (Makaja, 2000), inspired on one hand by the Croatian words *za* (for) and *jedno* (the one), i.e., "for the one," and on the other hand by the Croatian word *zajedno*, which means "together, mutual, in common."

As mentioned before, the conflict between desiring personal development and freedom and an emancipated sexual life, on one hand, and the need for lasting intimacy, depth of relationship and a secure home life, on the other, poses a very difficult dilemma for the people of our time.

By instituting *zajedna*, Komaja created a concept of group marriage, which resolves this conflict: *zajedna* is the term for the most intimate, lasting, loving relationship between at least two people (be it of the opposite or the same sex) who are open at any time to accepting new people as equal members into their life-companionship. An important element of the zajedna is that it is primarily based on the spiritual and psychological needs of its members. A prerequisite is open and honest communication among all members of *zajedna*, which should be a common characteristic of all mature adult sexual relationships.

Subforms of *zajednas* are the following.

Kajena, a term also created by Makaja, comes from *k, ka* (towards) and *je(d)no* (the one), is a subform of the *zajedna*, and means the form of living together of two people who are in the process of development towards becoming a *zajedna*. Also, the form of relationship between two people who have a strong and deep relationship, but who live in different zajednas (i.e., the strongest, lasting relationship) will "only" be a *kajena*.

Svejena, also a term created by Makaja, comes from the Croatian *sve* (all) and *je(d)no* and means "all is (the) one," "all is together," "all are together." It is a larger and, because of this, slightly weaker, lasting life-companionship, consisting of more individuals and/or *zajednas* and/or *kajenas*, for example the tantric groups Cherry Blossom, Small Door, Rhythm of Love.

THE TANTRIC GROUPS AS EXAMPLES OF ZAJEDNAS

The purpose of tantric groups is to enable interested people to work on human sexuality and relationships with the Art of Love, Komaja's program for the spiritualization of sexuality. Through their work together (most of them also live together in ashrams), the members of the groups became so close that they realized they were actually living in a *zajedna* (i.e., in its subform *svejena*) or group marriage.

Cherry Blossom is the oldest tantric group, founded in 1985. Today it has more than twenty members with an average membership length of ten years (in 2003). Almost all members of Cherry Blossom are members of the group marriage. To become a member of the tantric group one has to be a guest for one year and a candidate for the second.

The slightly younger tantric marriage, *Kamala*, founded in 1991, has 15 members. This group makes the core out of which in summer 2003 was formed Komaja's new tantric group Little Door, with more than 30 members. Rhythm of Love is the youngest tantric group; founded in 1996, it has 13 members.

The concept of the *zajedna* was presented at the 15th World Congress of Sexology in Paris 2001 (Milicevic-Sartorius, 2001). The results of a study on approximately 70 people who have, over several years, regularly attended Komaja's tantric courses were presented at the 16th World Congress of Sexology in Havana 2003. Participants' average age was 32 years, with an average duration of five years in one of the three investigated tantric groups. The Trier Personality Questionnaire (TPF), constructed by Peter Becker, consists of nine variables describing the construction of Mental Health, including behaviour-control; mental health; meaning-fulness; self-obliviousness; freedom from distress; expansiveness; autonomy; self-esteem; and capacity of love. The TPF results for this group show that the mental health of people practicing tantra is very stable, with a significant difference ($p < .001$) in 7 of the 9 TPF variables. This analysis demonstrates that people practicing Komaja's forms of tantra have higher values concerning mental health than the average population (Heil, 2003).

The most important psychological concepts influencing the sexual lives of people practising The Art of Love have also been measured. The same 70 people were tested with the Multidimensional Sexuality Questionnaire, an objective self-report instrument constructed by Snell, Fisher and Walters. Men and women attending Komaja's tantra appear to have a healthy sexual esteem and feel sexually satisfied. They are significantly more sexually motivated than other people. Women practicing Komaja's tantra are in many aspects significantly different from the female norm: they think more about sex, they believe that the sexual aspects of life are determined by their own personal control; they are more sexually assertive. The longer they attend the courses the more conscious they become about their sexuality. The men practising Komaja's tantra are more conscious about their sexuality than other men and more aware of the impression their sexuality has on others (Sartorius, 2003).

CHILDREN AND PARENTHOOD IN KOMAJA

If two Komaja people decide to have a child, it is completely their concern and not the concern of the community, as opposed to communities like Oneida or Kerista which had explicit communal approaches to this topic. In Komaja the responsibility for child rearing always remains in the hands of the blood parents. If people are living in a *zajedna* of more than two people, then the other members have the obligation to treat the children of the other *zajedna* members as if they were their own. As "assistants" to the children's blood parents they have to bring them up in accordance with the will of the blood parents and follow their instructions (Makaja, 2003). Not only partnership but also family are seen as part of the spiritual path and, together with the partners of the group marriage, education becomes for the zajedna one more place where to live spiritual values and pass these values on to the children in question.

MAKAJA: PROFILE OF A SPIRITUAL TANTRIC MASTER

Aba Aziz Makaja was born 1953 into a socially and spiritually prominent Herzegovinian family in Mostar, Bosnia-Herzegovina. He studied law before he undertook an intensive, disciplined study and practise of far eastern spiritual traditions (Yoga, Tantra, Vedanta), which led to a fundamental change and broadening of his consciousness. Makaja began to teach. He describes his motivation in the following terms:

> I feel the need to lead people to their source, to their Divine centre, to discover what is their own will as the children of God, regardless of all religions, all dogmas, all cultural achievements of the civilisations, nations and races which exist and have existed. (Makaja, 2003, 5)

In his view,

> the various religions, sciences, ideologies, philosophies are just clothes with which the human soul, on its long journey to God, covers the vulnerable nakedness of its own ignorance. If they are torn, the clothes are changed; the path however, remains . . . Know Thyself. (Makaja, 1994, Aphorism for 16th July)

As a result of his work with people, and with reference to the schools of tantric kundalini and Christian thought, he developed the teaching *Komaja*, answering the needs of western people today. In 1978 he founded the spiritual community by the same name, whose organizations now internationally promote and disseminate his teachings.

Makaja has become more and more well known in Europe through his original teaching, his previously mentioned activities in cultural and socio-political areas, and his numerous publications. The value of Makaja's teaching is also evident through statements like the following by W.S. Schneider, the editor-in-chief of *connection*, the leading spiritual magazine in German language. As Schneider explains in his review of *Eros & Logos*, on the back cover of the book:

> I consider Aba Aziz Makaja to be one of the greatest contemporary masters of Tantra. In a way that hardly anyone else has done, he recognizes the Sacred in the sexual and the panerotic in the life of the true saints. I admire his courageous statement on love and truthfulness, on a spiritual, fulfilled life without hypocrisy and false compromise as well as his teaching of the 'spiritualisation of sexuality' with discipline and devotion, which he advocates in his book *Eros & Logos* so eloquently and authentically. (Makaja, 2003)

THE SCHOOLING

This is my message and my teaching. I teach people and help them know how to preserve and extend love in order to become healthier in soul and body, therefore helping their surroundings at the same time. This is how the world develops and goes forward, regardless of the religion we belong to.

–Aba Aziz Makaja

Komaja Spiritual Schooling

In Komaja, every area of human life and coexistence is rethought, new concepts are worked out, tested and, ultimately, experienced. Whether one is interested in issues of health, of partnership as a path to spiritual development, or whether one longs to develop love and consciousness, Komaja offers an extensive program of ongoing education. Its profound spiritual schooling emphasizes education, communal living, meditation, theoretical work, the spiritualization of sexuality, togetherness, karma yoga (unselfish work for the community), mantra singing and spiritual sport.

The Art of Love

In addition Komaja offers The Art of Love, a complete system to heighten one's awareness, and to control and refine one's sexuality. This long-term program consists of courses in Komaja's Tantra which run over one or two weeks. They are geared towards the cultivation and development of the love-erotic life, as well as the spiritualization of it. Makaja points out: "Our basic intention is not to teach people love-erotic skills, but to teach them how to use love-erotic life and sexual intercourse for spiritual development in the same way an Indian yogin uses meditation or a Christian mystic uses prayer" (Makaja, 2003). The working method in The Art of Love is determined by the individuals, couples or groups themselves.

Love-Erotic Therapy

Makaja's Love-Erotic Therapy is a summary of his teaching regarding the refinement and spiritualisation of sexuality and has been received with great appreciation by scientific audiences, for example at the symposium "Youth and Drugs" (Makaja, 1999), to which he was invited by the University of Zagreb in 1999; and at the 15th World Congress of Sexology in Paris, 2001. Love-Erotic Therapy is supported morally and financially by organizations such as USAID, the Government of Macedonia and from the administration of the City of Zagreb. Up to now the Love-Erotic Therapy has been mainly used to help people with relationship problems and people with drug addictions but it is used in other fields as well.

CONCLUSION

Three and more in love–is this possible? "Can human beings love both men and women at the same time?" asks Klein (1993, 6). " They can if they can," is his answer (Klein 1993, 7). For moving psychosexually freely among men and among women and reaching love-erotic mastery, the training of love is necessary: The ability to love can be learned, is said in the teaching of the tantric community Komaja, where also methods of realization, as well as for spiritualizing sexuality, are given.

"By sex to enlightenment," summarizes Makaja (2003) shortly in a challenging way: The happiness of love and true sexual enjoyment is related to the bliss of the holy and the first step to it. By the love for the other human beings one will reach the divine love. That is the conviction of different communities presented in this article. Different models of group marriage like complex marriage of Oneida, B-FIC of Kerista and the *zajedna* of Komaja give a frame, they offer forms of relationship in which commitment and sexual freedom are integrated.

WORKS CITED

Anapol, D.M. (1998). *The New Love Without Limits.* San Rafael: IntiNet Resource Center.

Bowden, J. (1971). *Karl Barth.* London: SCM Press Ltd.

Constantine, J.M. & L.L. (1973). *Group Marriage.* New York: MacMillan Company.

Dorst, B. (1995): *C.G. Jung und die feministische Kritik.* Zurich: *Du* TA Media, 8, 74-80.

Fogarty, R.S. (2000). *Desire and duty at Oneida.* Bloomington: Indiana University.

Foster, B., Foster, M. & Hadady, L. (1997). *Three in Love. Ménages à trois from ancient to modern times.* San Francisco: Harper.

Francoeur, R.T., Cornog, M. & Perper, T. (1999). *Sex, Love and Marriage in the 21st Century.* New York: toExcel.

Heil, O. (2003). *The Mental Health of People Practising Tantra.* Abstract from the 16th World Congress of Sexology, Havana.

Holjac, O. (2001). Od zavisnost od droga do zavisnost od ljubov. In: *Ljubavno-erotska terapija,* 23-30.

Horx, M. (1999). *Die acht Sphären der Zukunft.* Seedorf: Signum.

Kinkade, K. (1994). *Is It Utopia Yet?* Louisa: Twin Oaks Publishing.

Klaw, S. (1993). *Without Sin: The Life and Death of Oneida Community.* New York: Penguin Books.

Klein, F. (1993). *The Bisexual Option.* New York: The Haworth Press.

Lawrence, R. (1989). *The Poisoning of Eros. Sexual Values in Conflict.* New York: Augustine Moore Press.

Makaja, A.A. (1994). *Komaja Agenda 1995-2000.* Komaja: Zürich/Konstanz.

Makaja, A.A. (1998). *Komaja, die geistige Liebes- und Lebenskunst.* Komaja: Zürich/Konstanz.

Makaja, A.A. (1999). Ljubavno-erotski (ne)odgoj i narkomanija. *Anali studentskoga centra u zagrebu,* 1, 185-193.

Makaja, A.A. (2003). *Eros & Logos. The books for Saints and Sinners.* Komaja: Skopje/Zürich/Brighton.

Makaja, A.A. (2001). Ljubavno-erotsko (ne)vospitanje i narkomanija. *Ljubavno-erotska terapija, 11-22.*

McCullough, D. & Hall, D.S. (2003). Polyamory—what it is and what it isn't. *Electronic Journal of Human Sexuality,* 6, Feb. 27.

Milicevic-Sartorius, Annina (2001). *Three and more in love: the group marriage as a possibility to unite the need for commitment and sexual freedom.* Abstract from the 15th World Congress of Sexology, Paris.

Murdoch, G.P. (1986). *Ethnographic Atlas.* World Culture, Vol. 2-4.

Rauchfleisch, U. (1997). *Alternative Familienformen, Eineltern, gleichgeschlechtliche Paare, Hausmänner.* Vandenhoeck & Ruprecht.

Sartorius, Annina (2003). *What Psychological Tendencies Associated with Sexuality Are Dominant in People Practising Tantra?* Abstract from the 16th World Congress of Sexology, Havana.

Saum-Aldehoff, T. (2000). Die neue soziale Offenheit. *Psychologie heute,* 4, 16.

Sill, J.S. (1990). Utopian Group Marriage in the 19th and 20th Centuries: Oneida Community and Kerista Commune. *Free Inquiry in Creative Sociology*, 18 (1), 21-28.

Slomiak, M. (1997). The Shadow Side of Community. Denial and Demise of Kerista. *Communities. Journal of Cooperative Living*, 97, 52-58.

Spring, J.A. & Spring, M. (1998). *Seitensprünge*. Frankfurt: Fischer.

Sun, W. (1986). Religion of equality. *Kerista*, 3/1, 105-106.

Talese, G. (1993). *Thy Neighbor's Wife*. Ivy Books.

Tillich, H. (1973). *From Time to Time*. New York: Stein and Day.

Remembering the Kiss . . .

Suzann Robins

http://www.haworthpress.com/web/JB

Digital Object Identifier: 10.1300/J159v04n03_07

[Haworth co-indexing entry note]: "Remembering the Kiss . . ." Robins, Suzann. Co-published simultaneously in *Journal of Bisexuality* (Harrington Park Press, an imprint of The Haworth Press, Inc.) Vol. 4, No. 3/4, 2004, pp. 99-108; and: *Plural Loves: Designs for Bi and Poly Living* (ed: Serena Anderlini-D'Onofrio) Harrington Park Press, an imprint of The Haworth Press. Inc., 2004, pp. 99-108. Single or multiple copies of this article are available for a fee from The Haworth Document Delivery Service [1-800-HAWORTH, 9:00 a.m. - 5:00 p.m. (EST). E-mail address: docdelivery@haworthpress.com].

SUMMARY. This article traces the history of the polyamory/poly-fidelity movement through the experiences of a bi and poly woman who has participated in the formation of it. The article outlines the transformations from 1970s style communes, where polyfidelity was practiced, to the current polyamory movement, more multifaceted, open, and porous. The author presents her childhood innocence as proof that loving more than one person and of different genders is natural and healthy. *[Article copies available for a fee from The Haworth Document Delivery Service: 1-800-HAWORTH. E-mail address: <docdelivery@haworthpress.com> Website: <http://www.HaworthPress.com> © 2004 by The Haworth Press, Inc. All rights reserved.]*

KEYWORDS. Kissing, Kerista, Church of All Worlds, Loving More, intimate network, commune, polyfidelity, group marriage, Pepcon, *Green Egg*

I remember the kiss. We were in the backseat of a car with a couple of other 12-year-old girls in the front. One was pretending to drive, the other said "Yuck" when she realized what we were doing. I couldn't figure out why, I liked the kiss and it seemed the other girl did too. Later, we played spin the bottle with the boys. If a girl was spinning and it pointed to another girl, you had to spin over, the same for the guys, of course. I didn't like that rule, because I liked kissing the girls as well as the boys. And I didn't mind when a boy or girl I liked kissed some one else. I even liked watching and/or hearing about it, but quickly learned this was an unexpected reaction others did not understand or approve of.

These are my first memories of being judged about who I wanted to kiss, and finding out I was different, *queer*, the word we used then for someone who was "odd." All my friends were attracted only to the opposite sex, and they felt angry, and even cheated-on, if someone they liked also liked someone else. Not much of this made any sense to me, but there was no one to talk to about how I felt. Many things have changed since the 1950s, but some things remain the same. Although we live in an era of more freedom and open sexuality, it is important not to forget how these things came about. This article will relate some historical facts about the movement we now call polyamory. The etymology of the word polyamorous, meaning "loving many," is parallel to the word polygamous, which means "married to many," and is most often used to refer to men who have several wives. The term polyamory first appeared in *Green Egg*: 89 (May 1990) in the article "Bouquet of Lovers," by Mourning Glory Zell, who coined it with her partner Oberon. Experimental lifestyles had existed long before, and became especially prominent with second-wave feminism and the onset of the gay and lesbian movement. The traditional concept of "marriage," and loving only one in a lifetime, is partly a result of women being viewed as property of males. But committed relationships, no matter the number of partners or their sexual orientation, often have had little to do with the state of matrimony. Feminism, the gay movement, and some of the 1960s communal ideas were influential in making modern "poly" possible.

* * *

Founded in the 1970s by a man called Jud, the Kerista commune was a scientific utopian experiment with "families," or Best Friend Identity (BFIs) Clusters. The structure of their relationships involving multiple adults was referred to as polyfidelity. Most people who were attracted to this communal living option were in their 20s or 30s, except for the founder, who was in his 60s and had first choice of who was in his family group. Members, who numbered about 30, would sleep with a different person every night within the six or seven others in their cluster, which had equal numbers of men and women. Only heterosexual partnering was allowed, and there were no public displays of affection, referred to as PDFs.

Kerista rented half a dozen buildings and apartments in the Haight-Ashbury district where members cleaned houses, fixed up gardens, and published a free advertising newsletter. The commune was not only promiscuous in ordinary terms, but also extremely industrious. The strict rotating sleeping schedule was drawn up on a Mac computer, and in the span of about five years, the commune transformed a modest housecleaning business into the biggest Macintosh dealership and consulting firm in Northern California. For three years in a row, the company, called Abacus, was featured in *Inc. Magazine*'s annual list of the fastest-growing enterprises in America.

"All we wanted to do was change the world," Eve Furchgot, a former leader of this group, reported in a 1993 article in *Communities Magazine*. To join Kerista you had to accept polyfidelity as a lifestyle preference–if you didn't agree you couldn't join. A peculiar aspect of their polyfidelity was the numbers game. Members had decided, mainly on the force of Jud's conviction, that the families would eventually reach 36 people each: 18 men and 18 women. Eve remembers,

> The upshot of it was constant cruising, unceasing efforts to look for and recruit interesting and attractive people. Even though, at least in some cases, we had a number of good relationships going, we could not rest on that and be satisfied with nurturing those relationships. We were always looking for that next person. It became a kind of obsession and game, and, in its own way, a distraction from our other problems. In the end, it became exhausting. (*Communities Magazine*, 1993)

Many members found themselves in bed with people they were not attracted to, for the community believed all members were equal. Eve continues,

> Sometimes a newcomer would feel attracted to some members of a group and not others, but would decide to join anyway–on the grounds that we were all nice people and all relationships are unique, so it was OK if closeness developed quickly with some members and more slowly with others. (1993)

If a severe problem developed within a family group, one might be pressured to leave and end up separated from the loved ones well as the others. It was not always clear what was best, since there was no other model to follow. Eve relates,

> It took courage to hold on and try to work things out, trying to hang onto relationships that were dear in spite of the other difficulties. . . . [some of us] managed to connect with each other and form the beginnings of real love relationships. All of us in Mariah, my six-person family, played a leading role in initiating the sequence of events that led to the commune's disbanding [in the early 1990s]. I believe one reason it happened is that we finally reached a level of trust and closeness among ourselves that gave us enough motivation and confidence to take the stand we finally took [at the end]. (1993)

To be in a commune, group marriage, polyamorous or open relationship has its own inherent drawbacks and advantages, as any lifestyle does. To choose one is to let go of other possibilities. But Eve reflects,

> that's just the way life is. . . . We are three men and three women [in my current group marriage], and very satisfied with this arrangement. We have no ambitions to recruit additional members. In Kerista there was some trade-off between quantity and quality. I'm done with that. (1993)

Another California group, called Church of All Worlds (CAW), was founded in 1962 after Oberon Zell (who went by Tim at the time) and Lance Christie read the novel *Stranger in a Strange Land*, shared water and formed a water-brotherhood. It was "dedicated to the celebration of life, the maximal actualization of human potential and the realization of ultimate individual freedom and personal responsibility in harmonious eco-psychic relationship with the total Biosphere of Holy Mother Earth." During this time the Neo Pagan movement developed which embraces open sexuality and multiple relationships, and finds its roots in other sex positive traditions such as Wicca. The charge of the Star Goddess says "all acts of love and pleasure are my rituals." Many take that statement very seriously, including those involved in the publication of *Green Egg Magazine*, and in the Church of All Worlds, or CAW (Gabriel, 2003).

Green Egg Magazine was founded around 1968 and is widely credited as having been the most instrumental publication in the coalescence of the Neo Pagan Movement. For ten years (1984-94) Oberon Zell and his partner Morning Glory were in a three-person relationship with Dianne Darling, editor of *Green Egg*. In 1994, Dianne left and three others joined Oberon and Morning Glory to form the current expanded family, the Ravenhearts. The men in this group are heterosexual and the women bisexual, which is not atypical. In 1997, the Ravenhearts were featured on the TV show *Strange Universe*, and in 2000 they were a part of A&E's documentary series, *The Love Chronicles: Love in the '60s* (CAW Web site). In a recent conversation, Oberon Zell has commented,

> The best thing The Church of All Worlds did regarding the polyamory issue was declaring its affirmation and support for people wishing to marry, regardless of their gender or number, in an Amendment to the Church's Bylaws in 2001. CAW specifically declared ALL marriages to be a Sacrament, and authorized its Clergy to perform the ceremonies. I believe this was an historical first–a legally-recognized international Church to declare its support for marriage between any and all consenting adults who wish to marry each other. (2003)

As a result of these models, others decided to take the concepts and apply them under different circumstances, allowing more choices, more freedom and even hints of bisexuality. Two of the most notable leaders are Dr. Deborah Anapol in the San Francisco Bay Area, and Ryam Nearing, who then lived near Eugene, Oregon, with her husband and second male partner. Ryam's threesome also followed a strict rotating sleeping schedule with Ryam changing each night between Barry, with whom she had been partnered for 20 years, and A.J., who joined them years later. The three of them began a business called Polyfidelity Education Productions (PEP) and began a group marriage conference they called PEPCON. In 1985, they published a first edition of *The Polyfidelity Primer*. The revised and expanded third edition in 1992 carries the note: "Caution: This book contains radical ideas." An endnote quotes Way Konigsberg who suggests the ideas in the primer will appeal to sexually active singles who are tired of superficial sexual involvement and "people whose nature is too gregarious to fit into the nuclear family or loner lifestyles." The book suggests that the biggest single factor impeding the growth of this idea is ignorance and the fact that the vast majority of people assume it can't work due to jealousy and possessiveness, which many still believe to be insurmountable obstacles. Yet, Way concludes, "The fact that it does work is one of the best kept secrets around" (Nearing, 92).

Ryam and Deborah met on the set of a Playboy Channel talk show called *Women on Sex*. In 1984, Anapol had founded the IntiNet Resource Center (IRC) "to help inform people about new models for sexual intimacy and family design" (Anapol, 1992, back cover). IRC was intended to be a clearinghouse for information on ethical nonmonagamous relationships, and a network to link people and organizations. In 1988, Anapol, who now goes by the first name Taj, married Paul Glassco, a computer programmer particularly interested in the building of communal living. Their wedding ceremony for a group marriage provided for stand-ins for future partners.

In the fall of 1991, these two networks came together for the first PEPCON in Berkeley, California. The heterosexual focus included being married to a primary partner or partners, usually of the opposite sex. Any of the partners could also have one or more secondary or tertiary relationships, most commonly—but not always—of the opposite sex. This perspective began to move away from the ideas expressed in *Open Marriage,* a popular book by George and Nena O'Neill (1972) that reflected the practices of the swinging community, often called referred to as "the lifestyle." There, married partners look for other sexual partners while retaining their primary bond, but avoid emotional involvement. Emotional involvement and the building of long-term relationships are, on the other hand, the theoretical base for polyamory, which advocates long-term emotional connections with a variety of sexual partners. This made it interesting to me for I wanted to sleep with others without being sexual.

In 1992, with the publication of *Love Without Limits: The Quest for Sustainable Intimate Relationships*, Deborah Anapol defined "responsible nonmonogamy," or polyamory. In Ryam and Anapol's view, polyamory includes relational modes like polyfidelity, open marriage, group marriage, and intimate networks formed by "singles who desire friendship and perhaps sex, with their lover's other friend(s) and lover(s), forming a web of varying connections within a social circle" (Nearing, 1992). Rather than advocating faithfulness to more than one, as implied by polyfidelity, Anapol's book provided facts, definitions, forms, and guidelines for responsible, long-term nonmonogamous relationships that aren't necessarily group marriages. In a spirit of building community, Anapol's book also includes information on a variety of poly resources.

Both Anapol's and Nearing's books elaborate on the central concept of "triad," a three-person relationship also called "V." As they explain, a triad or V can include partners of either gender of sexual orientation. By way of example, Anapol's book included one of my letters to my sons where I called myself "trisexual," because I wished to make love in threes. I also observed that while many men liked the idea of having two women at once, others were intimidated. Most women wanted to be with two men, not necessarily simultaneously. I did the math and realized it wouldn't work, but at that time the community was relatively small and few women were interested in a relationship with both a man and woman–my ideal triad.

As the community grew it became more open to the idea of multiple relationships which might include same sex as well as opposite sex attractions for both men and women. After appearing on *Donahue* and several other TV talk shows, Taj, Paul, and I began to present small, experiential workshops on *Love Without Limits* in various east and west coast locations, including Harbin Hot Springs, near San Francisco, where I was living at the time. Harbin was known for its acceptance of open and multiple relationships, both same sex and opposite sex. It was also home to the Human Awareness Institute (HAI), begun by Stan Dale in the 1980s, who was out about having two wives. In this relationship, the women weren't necessarily sexual with each other. Their "Sex, Love, and Intimacy" workshops continue to be another avenue for people to find both gay and straight people interested in loving more than one. Some people in this network practice serial monogamy, but others are more interested in responsible nonmonogamy or polyamory. I seldom hear the word polyfidelity in today's discussions. And I know that although some polys still shy away from bisexual interactions, many embrace them.

Amongst the resources listed in the 1992 edition of *Love Without Limits* one finds communities like the Delaware Valley Synergy, Family Tree, Family Synergy, Live the Dream, Loving Alternatives, More University, and National Organization of Sex Enthusiasts (NOSE). Several of these are still active today as "polyamorous," while others have become more involved and open to the "the lifestyle" of swinging. Others still, including the Chesapeake Poly Network (CPN), have developed and appear to have blended these boundaries.

Resources that have helped the poly community grow include *Loving More Magazine*, a periodical that grew out of PEP, *Flood Tides*, published by IRC, and the online connections made possible through the World Wide Web. Many groups in today's vibrant poly community have become more open to sexual and romantic responsiveness not specifically tied to gender. In many cases, biphobia has been discussed at length and people have become more open and cognizant of their own "queerness," which has contributed to a positive reclaiming of this label. Networks of people can be found in major cities who meet on a regular basis to discuss issues relating to bisexuality and polyamory, as well as to make connections. The east and west coast Loving More conferences have continued to be more bi-friendly, and a group called Network for a New Culture, loosely modeled after the ZEGG community from Germany, is emerging. Other sex-positive group practices, such as Tantra, have also become less esoteric and grown into community in many places. Body Sacred, which began on the east coast in the early 1990s, has evolved into a community of people and a training ground for erotic exploration based on explicit negotiations and consents. More University, based in Lafayette, California, with a branch in NYC, is another avenue for learning about open, intimate relationships, both sensual and sexual. All provide opportunities for meeting other people looking for change to the dominant paradigm of hetero-sexual marriage.

Communities, organizations and relationships, as well as words to describe them, can and do evolve. Alternative relationships, including LGBT, serial monogamy, or responsible nonmonogamy, are much more acceptable and acknowledged than they were ten years ago. Eve, from Kerista, quoted above, concludes: "I know what makes [our idealistic lifestyle] work are the same things that make other relationships work: commitment, communication, compatibility, trust, love, and so on" (1993).

It is important to remember that social movements influence each other. "There is more cross-fertilizing than people think," says Loraine Hutchins, a leader in the feminist and bi communities, and co-author of *Bi Any Other Name*. In 1972 she lived in an east coast commune which included gay people interested in exploring their hetero feelings. As she explained in a recent conversation,

> Gay people influence heterosexuals and vice versa. In the gay community, poly is considered a non-heterosexual way of relating, but at the same time, not compulsory for any same-sex couple. Lesbians and bisexuals within the women's movement have tried many varieties of openness and different agreements. Gay/Bi men are famous for working out various open styles without needing a specific word for how they choose to live and love. (2003)

Recently, I heard some younger members of this large community talking about poly-intimacy, which I thought implied deep friendship with some nonsexual, but perhaps sensuous, interactions. I was corrected by the young polys that they were open to the sexual intimacy, even anal or oral, but not to the "amory" because they weren't necessarily "in love." I realized that a variety of definitions are now floating around. While the current idea of polyamory was established in the context of a movement prevalently of white, middle-class people, a great deal of overlap with the gay communities was there from the beginning, which now allows much room for growth in all directions.

* * *

What I know is I still love kissing, both women and men, and that probably isn't going to change. I have written my story in "Three in One Body" (Francoeur, 1995), and continue to search for my own group marriage. For seven years I have been living with a woman who is also open to being bi and poly, but isn't as interested in the sexual aspect as I am. We appreciate the communal idea of sharing meals and material goods with others, as well as having intimate emotional connections, if not physical ones. Since many Websites, chat rooms, and lists have helped to expand poly communities, other people have developed relationships with one partner identifying as poly and the other as "mono." People connect through the continuation of conferences, workshops, and meeting places such as those mentioned above. In 2000, The Institute for 21st Century Relationships took on the task of becoming an umbrella organization where those interested in a variety of lovestyles can come together, including poly, swinging, BDSM, and all varieties of LGBT. I am proud to have contributed to these resources. My goal has always been for the next generations to have more options, so that we may each kiss whomever we like.

WORKS CITED

Anapol, Deborah. *Polyamory: The New Love Without Limits.* IRC, 1997.
Francoeur, Robert T. ed. *Sex, Love & Marriage in the 21st Century.* toExcel, 1999.
Furchgot, Eve. *Communities Magazine.* 1993 (found online: www.ic.org).
Gabriel, Liza. Conversation. December 2003.
Hutchins, Loraine. Conversation. December 2003.
Nearing, Ryam. *Loving More: The Polyfidelity Primer.* PEP Publishing, 1992.
O'Neill, Nena. *Open Marriage.* Avon Books, 1972.
Zell, Morning Glory. "Bouquet of Lovers." In *Love Without Limits*, 1992.
Zell, Oberon. Conversation. December 2003.

WEB SITES

www.ic.org
www.caw.org
www.lovewithoutlimits.com and
www.lovethatworks.org

A Glimpse of Harmony

Deborah Taj Anapol

http://www.haworthpress.com/web/JB

© 2004 by The Haworth Press, Inc. All rights reserved.

Digital Object Identifier: 10.1300/J159v04n03_08

[Haworth co-indexing entry note]: "A Glimpse of Harmony." Anapol, Deborah Taj. Co-published simultaneously in *Journal of Bisexuality* (Harrington Park Press, an imprint of The Haworth Press, Inc.) Vol. 4, No. 3/4, 2004, pp. 109-119; and: *Plural Loves: Designs for Bi and Poly Living* (ed: Serena Anderlini-D'Onofrio) Harrington Park Press, an imprint of The Haworth Press, Inc., 2004, pp. 109-119. Single or multiple copies of this article are available for a fee from The Haworth Document Delivery Service [1-800-HAWORTH, 9:00 a.m. - 5:00 p.m. (EST). E-mail address: docdelivery@haworthpress.com].

SUMMARY. This article discusses what relationships might be like in a culture where men and women honor and respect each other, where dependency is not such a big component of man/woman relationships, and where traits associated with the feminine are encouraged. Pre-European contact Hawaii is used as an example of such a culture. The article covers child rearing practices in old Hawaii, particularly those that relate to sexuality, and compares these "sex positive" customs with the "sex negative" customs of our own culture. It goes on to consider the amazing variety of relationships that were part of village life in old Hawaii. We discover that the diversity of options for opposite sex and same sex friendships, as well as close ties between people of different generations, wove a tapestry of support that took the pressure off of spouses and biological parents. *[Article copies available for a fee from The Haworth Document Delivery Service: 1-800-HAWORTH. E-mail address: <docdelivery@haworthpress.com> Website: <http://www.HaworthPress.com> © 2004 by The Haworth Press, Inc. All rights reserved.]*

KEYWORDS. Community, polyamory, child rearing, family, friendship, sex roles, sex education, relationship, Hawaii, Ho' opono pono, Punalua, initiation

Some day, after we have mastered the winds, the waves, the tides, and gravity, we shall harness the energies of love. Then, for the second time in the history of the world, we will have discovered fire.

–Teilhard de Chardin

It's Sunday afternoon at Little Beach on Maui's south side. I have fled the torrential rains on the north side of the island, to soak up some sun. I long to immerse myself in the ocean and see what this weekly tribal gathering at Maui's only nude beach will bring. Nearly an hour's drive over to this side of the island but it's miraculously warm and dry here. I notice a few acquaintances but choose to spend the afternoon alone, contemplating the puzzle of sexual harmony–how do we find our way back to the garden?

Two young women arrive with palm leaves they're weaving into sun hats. They sit down next to me. A crowd of children quickly gathers to watch in fascination. I notice a beautiful slender blonde woman wearing an off the shoulder shirt over a faded blue bikini strolling arm in arm down the beach with a dark handsome man. His perfect muscular body, her happy smile and sparkling blue eyes give the impression of the perfect couple. She turns to wave to someone down the beach. He plunges into the turquoise ocean and she comes to squat behind the palm weavers.

I return to my own thoughts but after a bit I can't help overhearing their conversation. The blonde woman, who has a slight accent–Scandinavian, I think–is describing the birth of her child.

"It was the most incredible experience of my life," she exclaims. "My baby was born underwater here on Maui!"

"Where did you do that?" one of the young weavers inquires.

"In a hot tub at home," is the reply. "It was great for labor, too. Once I got out to see how it would be on land, but at the first contraction I headed right back to my water cave. Seven hours in the water and he was born. After a while I began to feel I had the hang of it, breathing and letting go through each contraction, and I would say to myself, 'Oh, this is not so hard!' but then one would come and let me know just how hard it could be. There were times when I felt I wouldn't make it, just breathing, but my midwife kept me going. And the warm water helped so much with the pain.

"When he came out, we let him stay under the water for five minutes!"

"Weren't you afraid he would drown?" the other young woman asks.

"No, we just watched him and he seemed to be doing fine, waving his arms"–she demonstrates with fluid undulations– "and you know the umbilical cord was still attached so we knew he was getting oxygen. Then we brought him up onto my chest and he took his first breath! I was just in bliss, it was the highest experience of my life," she continued excitedly.

"I want to have my babies underwater!" one of the young women interjects enthusiastically.

"After a bit the midwife said, 'Don't you want to see what sex your baby is?' because I had forgotten all about that, I wasn't at all interested, it simply didn't matter. The midwife told me I was the first woman she'd ever seen who didn't ask if it was a boy or a girl, but I just didn't care."

Her male companion has come out of the water while she is telling her story and squats silently beside her, stroking her bare arm in a familiar way. I am wondering if he is the father and noticing a wide gold diamond studded band on her left hand (and none on his), when she again waves at someone down the beach. Soon, she is joined by a tall blond man with a naked brown skinned toddler on his hip. His cheerful presence radiates like the blazing sun above.

"Mommy, mommy, mommy," the man says with a German sounding accent as he hands the little boy over. "He wants you, Marissa!"

"Will you have more children?" the young woman asks.

"I don't know," is the reply, "this one is a full time job." And Marissa turns to run after her son who is halfway down the beach and dangerously close to the water's edge.

The child's father takes up the tale. "She went into labor while we were watching the whirling dervishes."

"Whirling dervishes, here on Maui?" the young woman asks, sounding surprised.

"Yes, the Sufi dervishes, they come every year to Maui. And later I realized, my son was conceived in Florida when we were on a retreat with a Sufi sheik. At first I didn't see it, the connection, but then I thought, oh, the circle completes itself! The Sufis say that the child's soul chooses the parents, several months before conception. The soul begins to communicate and ask to come in.

"I never thought I wanted to have children, but at a certain point that changed and I'm so glad. Marissa always wanted to, and we thought maybe we would separate, but then this being began communicating with me and telling me I was chosen to be his father, and I felt that I wanted to do this. And I realized we are so blessed that Marissa didn't have to work outside the home, that my business could support us all. So we decided to conceive," he concludes jovially. His broad smile communicates his delight in his choice.

Marissa has returned and joined the conversation. She is arranging for the young women to baby-sit for her the next evening. She asks me to borrow my pen so she can write down the directions to their house. I want to ask her if the dark man is her lover and what his relationship is to the child's father, but the little boy is stuffing a tortilla chip into my mouth. By the time I've chewed and swallowed I've decided not to pry.

I realize it's no accident I've overheard this conversation. This scene perfectly expresses the essence of sexual harmony, just as last week's encounter with Eve and Jeff represented its opposite. Where is the bridge between these two worlds?

A BRIDGE FROM PAST TO PRESENT

Maui in particular and the Hawaiian Islands in general are well known as lands where the Feminine is very much in evidence, lands where the Spirit of *Aloha* prevails. *Aloha*. This common Hawaiian greeting is often translated as love. Literally, it means "let the light continue." The warm, moist breeze, the softly scented air, the silky smooth water, the tropical sun, the sudden rain showers with their brilliant rainbows–these combine with the power of the land, to create a sensual, even erotic, atmosphere. An atmosphere favoring relaxation and play over ambition and linear thought.

While we often think of love, sensuality, and beauty as the essence of feminine power, the Divine Feminine is not all sweetness and light. Madame Pele, Goddess of Fire, famous the world over for her volcanic temper, is revered here in Hawaii. Other Goddesses embody the protective warrior, the chaotic impersonal force of Mother Nature, the transformational power of death and rebirth, and the ruthless compassion of essential truth.

Nevertheless, at its core the Feminine is concerned with connection. She is the Source of interconnections among all living things, as well as between men and women. The power of the Feminine is still strong in Hawaii. I'd heard for years that Maui attracts those who seek to strengthen and nurture their feminine self, who are ready to embrace their receptive, feeling, intuitive side. I'd come hoping that communing with the *'aina*, with the spirit of this land, would help me come into balance myself, but it turned out to be incredibly uncomfortable for me. At the time I didn't fully understand why. Looking back I realize it was because the internal male support I needed so badly was difficult to find amidst all this softness!

I closed my eyes and saw an image of Maui's birthing pools, shallow depressions in the cliffs by the ocean where high tides bring salt water that becomes warmed by the sun, where legend says the Hawaiian women went to give birth before the haoles came. Haoles, the Hawaiian name for white people, means literally people without breath, without spirit, because, the story goes, the white people's words were not congruent with their energy. In other words, the native Hawaiians viewed the American and European newcomers as liars and openly said as much. And yet they tolerated their presence.

According to my library research, if Marissa's son had been born in old Hawaii, his parents would have begun preparing him for the future enjoyment of intercourse by gently blowing into his foreskin each morning.[1] Most likely, this treatment provided a secondary benefit of keeping the head of the penis clean and free of adhesions, which are often the rationale for infant circumcision in our culture. Later, when he entered middle childhood, he might be taken to a special temple or *heiau* for a ceremony in which the foreskin was slit (not removed as in circumcision) to allow it to slip back more easily during arousal. The priest and priestess might then suck the penis before applying healing herbs to the wound.[2]

A girl child would have mother's milk squirted into her vagina and the labia pressed together.[3] Again, this practice might well have hygienic benefits as well, due to the immune enhancing properties of breast milk. Her *mons veneris* would be rubbed regularly with kukui nut oil to encourage attractively rounded curves and to bring out her passionate nature.[4] When both boys and girls entered puberty, they would be sent to the *heiau* or temple for an ancient rite of passage to help them adjust to the joining of Heaven and Earth in their bodies. This work included a special form of massage which continued day and night until their sexual, spiritual and creative energies were fully integrated.[5]

These practices may seem strange, or even abusive, to those of us who've been raised in a sex negative culture where parents believe it's their duty to discourage every vestige of their children's sexuality. But from the viewpoint of a sex positive culture that values and honors the sexuality of both genders, Western customs of ignoring or even punishing children's sexual exploration might be considered neglectful and barbaric.

As author and healer Michael Sky asserts, "We are especially harsh and abusive toward a child's innate sexuality. Our own sexual confusions and abusive patterns are projected into every act of diaper changing, bathing, feeding, dressing, and toilet training and can leave an indelible trail of shame within the child's body. The idea that masturbation is sinful, when forced upon a growing child whose fingers *must* explore, creates an insidious self-hatred. Likewise, the failure to positively prepare a boy for wet dreams or a girl for menstruation can turn these basic human events into utter tragedies."[6]

In contrast, the old Hawaiian practices of blessing and perfecting of the infant's genitals acknowledged the sacredness of procreation. The genitals of the firstborn child, whether male or female, were considered especially significant as they were the link between past and future generations. This awareness is reflected in the Hawaiian language, which uses the same term, *piko*, for genitals, umbilicus, and the crown of the head.[7] Before the haole invasion, sex was accepted without shame and recognized as a supreme pleasure. Hence "beauty and pleasure in all ways and forms were blessings with which loving relatives desired to endow the first-born throughout life."[8]

In old Hawaii, family members slept in a common sleeping hut, and anatomical differences and the reproductive process, not to mention the sex lives of family and community members, were never kept secret from the children. Sex play among children was not forbidden, and most children had considerable sexual experience by the time they reached puberty.[9] People casually discussed, joked, and even sang about each other's sexual liaisons. Sexual activities of gods and goddesses and kings and queens were common subjects for storytellers and hula dancers. The *mele ma'i* chants particularly were dedicated to the sex organs, their appearance and their use.[10] These *mele* were more than just poems of praise, the chanting conveyed *mana* or spiritual powers of charm and potency.[11]

A RAINBOW OF RELATIONSHIPS

If Marissa had lived in old Hawaii, the two men whose relationship I had been so curious about might have been that of *punalua*. There is no English translation for this word because it refers to a concept that has not been an accepted part of our culture, although the relationship is described quite eloquently in Amy Bloom's short story, "Love Is Not a Pie."[12] However, it was the Hawaiian custom at one time to permit both men and women to have more than one mate. A man's wives or a woman's husbands are *punalua* to each other.[13] The term is also used to refer to the relationship between two people who share a longtime lover, regardless of marital status, or between a person's former and current mate.

Punalua treated each other's children as their own, and were an accepted part of the extended family or *ohana*. Jealousy of a punalua was considered disgraceful. According to one source, the existence of a social code, which taught that it was bad manners or *maikai ole* for *punalua* to "hold malice in their hearts towards each other" and which recognized and spelled out the responsibilities of the relationship, supported positive feelings between *punalua*.[14]

Hawaiians had another recognized form of man/woman relationship, which is so alien to our culture, it's often said to be impossible. In this instance, a man and a woman, who might be either married or single, are united in a ritual as platonic husband and wife. The partners treat each other with great respect and affection, bringing each other gifts and looking out for each other, but they are not lovers and do not live together.[15] Similarly, relationships between people of different generations who felt an affinity with each other and informally adopted each other were called *ho'okama*.[16]

The Hawaiian language also has an abundance of terms to describe friendship between people of the same gender. *Pili aikane* is comradely friendship, *pili hoaloha* is devoted friendship, and *hale kipa* describes a friend who is always welcome in one's home.[17] In all of these relationships it was common for the friendship to be integrated with and on an equal footing with blood and marital relations. Unlike our culture, in which your spouse is expected to be all and everything, the value placed on these different types of bonds no doubt helped to support sexual harmony by taking the pressure off the mate to be the only source of love and companionship.

UNRAVELING THE MYSTERY

The sexual norms from pre-contact Hawaii were not perhaps so different from those of early medieval Europe, prior to the full conversion of the country folk by the Church fathers. But one custom retained by the Hawaiians seems to have disappeared early from Western peoples, with the exception of the Orthodox Jews. The practice of isolating menstruating women in a special hut was rigorously enforced in old Hawaii. Here at the *hale pe'a*, or menstrual hut, women were freed from their usual tasks, their meals were brought to them, and their sacred blood was buried nearby.[18]

I remember learning about cultures with taboos about menstruating women as a young woman, and assuming they represented a sexist attitude. Indeed, Hawaiian culture, while still sex positive, seems to have taken a patriarchal turn even before the arrival of the European explorers and the Christian missionaries.

However, it is evident from reports of the Hawaiian women's sexual freedom, their defiance of certain taboos, and other indications of women's power in Hawaiian society[19] that the suppression of the feminine in Hawaii was never as successful as in Europe and the Americas. What could account for this, I wondered? Was it the Inquisition in which millions of powerful and independent wise-women were burned and tortured for "witchcraft"? Was it the Hawaiian *'aina,* the land itself, which legend says was once part of the ancient Lemurian civilization of Mu?

In any case, now that I have come to appreciate more fully the mystery of my womanhood, I wish I'd had such a sanctuary to retreat to, whether or not men initiated this practice. I longed for permission to leave family and work responsibilities behind and follow my natural inclination to use this sacred time to pray, meditate, and dream in peace.

I imagine that the notorious ill temper and hyper-emotionality associated with the premenstrual syndrome which plagues so many women–and their families–these days is a reaction to the disappearance of the practice of this monthly retreat. In fact, premenstrual syndrome could be viewed as an instinctual effort to regain this necessary solitude by chasing others away. I suspect it's also related to sexual frustration and the absence of an affirming attitude toward menstruation, our bodies, and sexuality in general.

Just as I was wondering how to account for the perplexing tangle of extraordinarily loving and harsh aggressive practices that seemed to be part of Hawaiian history, I found myself attending an evening talk given by a native Hawaiian teacher named Mahealani Kuamo'o Henry. A woman I'd met at a friend's birthday party had recommended Mahealani's class when I'd said I was looking for firsthand information about the old Hawaiian sexual practices. But before I had the opportunity to ask any questions, I was given so much valuable information that I completely forgot my own agenda.

First, Mahealani explained that the *Aloha Lokahi* Era lasted from 342 AD to 1299. *Aloha Lokahi* means love and unity or Oneness, acceptance of All. Before the war-like Tahitians came to Hawaii in 1299, there were no chiefs, no rules, no separation or fighting among the people, and no sense of spiritual power outside oneself. Each person was a law unto themselves, she told us, because they all understood *Kanawai Moakaako,* The Law of the Universe, which in Christian terms might be stated, as you sow so shall you reap.

Long before Captain Cook's arrival in 1778, a time of darkness prophesied by the ancient *kahunas* or spiritual teachers had begun. By the time European and American influences began to shape Hawaii, this *Na'aupo mana,* or divine darkness, had caused the spiritual values of the original culture to be nearly forgotten. Additionally, since the Hawaiian tradition was oral rather than written and because of the need to "go underground" when the missionaries demanded the Hawaiians adopt their beliefs, much of the surviving culture was distorted by white social scientists.

Take for example the use of the word *haole,* which I referred to previously. Auntie Mahealani told us that when she was a young girl, her grandfather reprimanded her because she called another child *haole.* Her grandfather told her with tears in his eyes that it was ridiculous to talk about a person with no breath because a person without breath would be dead. Instead, she was instructed to call foreigners *hanai po'e*, or adopted people, with the understanding that we are all one family.

I was moved and uplifted by both the words and the energy that Aunty Mahealani shared with us. I quickly realized that the *ho'opono pono* teaching she was offering was indeed the traditional Hawaiian way for maintaining harmony in the *ohana* or family clan and that it is based on reminding us of *uhane hui*, of the greatness of the spirit that we are.

Having studied many systems of psychological and spiritual healing over the past twenty-five years, I appreciated the simple elegance and profundity of the *Aloha Lokahi* philosophy Auntie was teaching. My instincts told me that this was the vibration that had drawn me to this beautiful land, and I was delighted to have the opportunity to learn more about the Hawaiian way of creating harmony.

MAKING RIGHT

Growing up in my family, I learned far more about making wrong than making right. While I knew that my family was far from unique in this respect, I hadn't really grasped the pervasiveness of the blame game in our culture as whole prior to hearing Auntie Mahealani's perspective on *ho'opono pono*. The term itself, she told us, had been incorrectly translated as "making right the wrongs," when the Hawaiian word for wrong, *hewa*, is not used at all in this expression.

She maintains that the traditional Hawaiian practice emphasizes rightness or excellence and stays away from the concept of "wrong" entirely. Rather it is literally "making right more right." In fact, some prefer to translate *pono* as harmony,[20] so *ho'opono pono* would be making harmony more harmonious! The flip side of *pono* is not wrong but *pilikia* or trouble.

Through this traditional practice, family members are guided to be conscious that they have a choice in every moment to choose trouble and melodrama or to choose harmony. Making right is the key not only to creating harmony with the opposite sex, but also to creating harmony within.

NOTES

1. Kahuna La'au Lapa'au: The Practice of Hawaiian Herbal Medicine by June Gutmanis, Aiea, Hawaii: Island Heritage, 1976, p. 42.

2. E.S. Craighill Handy and Mary Kawena Pukui, The Polynesian Family System in Ka-'u, Hawai'I, Rutland, VT: Charles E Tuttle Co, 1996, p. 94.

3. Ibid., p. 94.

4. Kahuna La'au Lapa'au: The Practice of Hawaiian Herbal Medicine by June Gutmanis, Aiea, Hawaii: Island Heritage, 1976, p. 42.

5. Powell, Wayne Kealohi, The Way of Aloha, http://www.hawaiiheart. com/wayne. html

6. Michael Sky, Sexual Peace, Santa Fe: Bear & Company, 1993, p. 112.

7. Mary Kawena Pukui, EW Haertig, MD, and Catherine Lee, Nana I Ke Kumu, Vol 1, Honolulu: Hui Hanai, 1972.

8. Craighill Handy and Mary Kawena Pukui, op. Cit. p. 94.

9. Ibid., p. 95.

10. Gutmanis, pages 31-32.

11. Craighill Handy and Pukui, p. 93.

12. Amy Bloom

13. Handy and Pukui, p. 56.

14. Ibid., p. 58.

15. Ibid., p. 55.

16. Ibid., p. 71.

17. Ibid., p. 73.

18. Gutamis, page 31.

19. Sacred Queens and Women of Consequence, Jocelyn Linnekin, Ann Arbor: U of Michigan Press, 1990, p. 5.

20 Op. Cit. Powell, page 1.

21."Breastfeeding and Bedsharing" James J. McKenna, Mothering Magazine #114, September/October 2002.

WORKS CITED

Craighill Handy, E.S., and Mary Kawena Pukui. "The Polynesian Family System." In *Ka-'u, Hawai'I*. Rutland, VT: Charles E Tuttle Co, 1996.

Kawena Pukui, Mary, EW Haertig, and Catherine Lee. *Nana I Ke Kumu,* Vol. 1. Honolulu: Hui Hanai, N. D.

La'au Lapa'au, Kahuna. *The Practice of Hawaiian Herbal Medicine by June Gutmanis*. Aiea, Hawaii: Island Heritage, 1976.

Linnekin, Joycelyn. *Sacred Queens and Women of Consequence*. Ann Arbor: University of Michigan Press, 1990.

McKenna, James J. "Breastfeeding and Bed Sharing." *Mothering Magazine*: 114 (September/October): 2002.

Powell, Wayne Kealohi. "The Way of Aloha." http://www.hawaiiheart.com/wayne.html

Sky, Michael. *Sexual Peace*. Santa Fe: Bear & Company, 1993.

Part Two: Testimonials and Reports from the Field

In the Forecourt of Paradise: A Report on the Possible Love-Erotic Future of Humankind

Konstanza

http://www.haworthpress.com/web/JB
© 2004 by The Haworth Press, Inc. All rights reserved.
Digital Object Identifier: 10.1300/J159v04n03_09

[Haworth co-indexing entry note]: "In the Forecourt of Paradise: A Report on the Possible Love-Erotic Future of Humankind." Konstanza. Co-published simultaneously in *Journal of Bisexuality* (Harrington Park Press, an imprint of The Haworth Press, Inc.) Vol. 4, No. 3/4, 2004, pp. 121-132; and: *Plural Loves: Designs for Bi and Poly Living* (ed: Serena Anderlini-D'Onofrio) Harrington Park Press, an imprint of The Haworth Press, Inc., 2004, pp. 121-132. Single or multiple copies of this article are available for a fee from The Haworth Document Delivery Service [1-800-HAWORTH, 9:00 a.m. - 5:00 p.m. (EST). E-mail address: docdelivery@haworthpress.com].

SUMMARY. In a combination of personal narrative and theoretical presentation, the life of the polyamorous tantric circle "Cherry Blossom" (founded in 1985) and the teaching of the tantric Master Aba Aziz Makaja are presented. The disassociation of body and mind and consequent separation of sexuality and spirituality are left behind through a concise presentation of Makaja's "Theology of Sexuality." The narrative shows how, on the one hand, sexual intercourse can support a person's spiritual efforts and accelerate his or her self-realization or realization of God; on the other hand, how spiritual growth increases one's ability to love and therefore enjoy. Through the example of her intimate life, the author, who lives polyamorously, shows that the essence of Tantra is the disciplined training of virtues, including love, truth, and consciousness. Through this training jealousy is transformed into joy as a result of one's partner's happiness. Sexuality becomes conscious and ecstatic, and the realization of God is accelerated. *[Article copies available for a fee from The Haworth Document Delivery Service: 1-800-HAWORTH. E-mail address: <docdelivery@haworthpress.com> Website: <http://www.HaworthPress.com>* © 2004 by The Haworth Press, Inc. All rights reserved.]

KEYWORDS. Aba Aziz Makaja, enjoyment, enlightenment, ecstasy, jealousy, polyamory, love, self-realization, spiritualization of sexuality, tantra

25 years ago Aba Aziz Makaja founded the international spiritual community Komaja; the spiritualization of matter, including one's own bodyliness, is one of the basic characteristics of Komaja's spiritual philosophy and practice. Through these efforts three tantric circles have been founded over the years, including Cherry Blossom, Kamala, and Rhythm of Love. Here a successful model of "responsible non-monogamy" is lived. Konstanza from Cherry Blossom reports.

THE PAST

The less love, the more monogamy.

–Aba Aziz Makaja

"Well, who are you in love with?" my uncles and aunts asked me when I was 14. In their voices I could feel a longing for their past youth and for its

lighthearted bliss, their wish to catch a little bit of "those days" through me . . .
I thought about their question. There was Peter, Steven, well–and Igor, and
Michael, and daring Daro, and much older Roman. And my married cousin.
Well, I'm in love with approximately seven friends, was my hesitant answer.
Joyful laughter. "But still, you have to DECIDE on one of them!" they said.
That was difficult–with each of them it was so beautiful and sweet, with each
of them I was happy. After all, lots of times we were all together–them, my
girlfriends and me in the evening, sitting on the railing of the bridge. I felt I
was in love with all of them, I was blissful in their presence. Why make a decision?

Years later, when I had learned to make decisions and I was living in a monogamous relationship, the "others" were still there. They just had different
names and had also learned to make decisions. Adultery? A change of partner?
These possibilities were out of the question: I had been raised to believe in a
strictly Christian ethic and value system, and I placed ideas like honesty, truth-
fulness, and willingness to sacrifice above my personal wishes and needs.

But the tension inside of me was growing; on one hand was my longing for
freedom, for a love-erotic exchange with other beloved souls and bodies, on
the other my need for safety and security . . . I did not know how to bring them
together. I was getting more and more dissatisfied and tense, while love in my
life was diminishing . . .

Again I thought I had to make a decision between freedom and security.
Freedom won and so I broke up with my partner.

What I did not know in those days was that love never makes decisions,
never excludes, and never builds borders. Love never expects, never demands
and never separates. Love gives itself, love saves, nourishes and unifies. It creates a synthesis of freedom and security. And it is because we lose our love
that we make decisions–either for freedom or for security.

Then, one day, I saw a blossoming cherry tree by the wayside . . .

CHERRY BLOSSOM

> To achieve this surrender, this disintegration of oneself through
> love–this is in fact the greatest and the only real spiritual effort. There is
> no other.

> –Aba Aziz Makaja

We are 24 people, mostly academics–doctors, psychologists, artists, social
scientists and others. Our longing for knowledge of all-embracing life, for the
meaning of our existence, and, for many of us, a longing for God also, has
brought us together and is still keeping us together. We live in a so-called
"group-marriage," even though we don't especially like this word for it re-

minds us of the institution of marriage, which seems outdated to us, for reasons more complex than high divorce rates. Our name for our form of living together is *Svejena*, the Croatian neologism for "everything is one, the One; everything is together, everybody is together, we all are a community."

The spiritual teacher Aba Aziz Makaja is our guide, he is our teacher and model. He is a fully accomplished tantric teacher, one of the greatest living masters of Tantra, as experts say. We are very happy that we are able to live so close to such a source of love and knowledge. But what is special about our tantric circle Cherry Blossom (and the other tantric circles as well as the Komaja community altogether) is that all of us are teachers and examples for each other. Maintaining and developing forms of communication and interaction is an essential part of our methodology for personal and spiritual growth. I admire and I learn from Jane's[1] enrapture, Anne's awareness, Christopher's patience, Kathrin's power, Andrew's joy, Marie's loveliness and so on. Each of my husbands and wives is an example and teacher for me, each is a support in my efforts for self-completion.

THE RECONCILIATION OF OPPOSITES

If you would really understand that spirit is also the spirit of worldly life and worldly pleasure, you would all be, without exceptions, as diligent and as disciplined in your spiritual efforts as I am.

–Aba Aziz Makaja

We, children of the Western Christian tradition, inherit a legacy that strains further development, which L.L.Whyte calls it "the European Dissociation of Body and Mind."[2] In his view, dissociating the mental and physical levels of exchange results in disturbing and deforming each exchange system. It strains them with overcompensating activities, which are driven by the systems' dissociation, rather than by their internal qualities. As Ken Wilber put it: ". . . both, an obsessive emphasis on the sensations of the body and sexuality, and the Ego's obsessive need for power and abstract truth or future aims are often typical for the dissociated I."[3]

Therefore, in Western culture and in the organized religion of Christianity, sexuality and spirituality are constructed as irreconcilable opposites. This alleged dualism is deeply anchored in the subconscious of Westerners: sex has its place in the bedroom, spirituality in the silence of one's chosen place of contemplation. It is not thinkable to put them together. There is no answer to the question of the reconcilability of sex and spirituality. Mutual support and stimulation are even less plausible. But in the human being both aspects are present in different percentages and different forms of expression: the "earthly"

longing for a love-erotic merging with others and the transcendental longing
for becoming one with God.

TAKE THE MAGIC WAND OF LIFE!

Take the magic wand of life!
Awaken Kundalini!
You are the Lingam between heaven and earth!

–Aba Aziz Makaja

The basic concept of Makaja's teaching about personal and spiritual development is so obvious and logical that it seems amazing that Cherry Blossom and the other tantric circles of Komaja should still represent the
exception.

We human beings are channels of spiritual or life energy, also called
Kundalini. This basic energy moves through our energetic body and causes
various psycho-physiological phenomena. In the region of the sexual organs,
these include sexual arousal, fear, hate, depression; in the area of the stomach
they include analytical abilities, but also lust for power, self-obsession and
criticism; in the area of the heart love, joy and enrapture; in the throat area,
courage and devotion; in the forehead reagion creative and spiritual intelligence and consciousness; in the crown *chakra* highest orgasmic ecstasy and
bliss of the saints. Normally our life energy is not under conscious control, it
moves through the body as it likes, reacting to energetic influences from outside, which are also unconscious. Thus we get "infected" by the anger and joys
of others. On the other hand, if we are strongly anchored in love, we can suc-
ceed in disarming someone else's rage.

Our experience, as well as psychological and philosophical research work,
shows that the human being is most happy when it is in the state of love or being in love; then one is physically and psychically healthy, one feels fulfilled
and creative, one's efficiency in general and one's social consciousness are
also increased. In this state we use our abilities to the maximum. With love's
great inspiration we can even rise above ourselves and unique intellectual and
artistic results follow. If we want to live happily and completely develop our
human potential, we have to become masters of love and being in love, which
implies bringing the mighty basic energy of life under our conscious control,
and guide it wherever we want.

This is the principle. How a person acquires it is not really important. Our
disciplines include meditation; the *Seven Conditions*; the *fourfold impeccabil-
ity* (in thoughts, feelings, words and deeds); as well as our training in the virtues. Tantric work is a methodology as well as a touchstone of success in the
practices mentioned above.

THE TECHNOLOGY

Instead of using sex, you abuse it.
It is Divine.

–Aba Aziz Makaja

In the part of the meetings related to the spiritualization of sexuality, we teach people how to use their sexual center as a trigger to activate their higher centers of energy and consciousness. Both theoretically and practically, these centers are activated in the same way as dynamite is activated by inserting a capsule containing explosive which is lit via a wick. When the capsule explodes, it sets fire to the dynamite. When we activate a person's sexual center in the right way, it is like the explosion of a capsule. This means that one's intercourse should last quite long without orgasm, but at the same time one's energies should flare completely and be released. One's movements, grimaces, voice and words express everything–everything good, everything bad, all of one's wishes, fears and deviations–not only the sexual ones, but all possible ones. In this way one expresses also all one's ideals and longings for paradise completely freely, as well as one's visions for one's ideal life, partnership and community. When we manage to do everything the way it should be done, when one's sexual center is kindled in this way, there is the explosion of one's sexual center capsule.

When this "explosion" happens, one's energy naturally moves to one's higher centers and one experiences enlightenment. The prerequisite for this is that intercourse lasts at least one to one and a half hours, that it be completely inflamed. Naturally, sincerely and truly, from earth to heaven, everything should be open. Then one's higher centers of energy or consciousness open up and become activated. The person experiences him or herself like an aura, a being made of energy, spirit and consciousness, and as such, the person transcends sexuality. People do not care whether they will have an orgasm or not, because they are in complete delight, in the bliss of consciousness which is in fact our core.

The intensity of the ecstasy depends on how much one's *nadis*, or channels in the etheric body, and one's nerves and endocrine glands are purified. Also related to this is how long one's state of heightened energy, one's heightened enjoyment of life, will last. For some people it stops at the end of intercourse, and for others it lasts for another day or two, or even five or six more days. There are different techniques, methods and teachings that help to enter the state of extended, or Divine, consciousness. One can enter these exalted states via different centers, one of them being the sex *chakra*."[4]

As a result of this approach the quality and purpose of sex changes completely. Instead of it being "occasionally" ecstatic, one willingly, systematically makes it ecstatic. Love's play no longer results in mere physical satisfaction or exchange of love between partners, but it helps to broaden the lover's consciousness and their knowledge of all embracing life. It transforms itself into lovemaking with God.

Typically, this kind of lovemaking can go on for hours with a minimal loss of energy and a huge increase in love, happiness, joy and an all embracing satisfaction of body and soul. The longer love's play goes on, the stronger it becomes, as in a meditation. At the same time, each part of the body becomes highly sensitive, like a vagina. Spontaneous animalistic impulses are set free, including "grunting" without mental mediation. This setting free of such animalistic or "demonic" energy is usually followed by strong eruptions of love and devotion, accomplished by the feeling that one has become closer to God and the secrets of his creation.

Over and over again, when I have *Maithuna* with Makaja and I look at him, his face seems to be "age-old" and timeless at the same time, as if it bore the writing of the experience of a million years. Through this face I dive into creation. Eternity is in the room. It is unity between my life and his, and with all life surrounding me. No more "I," no more "you"–all of God is revealed through our bodies and souls.

WHAT MAKES THE WISE MAN RISE, MAKES THE FOOL FALL

Not a big cock but a big heart, this is what the women go crazy for!

–Aba Aziz Makaja

Some people think that tantric work is about sex. This is partly due to some Tantra teachers who focus on the expression of suppressed and forbidden erotic desires and sexual needs. Also at cause is our anti-sexual or hyper-sexual consciousness formed in the occidental tradition. The basic principle of Tantra is that all manifestations of life are integrated, including the animalistic, the sexual, and the higher manifestations of love and spirit–but dominated by the latter. In the occidental tradition, all this has been reduced to a sexual principle.

But Tantra is not about sex. It is about virtues! It is about love, truth, honesty, consciousness . . . We live together to practice these virtues and the one who is the best in virtues is ultimately the best in sex. There is no enjoyment of sex without virtues. We enjoy when we love. This is what it is about. LOVE! Is your soul in erection with love and longing? Is it open and devoted? Are you free from your ego and thoughts? In short: do you love? Do you love your counterpart, do you see the Divine in him or her and are you devoted to them during this act so Divine, that sexual unification is supposed to be?

I especially enjoy when we make love and there are several men and women and especially when my partner and I are together with several women. The multiplicity of forms and colors, the beautiful clothes and textiles, the different voices and cries, the different souls with their character and fondness, excite me. But the heights of such love play are unreachable to me when I have lost balance due to a violent quarrel, or I've constantly had a critical attitude against my fellow human beings, or suffered from jealousy and fear for my partner. In such situations, I cannot forget my ever important "I" and I stay captured in the layers of my ego, separated from my beloved ones. There is a certain sexual enjoyment, but it is merely physical and therefore superficial, unsatisfying, the soul stays closed in sadness and is hurt. Spirit cannot manifest.

However, things are different when my daily routine is filled with unlimited, joyful openness and acceptance. At that time, enjoyment is increased by the sexual excitement caused by contact with electrified bodies. Due to my self-oblivion and devotion, each wave of sexual excitement turns into a wave of heavenly delight for my body and soul, a wave of bliss and ecstasy. The higher my enjoyment and feeling of happiness, the more perfect is my self-oblivion and love for all those present, the more perfect my awareness of the unity of all of Divine life–through me and them.

MAITHUNA is exactly this–sexual unification finalized to divine awareness. We are striving for love, we are looking for knowledge, we live in spiritual inspiration. Our lovemaking is but a continuation of this journey, yet now, due to activated vital power, the journey is accelerated. We do what mystics or yogis do: strive for knowledge, the experience of God, but we want to ride there on the flying dragon of our vital power. But this flying dragon can lead us to "devil" if we do not keep the reins in our hands as loving and conscious beings.

I once asked Makaja, "What do you do during lovemaking?"

"The same as during any other activity," was his answer. "I use the mobilized energy to fly to God like a rocket." But this he does, because he ALWAYS "flies to God." In his view sex is the expression of a whole being. What we usually are, is also what we are during sex. Wherever we usually "fly" to we also "fly" during sex. If we usually strive for truth, love and rapture, then we do during sex as well. If we quarrel, if we are critical, if we have bad feelings and thoughts, if we are closed up or egotistic–that's how we are during sex as well. There is no "good" or "bad" sex. Sex is just the setting free of our vital power. And then anything that is living inside of us, what we "cultivate," is what acquires this power. And so my spiritual teacher becomes more and more spiritual and mighty due to his intense tantric activity while the average man becomes more and more material and weak as a result of his sex.

THE GREEN-EYED MONSTER

In their love, worldly lovers forget about the whole world. Spiritual lovers, through love for each other, arrive at love for the whole world.

–Aba Aziz Makaja

Jealousy, or fear for oneself, is a green-eyed monster we look at with open eyes. I used to believe jealousy to be the evidence of the sincerity and strength of one's love: s/he who is not jealous does not love, because people worry only about what is precious to them. In a certain sense this is true. It is a level, a stage we have to pass on our way to complete love. In the end, jealousy indicates lack of love and trust in life.

Most people do not confront jealousy out of fear of its green-eyed, devouring monstrosity. But how can one confront it? One way is loving one partner absolutely, being always totally open to him or her, and giving them unlimited freedom from the bottom of one's heart: "It is a great experience to watch your partner being with someone else. It is a deep meditation, if one wants to go through oneself and get to know oneself. One does not need to be a psychologist nor to psychoanalyze oneself. It is the work of one moment, a direct struggle with the contents of one's subconscious, most of which become conscious in a second! Therefore, for those committed to their spiritual activity and goals, this experience is an opportunity for expanding their consciousness in an accelerated way."[5]

All of us in Cherry Blossom had the courage to take this step. We love our partner and give freedom to him or her. And we watch them being happy, being ecstatic with another person–with or without us. In some couples or triads one partner can focus on one person for a certain period, at which time this person becomes their "most important" relationship. However we do not separate because if one has truly loved once, one loves eternally: Hence the duration of the average membership in Cherry Blossom is more than ten years.

Fifteen years ago I would not have believed that the love-erotic happiness which my loved one experiences with another person could make me happy. But it's true and I have lived in a *Zajedna*[6] with him now for thirteen years. He is in love with them, he embraces them ardently, gives them his heart, brain and sex. I stand or lie beside them, or remember his devotion and their happiness and the same love and devotion flows out of myself as if I were an extension of his hand, a part of his soul. What his soul does, mine does too. And when the "other person" is ready, she will become part of us. With some women this has already happened while some are still standing "outside."

Sometimes I still cry because of their happiness, unfortunately. Actually, this is not because they are happy, but rather because I am not. Suddenly, I am standing "outside," I have lost love–due to fear or lack of discipline.

IN THE FORECOURT OF PARADISE . . .

The art of living is primarily the art of loving!

–Aba Aziz Makaja

Nearly half of the members of Cherry Blossom live together on a large property in the country, while three-quarters of the remaining members live in the immediate vicinity. Three times a year we all gather. We share, practice our disciplines, get support from our spiritual master, learn from one another's experience, gain new knowledge, go deeper, and love and enjoy each other.

It is an atmosphere of understanding and trust. Nothing remains unspoken or unexpressed. Nothing is left unattempted for us to reach the heights of love. We talk to each other a lot–communication being a central point.

We explore the depths of sex. What is so fascinating about sex? Why does it keep people so busy–in a positive as well as negative sense? Why have we lost our naturalness and become obsessed? How can we become free from slavery to this dragon, or better, how can we turn sexuality's dragon into a companion and servant?

We enjoy each other. We celebrate love (with no aphrodisiacs or narcotics). Those who practice their training in radiant love most diligently and successfully enjoy the best. Cherry Blossom satisfies our need for multiplicity, a love-erotic exchange with many souls and bodies, as well as for safety and family. This especially interesting and fulfilling combination enables us to share with many and at the same time deeply. Every year each member of Cherry Blossom defines which percentage of an ideal civil marriage he or she has actualized with the other members of Cherry Blossom. In the year 2002 the group actualized 53% of an ideal civil marriage with each other on average. But many of us, above all those who have been members for a longer time, have actualized about 70%, and with more than 20 persons! These figures show the vividness of our relationships. Makaja, an enlightened tantric master, irresistible and attractive to women and men, because of his realized constant love, is but one of us. Everybody is desired, everybody communicates. Differences in intelligence, beauty and character lose their meaning in our atmosphere of love and multiplicity.

In our meditations and prayers, in our everyday life, at work, in our families we practice the training of love and being in love developed by Makaja. Everything arose out of this basic activity, and thanks to it all exists and grows. When we fall in love again, every time the phase where I feel like "I could embrace the whole world!" arises first. It lasts longer for one person and less for another. It is exactly this ecstatic initial phase of self-oblivion and "disintegration of ourselves through love" we master more and more and make it increasingly durable and independent of the "object of love." This brings us in love with the whole world and finally in love with God.

NOTES

1. Names have been changed to maintain the privacy of the members of Cherry Blossom.

2. Cp. L.L. Whyte, *The Next Development in Man,* New York 1950.

3. Ken Wilber, *Halbzeit der Evolution*. (Up from Eden.) Frankfurt a.M. 1996, S. 244 f. (My translation.)
4. Aba Aziz Makaja, *Eros & Logos*. *The Book for Saints and Sinners*, Skopje/Zürich/Brighton 2003, p. 247 ff.
5. Ibid., S. 151.
6. The term *Zajedna*, from Croatian *za* (for) and *jedno* (the One), th.i. "for the One" but also from Croatian *zajedno* (together, common, with each other), is a new creation (neologism) of Aba Aziz Makaja.

WORKS CITED

Makaja, Aba Aziz. *Eros & Logos: The Book for Saints and Sinners.* Skopje/Zürich/ Brighton: Komaja Stiftung, 2003.
Makaja, Aba Aziz. *Komaja–die geistige Liebes- und Lebenskunst* (Komaja–the spiritual art of loving and living). Zürich/Konstanz: Komaja Stiftung, 1998.
Whyte, Lancelot Law. *The Next Development of Mankind.* Somerset: Transaction Publishers, 2003.
Wilber, Ken. *Halbzeit der Evolution* (Up from Eden). Frankfurt a.M: Fischer, 1996.

Love Is Born from the Pulse of God's Heart: An Insight into the Polyamorous Circle Kamala

Numa Ray

[Haworth co-indexing entry note]: "Love Is Born from the Pulse of God's Heart: An Insight into the Polyamorous Circle Kamala." Ray, Numa. Co-published simultaneously in *Journal of Bisexuality* (Harrington Park Press, an imprint of The Haworth Press, Inc.) Vol. 4, No. 3/4, 2004, pp. 133-139; and: *Plural Loves: Designs for Bi and Poly Living* (ed: Serena Anderlini-D'Onofrio) Harrington Park Press, an imprint of The Haworth Press, Inc., 2004, pp. 133-139. Single or multiple copies of this article are available for a fee from The Haworth Document Delivery Service [1-800-HAWORTH, 9:00 a.m. - 5:00 p.m. (EST). E-mail address: docdelivery@haworthpress.com].

SUMMARY. By constantly developing the ability to love consciously and unconditionally, it is possible to transcend the problems of a monogamous partnership, as well as the jealousy that often accompanies it. Here is a personal account of the transformational process of one of the first members of Komaja's tantric circle Kamala, which has existed for thirteen years and has fifteen members. This demonstrates her struggle to be free from the limitations and expectations acquired from parental and social belief systems, as well as the illusions surrounding sexuality. Included are several practical examples of how the spiritual schooling of Aba Aziz Makaja, founder and spiritual master of the international community Komaja, assists in the cultivation and spiritualization of sexuality, as well as the development of conscious love. The fruits of this transformational process lead to intensive spiritual development, a happier and healthier love-erotic life, and long lasting relationships. Here is a glimpse of what could be the possible future of marriage. *[Article copies available for a fee from The Haworth Document Delivery Service: 1-800-HAWORTH. E-mail address: <docdelivery@haworthpress.com> Website: <http://www.HaworthPress.com> © 2004 by The Haworth Press, Inc. All rights reserved.]*

KEYWORDS. Tantra, love, group marriage, spiritualization of sexuality, Komaja, polyamory

Kamala–
Lotus flower,
The queen of erotic love that shared the beauty of her art with Siddhartha in Herman Hesse's novel about a young man's journey to enlightenment.

Kamala–
A flower on the way to self-realization,
Komaja's second oldest tantric circle,
An adventure on the path to the spiritualization of body and soul.

We are a group of men and women learning together about love, freedom, and responsibility through our efforts to make conscious and spiritualize our sexuality. With Makaja as our mirror and guide, we have come through personal and group crises, growing in love and trust, and glimpsing the divine. Our wish to grow in love and spirit is the glue that holds us together. While two out of three marriages break apart because people act upon their wishes to share love and have a sexual encounter with a new person, the core of Kamala has been together for thirteen years, learning how to share our love with many people in a responsible, truthful way.

I came to Kamala in 1991, rich with the experiences of being a part of two avant-garde communities in New England, which experimented with different ways of living human relationships.

Before that, I spent several years leading what could be called a 'free' sexual life in New York City, where I was born. My goal during this time was to gather as many different kinds of experiences as possible, beautiful and ugly, while at the same time breaking every taboo that I possibly could. I use the word 'free' rather loosely, because although it looked like freedom from the outside, on the inside I was prisoner to much loneliness, always running, trying to fill up the huge dark hole inside my soul. Having one lover, or many, having one partner, or many, does not fill up the hole. My experiences in Kamala have given me the courage to see what is inside this dark hole, as well as the knowledge to fill it up with light and spirit.

My partner and I have lived for eleven years in community with several other couples from Kamala. Together we are its core group. In the early years, Kamala was an experiment for us to learn and grow from. We were unsure about how exactly the group would develop. Now we have developed enough love and trust for one another to say that we experience our relationships as a form of marriage.

Life in Kamala has shown me that love generates more love. When I fall in love I open myself, I become love. It is God's creative magic here in the material world. I love my partner more, I can love his lovers, the people I work with, the stranger on the bus.

When I make love with my new love, or a dear friend, I then experience a fresh wind in making love with my partner again. I bring to him my joy. Something new is born inside of me, therefore something new can be expressed between us. I forgive. Old grievances burn away in the fire of love, and we come closer to each other. It was hard to believe that this could be true until I experienced it myself.

So many of the old beliefs about love and relationships that we have been taught by our parents, established religions, and society are simply not true. It is not falling in love and having sex with someone else that destroys a relationship. Lying and deceiving, having secrets and withholding forgiveness, is what destroys love and trust between people, sometimes irreparably. Most people choose monogamy because they are afraid to face the pain of seeing their loved one enjoying himself or herself with another, afraid of speaking the truth, afraid of being alone. People are afraid to lose what little joy they have found, so they insist on monogamy while they think that they can be secure knowing that their loved one shares love only with them. Security is monogamy's biggest illusion! One must always choose between an old love and a new one, because two loves are not allowed! Therefore there is actually no security in a monogamous relationship. People are always falling in love with each other, it is a gift of human nature. In the polyamorous relationship that I now have with my partner, I have a feeling of security that was never possible before. We can love each other, and love someone new, and we never have to choose.

Although we have given our blessings to each new love that comes into our lives, we do not always accept it gracefully. Sharing is something that has to be learned, and it is not so easy. However, we have decided to go through all possible crises and painful situations and stay together, even when the impulse to run away from each other tempts us. We have decided to choose love, and to choose each other, and this decision makes what appears too painful to endure possible. Of course the understanding and support of a group of friends who have also chosen to face their fears and love each other with body and soul is crucial to the success of such an endeavor. However what has been most valuable is the love and guidance of our tantric guru Makaja. Through the teachings and exercises that his courses provide, and the suggestions and observations that he shares with us, we are led to a deeper understanding of our true nature. What has been a great inspiration to me is learning how it is possible to use our partnership as a method to develop into loving spiritual beings, instead of using the partnership only to satisfy personal, emotional and sexual needs.

One of Komaja's techniques that I found most helpful develops unconditional, impersonal love for all beings. In the love meditation, men and women sit across from each other and gaze deeply into each other's eyes, showing their souls completely, loving this person with their whole hearts. Then, after changing partners, they love the next one just as much. Practicing this, I have developed the ability to love consciously. Love no longer just happens all by itself out of my control, although of course it is wonderful when it does so happen. By deciding to open myself and give myself, by deciding to love, I can include many more people in my intimate life. I have seen that the ability to love is inside me, and not dependent on the qualities of the other person. By not making someone else responsible for my love, I can love my partner when he is in a bad mood, or when he lies to me. I can love his girlfriend when she is being selfish and thoughtless. (Well, at least some of the time!) For this is my spiritual practice. It is becoming easier to let go of the expectations that I have, that my partner must behave in a certain way in order that I can love him, for I have seen that these expectations are not of love. They are my old pictures of love, pictures inherited from my mother, and her mother, pictures that don't fit anymore with what I know to be true about the nature of love. My ability to love is a virtue that I can train by watching myself through different difficult situations, and after the first waves of fear and doubt are over, I can choose to love again. This is my spiritual practice.

During one summer course, I felt extremely betrayed by something that my partner did. I could not forgive him, and my anger and hate was poisoning the whole group. In response to my condition, Makaja said something that has helped me again and again. It doesn't matter what my partner says or does, my task is to remain in good feelings and to stay in love. Nothing else matters.

This is a very simple statement, but when followed, it makes happiness and success in life possible. I cannot always stay in good feelings, but I hold this as my goal. I remember this sentence every time I fall. It helps me to remember that which I know to be true; that love is born from the pulse of God's heart within me, and it is not dependent on something or someone from the outside.

These years of being in Kamala have dissipated so many old beliefs about love and relationships, that I am now a new person. I am learning not to define myself by my thoughts, feelings and beliefs, for I am a child of God. Before my experiences in Kamala, I believed that if my partner was interested in another woman and made love to her, that meant something was wrong in our relationship, I cannot hold his interest because I am not good, spiritual, young, or pretty enough. Now I see that when he is with another woman, I become more interesting to him if I remain in peace. Then he can share his joy with me, and he is very grateful for my openness and understanding. We become closer. What was really interesting to notice was that after I have made love with someone else, I become so much more interesting to him! Then he is especially kind and sweet to me, as long as he can remember to stay in love. Another common social belief is that it is simply not possible for more people to live together while sharing their lives, love, and sexuality, and still remain good friends. This is understandable considering the high divorce rate.

The tantric groups of Komaja are proof that this is possible, thanks to Makaja and his spiritual school.

The next big illusion about the nature of love that Kamala has dissipated for me is the illusion of jealousy. How jealous I am is not an indication of how much love I feel for a person, as is commonly believed. Actually it is a measure of how little I love that person, how little I trust our love, and how low my self esteem is at the time. The biggest cultural illusion around jealousy is that we are powerless against it.

Love, true divine love, impersonal love is the key. Where loves rules in the breast, there is no room for jealousy. Jealousy is always an indication of egotism.

I have helped myself here with an affirmation and visualization:

"I am free of jealous feelings . . ."

With all the power and longing in my heart, with all the passion in my soul, I picture with great concentration how my life is different when this is true. What does love look like when this is true, how do I act, how do I feel. I see it before me, I can feel it in every cell of my body, and then I become it . . . free . . . I picture this while peeling carrots, while meditating, while sweeping the floor, while my partner is making love with someone else.

I am not always free of jealousy, but more and more I can stay in peace, with love filling my heart, and sometimes I even catch a glimpse of happiness when he shares love with someone else. This happens easiest when I am also in love with the women he is with. I feel a very special connection with the women my partner loves. We share something very intimate, for our souls are bonded together through his body and soul. This is why in love and erotic relationships it is extremely important to be impeccably honest. All people involved are deeply connected, and without a person's permission, it is like stealing a part of their soul. When I allow this connection to flow between my partner, his lover and myself, it is something very beautiful. Making love as three, the awakened energies that are channeled through our bodies and souls are very intense, because three energy fields are merging together, three hearts, three souls. Being together in this way also helps to overcome jealous feelings. I love her, and she loves me, and together we love the man, transcending our physical boundaries, and flying up to heaven.

The tantric groups of Komaja provide a safe space for people to discover their erotic impulses towards members of the same sex. Through learning to trust each other, and learning to trust in love, all dreams and fantasies can be realized. This is one of the big advantages of such a group. Having the chance to live out our love-erotic fantasies in a loving and safe environment, we can become free of them, and so have more clear attention for developing spiritually. The people who find the courage to show the sides of themselves that have always remained hidden in the darkness free themselves of these dark sides, and develop a deeper intimacy together. In this way it is possible over the years to build intimate relationships with many people, that are on the same deep level as the marriage between one man and one woman.

Sharing my partner with several other women, I often find myself without him. In the beginning of our relationship, I often felt sad and lonely, needing him to give quality and happiness to my life. At first it was a trauma when he would leave me for five days to visit his lover, fears being stronger than love. Through the years positive experiences have vanquished the fears. After a time my emotional self began to realize that the world will not end when he is with someone else, I will not die because of it, and he will not leave me. As a direct result of our loving other people, our love continues to grow and change, instead of drying up and dying. Now I use my time alone to deepen the relationships with the other special people in my life, to go deeper into myself, and to create the life that I have dreamed of: A life built on discovering the unending source of creative inspiration that flows from my depths and finds expression in all thoughts, feelings and deeds, a life where change and growth are welcome, a life where the love of all people who touch my soul can find expression.

Kamala is the art of living together that the future promises to our generations to come. Kamala is the future born in the present.

Uncomfortable Bridges: The Bisexual Politics of Outing Polyamory

Nathan Patrick Rambukkana

http://www.haworthpress.com/web/JB
Digital Object Identifier: 10.1300/J159v04n03_11

[Haworth co-indexing entry note]: "Uncomfortable Bridges: The Bisexual Politics of Outing Polyamory." Rambukkana, Nathan Patrick. Co-published simultaneously in *Journal of Bisexuality* (Harrington Park Press, an imprint of The Haworth Press, Inc.) Vol. 4, No. 3/4, 2004, pp. 141-154; and: *Plural Loves: Designs for Bi and Poly Living* (ed: Serena Anderlini-D'Onofrio) Harrington Park Press, an imprint of The Haworth Press, Inc., 2004, pp. 141-154. Single or multiple copies of this article are available for a fee from The Haworth Document Delivery Service [1-800-HAWORTH, 9:00 a.m. - 5:00 p.m. (EST). E-mail address: docdelivery@haworthpress.com].

SUMMARY. This article discusses the relationship between polyamory and bisexuality in the context of the formation of the Trent Polyamory Society, a university discussion and social group. Through a discussion of the rationale and goals of the group, and the diverse reactions to its formation, this article explores the parallels between coming out as polyamorous and coming out as bisexual. Both polyamorists and bisexuals occupy liminal subject positions (most notably between straight and queer cultural values and practices). Just as bisexuality is an uncomfortable bridge between straight and queer culture, polyamory (or public polyamory) can be seen as an attempt to 'tame' a culture of radical sex, or to universalize a lesbian feminist practice. A pressure to be(come) bisexual within polyamory is discussed with reference to a similar pressure within 1970s feminism to be(come) lesbian. *[Article copies available for a fee from The Haworth Document Delivery Service: 1-800-HAWORTH. E-mail address: <docdelivery@haworthpress.com> Website: <http://www.HaworthPress.com> © 2004 by The Haworth Press, Inc. All rights reserved.]*

KEYWORDS. Polyamory, bisexuality, lesbian feminism, sex radicalism, coming out, identity politics, queer, non-monogamous relationships, monogamy

It all started at a potluck social over vegan food and the boisterous release of tension that can come only from serious essay procrastination. Basking in the starch-induced afterglow, we began wondering what kind of shit we could disturb if we put up a sign proclaiming ourselves "The Trent Orgy Club" at the next clubs and groups day of "Canada's Outstanding Small University." After some deadpan renditions of how we would answer such obvious questions as "Okay, so what do you guys *really* do at your meetings?" (Oh, we really have orgies–if you're interested, here's the sign-up sheet, and make sure to write down your contact info and indicate your three biggest turn-ons . . .), the conversation turned to how great it would be if we actually could have a polyamory group at such a small university. Even though I knew several people there that evening were polyamorous, or considering becoming so, I was surprised when people said they would be eager to join such a group, and in fact would be willing to help get it going. I was even more surprised, however, by the amount of controversy that would eventually be drummed up in the countercultural community by our group's existence.

As a novice polyamorist, I had noticed that though there seemed to be some public discussion of polyamory, it was nearly always on the margins of society, as part of queer or kink sexual subcultures (such as the BDSM[1] community) that saw it as part of their own individual discourses, and rarely discussed it on its own.[2] There were many issues that various people felt needed addressing. Some of us were in straight partnerships, and were disillusioned that we could not access the support of the queer community on poly issues. Others were not close enough to an organized kink scene to truly benefit from the poly discussion therein or else wanted to discuss it in a non-kink context. As a collection of individuals, we were concerned about the lack of a public forum for working through the issues surrounding non-monogamy and wanted a social group where people could talk, socialize, and share resources, as well as generally have fun. After a few more potluck-dinner conversations we decided to go ahead with it. The Trent Polyamory Society was born. We hoped the group's presence would create that which the name implied: a social network among non-monogamous people. What we didn't foresee (though perhaps we should have), was that to come out as polyamorous individuals would have further implications: it would out the issue of polyamory itself.

Coming out is a delicate issue. It has serious corollaries, and the ongoing examination of these is one of the topics that fuels a great deal of theory and debate among the (sub)culturally marginalized. The phenomenon of publicly coming out as polyamorous is particularly interesting as there can be many different responses and social consequences. The reaction to our group forming was partially a backlash, not from those necessarily opposed to polyamory, but interestingly, from other people who practice polyamory, or other forms of non-monogamous sexuality. These reactions and their consequences make up the first section of this paper. The second section deals with the existence of some commonalties that I have observed between coming out as polyamorous and coming out as bisexual. I believe that, to a certain extent, the politics of polyamory can be seen as similar to those of bisexuality. Both "polyamorous" and "bisexual" are particularly difficult social mantles to take on, partially due to the fact that their liminal nature–their position between conditions that many conceive of as mutually exclusive (i.e., gay/straight, radical/mainstream)–makes them uncomfortable bridges between discourses that, at the best of times, resist being bridged, and at worst, want nothing to do with each other.

We started our group slowly, posting notices around the university and in the student newspaper. After a few meetings, including a well-advertised movie night, we had a public image and a regular membership. There was no one factor common to everyone who attended these meetings and events. Some people were in couples or marriages, others were single or in more casual relationships. Some were obviously and actively seeking partners, while others were practicing poly-fidelity. Most of the people attending meetings were in their 20s, but not all, and the mailing list we maintained contained more than one older married couple. Many were polyamorists, but some were non-polyamorists who were either curious or just interested. Most were students at the university. Finally, there were a large number of members that identified as bisexual (both men and women), some as straight, and a few as lesbian.[3] In terms of membership, we were secure in the small but active community we were creating. Many people outside of our group, however, didn't seem to take us seriously. I found it disconcerting that the most openly polyamorous people at Trent (and here I am referring to a group of out and political lesbians, some of whom have talked about polyamory and non-monogamy in the school newspaper and on the radio) never attended any of our events or meetings. It's not that they didn't support our group's existence (a friend of mine in that group actually wrote an article about polyamory that mentioned us at the end), but they were conspicuous in their absence.

The most negative reaction (that I was personally in a position to observe) from a non-polyamorist was from a married student who was quite defensive about her own monogamy. However, once I explained that the attitude of our group (and of many people into polyamory) was not one of anti-monogamy, but rather of anti-*compulsory* monogamy, she was more accepting. The most damaging reaction came from an article in the sex advice column in our school's newspaper. This article portrayed our group as a bunch of "culty" sex maniacs who "[get] together to watch inspirational films, such as *Threesome*" (Raunchy 15). It implied that we were a polyamory recruitment machine, that we were "[sucking people in] with promises of sex and more sex" (15), and basically intimated that we didn't have a balanced view of what we were talking about. This article hurt our group for several reasons. First, publicly ridiculing our group's composition and mandate (with such comments as "Please god, don't give them a levy" [15]) was very demoralizing; I noticed a drop in enthusiasm in the group, and I personally started questioning what were doing, and why we were doing it. Second, it made others do the same thing, and stole back much of the ground of respectability that we had been slowly trying to accumulate through a variety of strategies, such as being very public and above board with our events, and hosting a successful (if sparsely attended) workshop on polyamory issues for a sexuality conference held at Trent. Finally, but probably most fundamentally, the article completely misrepresented the group's standpoint with respect to polyamory. If our group had been proselytizing–that is, if we had been radically political and had insisted that everyone ought to become polyamorous[4]–then the article's broad pronouncements about our "glorifying polyamoury [sic]" (15) (which were followed by a clichéd version of the contents of *The Ethical Slut*) would have been an appropriate chastisement of our group. We had, however, been proposing a balanced perspective on polyamory, discussing the negative as well as the positive aspects of the lifestyle during our meetings and events, and so we were baffled, and in fact quite angry, that we were being quite inappropriately accused of the opposite. This article, like many other opinions we heard in response to our new public visibility, was based not on a point of view gleaned from attending one of our meetings or workshops, nor from reading anything we had written, nor even from knowing us personally. We thus discovered the most insidious enemy in the battle to create a societally visible aspect to polyamory: preconception.

The most common criticism I heard was that some people were afraid that any group of openly polyamorous people would be nothing more than a pickup scene, and a straight pickup scene at that.[5] This could have had to do with an impression that the straight non-monogamous scene is the legacy of 1970s free-love, swap clubs, and swinging: all scenes that have been guilty of a large degree of male chauvinism and the reinforcement of traditional male/female sex-roles (Weeks 19). Gay male and lesbian non-monogamy, on the other hand, can be seen to have its roots in anonymous/group sexual experiences, and the extension of the lesbian feminist rejection of all things "patriarchal," respectively. Though there is certainly some merit to this reasoning, I believe that such direct social lineages are mythic. In reality, rather than an unbroken line from one group of sex radicals to the next, the acculturation of individuals into certain ways of being can be (and usually is) much more eclectic. My own acculturation into the world of non-monogamy was multifaceted. When I mentioned that my partner and I had decided to engage in an open relationship, a polyamorous lesbian friend of mine recommended *The Ethical Slut*. This led to many discussions with polyamorists and free-love advocates (young and old), to perusals of the Internet, to devouring even more books and articles, and finally to my own experiences. These experiences (especially the bad ones!) taught me my most profound lessons. All this has led to what I like to think is a multifaceted, multi-traditional practice of polyamory, and to the conclusion that there are as many styles of polyamory as there are polyamorists–with no single tradition being the sole factor influencing any one particular group.

So why was there a resistance to our group's formation among some polyamorists? I began to realize that much of it stemmed from a negative reaction to straight pickup scenes. A fundamental distrust of "straight" polyamory, due in part to the spectre of the harem, seemed to be an ineluctable consequence of being openly, and publicly, polyamorous.

If this is in fact the case, is there no way to reclaim straight polyamory? If non-progressive moulds are the only ones that people seem able to symbolically associate with this particular style of loving, is there no way to transcend that inheritance? Must straight polyamorists become gay, or at least bi so that they can fit into a "queer" discourse of polyamory? Why does this discourse seem more fundamentally "authorized" among the countercultural? Must heterosexual polyamorists remain closeted with respect to their multivalent desire, to avoid seeming like "players" or "sluts"?

I don't believe, however, that we were naive to think that a non-subculture-specific society would be a positive and progressive move for polyamorous politics. This might have been the case if the lack of our group's popularity had been the end of our group's impact, but this was not the case.

One of the most interesting consequences of starting our Society was the reaction of people who didn't join. Many of the most involved discussions about polyamory that I (and others) have had since we started the group have been in bars and coffee shops and even on the streets. They centre around either people who are intensely interested in polyamory, people who have had non-monogamous experiences in their past (good and bad) or else poly (or prospective poly) folk who, for one reason or another, don't want to or can't be an active part of our Society. For some it is that, though privately out, they aren't ready or aren't willing to be public with this aspect of their sexuality. For others, it is a desire to understand their friends' lifestyles that drives them to ask questions: they want to know how the dynamics of polyamory work so they can know things like how to relate to their friends' lovers, and their friends' lovers' lovers. Still others are just fascinated by the existence of a way of being so alien to their own as to be completely incomprehensible, if not completely inapplicable to their own lives and situations ("just how *does* one deal with jealousy anyway?"). These conversations are occurring more and more frequently. Non-polyamorous friends tell me of discussions they have had with others on the topic, and in the past year polyamory has been mentioned in our school newspaper at least four times and at least five times on the campus radio station.

Polyamory's presence in the public sphere (the discussing of its issues in the public realm) though not a direct result of our group forming, was a result of the "outing" of the issue of polyamory, combined with the social visibility of some of our group's members. The discussion and debate generated by posters announcing events for polyamorous people was truly fascinating. Many wanted to know about polyamory, even if they were skeptical, or even downright opposed to the precepts that underlie non-monogamous relationships. Taking a page from other fringe sexual political movements, we used the "p" word; vocally and often, and as a result, the *idea* of polyamory (that it existed as a choice and was a real thing) was reified. I see this as our greatest–and most ongoing–success.

But the question remains: is there no way for polyamorous people to transcend the image of the neo-hippie/swinger and the concomitant stigma attached to coming out? In order to explore this, the reasons for remaining closeted might bear further scrutiny, and a comparable example might lend a useful perspective. A similar crisis of coming out, and a similar fear of the negative consequences that could be caused by coming out, is perhaps present in another act of self naming: that which troubles people who identify as bisexual.

Kinsey's figures indicated that while only few of the men he surveyed self-identify as bisexual, 46% of them had experienced sexual acts with both men and women (Kinsey, "Human Male" 36).[6] There is a similar phenomenon with people who practice multiple partnerships. While most people do it sometime in their lives (though for most it is experienced in its less ethical form: cheating), few people want it linked to their identity. Being seen as someone who 'juggles' multiple relationships is often to be marked as a player, or a slut (Easton and Liszt 4). In addition, public polyamory can carry serious social and legal consequences, such as the loss of friends, jobs, and the custody of children (Easton and Liszt 206). Often, if a polyamorous person is single, or in couple, passing as non-poly is the preferred strategy.

Any act of passing, however, can be problematic. While with same sex partners, bisexual people can "pass" as gay or lesbian, with opposite sex partners, however, or while single (or if celibate), they might be questioned or accused of trying to maintain heterosexual privilege or conversely, in the former case, of trying to maintain "queer" privilege. In certain cases, this may be a valid accusation, but it needs exploring. What can be found in an analysis of the notion of "trying to maintain a privilege"? One could charitably attribute the above paradigm of "privilege-maintaining" to mean that a person who is actively engaging in a certain discourse-culture (such as a lesbian culture) wants to retain the ability to be seen as a member of another theoretically "opposite" discourse-culture for the purposes of reaping the social/personal rewards reserved for people who can claim membership in, or be positioned within, that discourse. This can be seen as a lack of solidarity with others who are struggling for the increased visibility of certain marginalized subject positions. From a certain political point of view, this is a justified position. As Jeffrey Weeks has remarked, modern Western homosexual discourse is to a large extent gated by the paradigm of "coming out," in that one's "outness" is seen to be crucial to having a valid homosexual identity (Weeks 50). This symbolic act marks, for many, their official entry into a lesbian or gay discourse-culture.

If we look at the phenomenon of coming out more closely, however, we can see a hidden conflation that occurs, one which is the key to the distinction that disallows the validity of maintaining heterosexual privilege. For many people, to fully come out it is not enough to publicly embrace same-sexual feelings, one must also *renounce* one's opposite sexual feelings. Not only that, but to be gay, according to a large number of people (both gay and straight), one must renounce one's connection to the (utterly alien) straight world:

> The heterosexual's erotic preferences and aversions usually do not permit an understanding of the homosexual. Homosexuals as well are baffled by attraction to the opposite sex. This creates two distinct camps from which banners can be flown. And though they may be ideological threats to each other, the two camps are distinct; they are as clearly different as the American eagle and the Russian bear. Their threat to each other is familiar, and the battle lines are clear-cut. (Klein 43)

For many, this move is quite natural. The minoritising trend in gay and lesbian politics[7] is a testament to the fact that many people do feel that they do not belong within straight culture, and actively reject large sections, if not all of it. Rejecting straight desire comes naturally for these people. This is not true for everyone, and it is this grey area between two vectors of desire that is a locus of bisexual desire.

Coming out as bisexual risks ostracization from essentialist segments of both straight and gay cultures that see such identities as mutually exclusive. Coming out can mean that instead of enjambing two fulfilling social discourse-cultures, one is barred from both. Is a bisexual woman welcome at the Lesbian Lunch Social, or the Dyke Hike? Maybe, but maybe not. And not with respect to the event's name, unless she passes. Despite the potential social awkwardness passing could engender (if it were discovered, for example), in situations like those exclusively for lesbians it could be quite tempting–especially if one is single, or happens to be partnered with a woman–to do so.

And if a bisexual man and his female partner happen to look like a straight couple and the family reunion might be a little easier if he doesn't wear his "Nobody Knows I'm Bisexual" T-shirt, then he may well choose to remain closeted in this situation. Greater visibility can help engender more positive feeling towards bisexuals and other marginalised groups, but it can simultaneously make one a target, and–the personal political aside–sometimes it's just easier, strategically convenient, or economically necessary to live under the radar. Not all of us can afford to be sex radicals–and for people in certain situations (like living in countries with harsh morality laws) it is not a choice at all.

The same is true for polyamorous people. To come out of the poly closet is to risk alienating oneself from the straight(-edged) world, but also perhaps from the sex radical community. This may be partially due to a phenomenon identified by Sarah Thornton in her book *Club Cultures*. Thornton identifies a tendency in subcultural groups to privilege the authentic, the anti-mainstream–in a word, the underground (Thornton 5). If something seems too mainstream, or seems in any way corrupted by outside influences, it is often rejected (6). Discussing "secret" sexual matters might make them seem less naughty, less exciting. It is possible that this was happening within the local sex radical community. The impression that our group was attempting to "train" just anyone in the art of polyamory might have been seen as a corruption of something pure, something authentic that arose in its essential form in the utter rejection of heterosexist culture, that is, in lesbian feminism.

Lesbian feminism can be properly thought of as a discourse-culture. Amanda Udis-Kessler traces the intersection of the discourse of radical feminism with lesbian culture in the 1970s/80s:

> There were serious questions as to whether lesbians could be good feminists. Lesbian feminist groups such as Radicalesbians and the Furies turned the tables [in the 1970s], arguing that lesbianism was a political choice indicating the willingness to prioritize women over men, and as

> such was exactly what feminism needed. Ti-Grace Atkinson had pro-
> posed that "feminism is a theory, lesbianism is a practice"; this aphorism
> spread in a slightly, but crucially, different form: "feminism is *the* the-
> ory, lesbianism is *the* practice." Over time, this idea was adopted among
> lesbian feminists, and came to permeate feminist culture to such an ex-
> tent that it was questioned whether heterosexual women could be good
> feminists. (20)

She speaks of a culture into which the price of full entry was to assume the
mantle of "lesbian," and she attributes this historical moment to the rise of
out/political bisexuality. In opening the door to same sex desire, many women
found that they could embrace it, but could not–or did not want to–fully aban-
don opposite sex desire (23). Being part of the lesbian-feminist discourse-culture, while also remaining true to one's self, necessitated a re-closeting of
desire, this time of straight desire (24). Caught between two options, both of
which would mean some sacrifice, some closeting, the movement of public
and radical bisexuality was born, the love child of lesbian-feminism and
straight desire. From groups such as The Boston Bisexual Women's Network,
the Chicago Action Bi-Women and BiPOL in San Francisco grew a vibrant international community, and a new way to think about sexuality (26).

While a more accepting, queer community now exists in many places (most
notably, perhaps, on university campuses where queer theory is in and
genderfucking and other still more liminal forms of expression are *de
rigueur*), there are still groups organized along very exclusive lines. The world
of woman to woman desire in many places remains very much the province of
the lesbian, and many lesbians stick to their own, and, if not taking issue with a
bisexual woman's identity, might not consider dating her.

This could have to do with the continual presence of stereotypical portrayals of bisexuality in the media. An episode of the popular television show *Sex
in the City* portrays a group of bisexual friends as immature, childish swingers
who cannot take relationships seriously, and who presumably play spin the
bottle every night after polishing it off (along with several others) in their
swank New York City apartments. Okay, so maybe it's not a thousand miles
off, but it still portrays bisexuals (and non-monogamous people for that matter) as frivolous, childish and somewhat shifty.

Now, one of the attractive things about recent, progressive, lesbian culture
has been the generation of an extensive discourse on the subject of polyamory,
to which the existence of books like *The Lesbian Polyamory Reader* is testament. The cultural cachet of this discourse (the strategies, joys and dangers of
polyamory, and–most importantly–their discussion) is not something to be
taken lightly, given up, or disseminated widely. And since this kind of sexuality is seen by some as an essential part of lesbian sexuality, there is a particular
resistance to disseminating this discourse to straight people. The *Reader*, for
example, is structurally exclusive (as the name indicates, it is a book about les-

bians and for lesbians) but it also contains an anti-monogamy and marriage bias (DeCrescenzo 2) that may alienate some straight people, as my married friend was alienated by just such an impression.

Just as "out" bisexuality is, in one of its many aspects, a liminal position between two fiercely opposed discourses, perhaps "out" polyamory is no longer countercultural (or perhaps exclusive) enough to be comfortably part of a sex radical discourse. I have been told that "polyamory isn't something you talk about, you just do it." Given that the same people who say this also purport to value communication within a sexual and romantic context, I find this attitude a little incongruous, and maybe a little defensive, too. If being caught between underground radicalism and public discourse is polyamory's first claim to liminality, the second might be its place caught between queer and straight discourses of desire.

I can perhaps be forgiven, here, for indulging in a little personal reflection. As a straight, male sex radical, I feel a kinship with certain radical feminists of the 1970s, and a resonance with their struggle. I feel as though in order to be a "good" sex radical, I need to be gay, or at least bi. This has not only a psychological and social aspect, but also a practical one. I believe that though my sexual orientation is straight, my ideological and political orientation towards sex is queer. I feel at home in and around the queer community, but I can only benefit indirectly from parts of it. As it is not *my* community, I have never fully been able to fit in. From my spectator status at Queer Collective gatherings to being questioned for speaking out about queer issues (how dare I?!), I feel a pressure to either come out or get out. I have even, at times, assumed that foot-in-the-door half-identity: "bi-curious." Which, to a certain extent, is true. I am bi-curious, but I am not *a* "bicurious" (whatever this strange animal would be). The pressure of holding a subject position, such as that of a polyamorist, that straddles aspects of both "queer" and "straight" forms of relationship is one that follows the path of least resistance: towards the more accepting queer discourse-culture, and the more established polyamorous discourse therein. But as much as ideologically and theoretically I might believe the opposite, to *be* poly is not enough to *be* queer, no matter how much it may be queering the concept of love or partnership. For me to claim queerness would weaken the definitional specificity of "queer," which, though slippery and resistant to definition by its very nature, does have one very clear vector of definition for most people: queer is not straight. I would feel uncomfortable claiming a heterosexual queer subject position as I think it is not politically viable with respect to current identity politics and might erode the radical potential of the queer subject position.

So where does that leave straight and bisexual polyamorists? I don't want to feel like I need to assume a put-on sexual identity to be a part of, and find solace and support in, the "right" kind of polyamorous discourse-culture. Nor do I want my bisexual partner to feel isolated from the queer discourse of polyamory, or any queer discourse, due to the fact that she is dating a man.

Ethical polyamory is about trying to transcend the space mapped out by such movies as *Threesome, Eating Raoul* and *Shampoo* where non-monogamy is either demonized, seen as frivolous and irresponsible, or leads to traumatic catastrophe–if not all three. I feel it is a shame that poly folk sometimes get lumped in with these stereotypical and dated images of non-monogamy. We're not perfect, none of us, but how well we "do" polyamory is certainly not organized along purely classical group lines. I think that some of the polyamorous lesbians I know are closer to a more *laissez-faire* swinger lifestyle than they would like to believe, while many of the straighter poly couples I know take their politics directly from lesbian feminist models of desire.

So I find myself, like the disillusioned lesbian feminists before me, stepping into that liminal space between comfortable opposites and staking a claim to it. As a straight, out polyamorist, I am exercising my existential right to self-name and forge a subject position for myself and for those like me. "Once forms of sexuality are named, then people find that their longings, which had previously been lonely, unspeakable, perhaps unformed, have a home" (George 101). Like the bisexual identity Sue George is referring to in this quote, a polyamorous identity has that power of organization. And perhaps for non-monogamous sexuality, this naming is even more important, since it already has a set of frames within Western consciousness–almost all negative.

If I can find *The Ethical Slut* shrink-wrapped in a garden-variety sex store in a small Canadian city, then something is happening. As individuals, I feel that those of us that can afford to have the label "polyamorous" linked to our identities have a responsibility to help guide the uncertain future of non-monogamy. As far as the Trent Polyamory Society is concerned, we are going into the second year of poly awareness-raising here in our small corner of the world. This year we plan to be even more public and open with our activities, in order to make it more difficult for anyone to judge us based on prejudices alone. Not only will there be posters announcing everything from "Polyamorous Pool Parties" and "Polyamorous Picnics" to "Polyamorous Potluck and Panel Planning Parties," but these events will be publicized and discussed as much as possible in the campus media before and after they occur. In addition we plan to put up a Website and forge contacts with other polyamorous groups in order to really push the envelope of poly community with some good old-fashioned networking.[8] Perhaps with time, people will become less inhibited about the public discussion of "secret" matters, and the queer and straight communities will decide they can share ethical polyamory. Solidarity has many facets, and sometimes the hardest step towards it is abandoning the belief that some people must be denied access to something worthwhile and special in order to retain its specialness.

NOTES

1. Bondage and Discipline, Domination and Submission, Sadism and Masochism.

2. With excellent and notable exceptions such as books like *The Ethical Slut: A Guide to Infinite Sexual Possibilities* by Dossie Easton and Catherine A. Liszt and *Polyamory: The New Love Without Limits* by Deborah Anapol.

3. These are only the orientations I am sure of. Though I am not sure that any gay men attended our meetings or joined our mailing list, I am not sure that none did. The preponderance of men that attended the meetings and events were bi or straight identified.

4. Which isn't to say that some members of our group don't think this as individuals.

5. So afraid were we of this interpretation of our motives that we started including the legend "We assure you, this is not an orgy club" in all of our meeting announcements.

6. He has obtained similar results with women (Kinsey, *Human Female* 472).

7. Though in many ways, the view that homosexually oriented people were a different race comes from a heterosexualist discourse of otherness, that is in many cases co-opted and taken up as a reverse discourse. For a further discussion see Michel Foucault, *The History of Sexuality, Volume 1: An Introduction*.

8. If you have a poly group, or just want to join our ongoing discussion about polyamory, drop us a line at <TrentPolySoc@mailup.net>; or join our discussion list at <http://groups.yahoo.com/groups/TrentPolyList/>.

WORKS CITED

Anapol, Deborah. *Polyamory: The New Love Without Limits.* San Rafael: IntiNet Resource Center, 1997.

"Boy, Girl, Boy, Girl . . ." *Sex and the City.* Dir. Pam Thomas. Episode 34. 25 June, 2000.

DeCrescenzo, Theresa. "A Look at Books," rev. of *The Lesbian Polyamory Reader* Marcia Munson and Judith P. Stelboum, ed., *Lesbian News*, Oct 1999, Vol 26 Issue 3: 41.

Eating Raoul. Prod. Anne Kimmel. Dir. Paul Bartel. Bartel, 1982.

Easton, Dossie, and Catherine A. Liszt. *The Ethical Slut.* San Francisco: Greenery Press, 1997.

Foucault, Michel. *The History of Sexuality: An Introduction.* Trans. Robert Hurley. 1976. New York: Vintage, 1990. Vol. 1 of *The History of Sexuality.* 3 vols. 1976-1983.

George, Sue. "Extracts from Women and Bisexuality (1993)." *Bisexuality: A Critical Reader.* Ed. Merl Storr. London and New York: Routledge, 1999. 100-106.

Kinsey, Alfred C., Wardell B. Pomeroy, and Clyde E. Martin. "Extracts from Sexual Behaviour in the Human Male (1948)." *Bisexuality: A Critical Reader.* Ed. Merl Storr. London and New York: Routledge, 1999. 31-37.

_____. *Sexual Behaviour in the Human Female.* Philadelphia: W. B. Saunders.

Klein, Fritz. "Extracts from The Bisexual Option: A Concept of One Hundred Percent Intimacy (1978)." *Bisexuality: A Critical Reader.* Ed. Merl Storr. London and New York: Routledge, 1999. 38-48.

154 PLURAL LOVES: DESIGNS FOR BI AND POLY LIVING

Munson, Marcia and Judith P. Stelboum, ed. *The Lesbian Polyamory Reader*. New York: Harrington Park, 1999.

Raunchy. "Raunchy Love." *Arthur*. [Trent University, Peterborough Ontario] 17 Mar. 2003: 15.

Shampoo. Prod. Warren Beatty. Dir. Hal Ashby. Rubecker, 1975.

Thornton, Sarah. *Club Cultures: Music, Media and Subcultural Capital*. Cambridge: Polity, 1995.

Threesome. Prod. Cary Woods. Dir. Andrew Fleming. Tristar, 1994.

Udis-Kessler, Amanda. "Identity/Politics: A History of the Bisexual Movement." *Bisexual Politics*. Ed. Naomi Tucker. New York & London: Harrington Park, 1995.

Weeks, Jeffrey. *Sexuality and Its Discontents: Meanings, Myths and Modern Sexualities*. London: Routledge, 1985.

We Are All Quite Queer

Betty Dodson

http://www.haworthpress.com/web/JB
© 2004 by The Haworth Press, Inc. All rights reserved.
Digital Object Identifier: 10.1300/J159v04n03_12

[Haworth co-indexing entry note]: "We Are All Quite Queer." Dodson, Betty. Co-published simultaneously in *Journal of Bisexuality* (Harrington Park Press, an imprint of The Haworth Press, Inc.) Vol. 4,
No. 3/4, 2004, pp. 155-163; and: *Plural Loves: Designs for Bi and Poly Living* (ed: Serena Anderlini-
D'Onofrio) Harrington Park Press, an imprint of The Haworth Press, Inc., 2004, pp. 155-163. Single or multiple copies of this article are available for a fee from The Haworth Document Delivery Service
[1-800-HAWORTH, 9:00 a.m. - 5:00 p.m. (EST). E-mail address: docdelivery@haworthpress.com].

SUMMARY. This article claims that solo sex could be viewed as queer sex because one loves a person of the same gender, and discusses the history of masturbation and its growing acceptance. The author explains how she became a teacher of solo sex to women who had difficulty reaching orgasm in the early seventies and, through years of teaching masturbation skills, defines solo sex as the kind of erotic meditation that enables more complete and creative forms of sexual expression. *[Article copies available for a fee from The Haworth Document Delivery Service: 1-800-HAWORTH. E-mail address: <docdelivery@haworthpress.com> Website: <http://www.HaworthPress.com> © 2004 by The Haworth Press, Inc. All rights reserved.]*

KEYWORDS. Solo sex, queerness, masturbation, hysteria, orgasm, vibrators, erotic meditation

If you have ever masturbated, you've had gay sex. Come on, it's a same sex activity no matter what you might be fantasizing. So get a grip on your clit or cock and enjoy being as queer as a three dollar bill. Whether you are straight, bi or gay, rejoice in your queerness because diversity is what sexual expression is all about.

As a woman who's been on the front line of liberating masturbation for over thirty years, I have often wondered why parents, clergy and politicians are so terrified that someone somewhere might be touching their own genitals for sexual gratification. Originally I thought the masturbation taboo was primarily created by organized religions. They put pleasuring oneself on their hit list to make us all guilt-ridden sinners in need of forgiveness so a few can control many. Of course those of us who were smart figured a way out–if God didn't want us to play with ourselves, She would have made our arms shorter.

Eventually I realized that there are other factors besides religion that have given the masturbation taboo its long shelf life. Take homophobia for instance. Many manly men feel that having to do their own dicks will make them less of a man so they have to get laid or have a woman "do them." What if he likes jerking off so much he stays home instead of going out to "score"? Maybe he's afraid that the immense pleasure he gets from working the hard shaft and swollen head with deft fingers will turn him into a queer. Or even worse, he'll end up in a gay bathhouse where he takes it up the ass "like a bitch" and there goes his hard earned masculinity down the drain along with his jism.

Homophobia affects men and women differently. Women are far less threatened by being gay or bi than most men. In many ways the image of two women having sex enhances a woman's feminine image while being gay devastates a man's masculine image. To me, a homophobe believes that being a gay man is being weak like a woman. One of the worst things any boy can be called is a sissy, but we think a girl acting like a boy is cute. We smile and say, "She's a tomboy." While most manly men want to fuck a woman up the ass, they refuse to let anyone get near their own.

The big social fear surrounding masturbating women is that once a woman masturbates and learns how to give herself fabulous orgasms, she will stop putting out for two-minute men, guys who ignore the clitoris and men who are threatened by vibrators. She might even prefer women. There are many manly men who don't want women to become sexually knowledgeable because down deep they know it would create a major change in heterosexuality. They would no longer be able to fuck her for a couple of minutes, blow a load, then roll over and go to sleep. Of course the exception to this is all the smart men who welcome a sexually sophisticated partner. They appreciate a woman who knows what she wants and is able to ask for it.

In my opinion heterosexuality is the one sexual preference that has the most difficulty in sharing equal orgasms. However, I recommend all committed couples whether they are straight, bi, or gay to include masturbation in their sexual repertoire. The most common complaint at the top of the list for married couples or domestic partners is living with a person who doesn't want sex as often as the other. When two people are living together it's important that masturbating separately remains part of each person's sex life. Those moments of sexual solitude allow us to focus on our own sensations and to explore our erotic minds without having to be concerned with another person's pleasure.

Still society resists embracing masturbation, teaching sexual skills and honoring sexual pleasures. Religious conservatives continue to view children as asexual and they discourage or condemn all bodily pleasures. For them, adult sexuality is a committed heterosexual relationship in a monogamous marriage. All other forms of sexual expression are seen as perverted and frowned upon by the church and punished by laws. But it wasn't always like this. When we worshipped the Mother Goddess, sexuality was revered and the human body was sacred.

When we take into account the entirety of humankind's recorded history, the masturbation taboo is relatively recent. Touching one's genitals for sexual gratification has been practiced since the Stone Age. Small clay sculptures of masturbating figures dating from that time show acceptance of this human activity. Greek pottery from the fourth and fifth century B.C. depict both women and men joyfully masturbating along with graphic images of dildo use. In ancient Egypt, the most popular creation myth was based on a daily masturbation ritual that took place in the Karnak temples built over 4,000 years ago–information long suppressed by scholars and religious authorities due to the embarrassment it still causes.

The following text was taken from a wall at Karnak: "In the beginning there was chaos. Chaos was darkness, the waters of the abyss. The first God, Amon, arose from the waters using nothing but his own strength to give form to his body. Amon existed alone. All was his. Yesterday and tomorrow was his. Alone he took his penis in his hand. He made love to his fist. He made his exquisite joy with his fingers, and from the flame of the fiery blast which he kindled with his hand, the universe was formed."

At dawn every morning, priests and priestesses passed through the processional hallways that linked the three temples, arriving at the last room that held the shrine of Amon Ra. There they reenacted the original creation of divine masturbation to raise the sun god for another glorious day. These ancient Egyptians self-created the source of their own spiritual power on a daily basis with divine masturbation–quite a departure from the majority of other religions that profane the human body and all forms of sexual pleasure.

While I realize the Egyptian creation myth doesn't mention a woman's phallus, her clitoris, and the fact that divine masturbation was practiced only by the male priestly caste, I have my own version. The last room is lit with scented candles. All the celebrants sit in a sacred circle passing a water pipe inhaling the sweet smoke from cannabis buds. While Amon is having a go with his dick, the priests and priestesses join in for a morning circle masturbation ritual that ends in orgasms, singing, dancing, playing tambourines and sipping cold Egyptian beer.

In ancient Ireland, the Gaelic word for masturbation was "self-love," but with the arrival of Christianity it was changed overnight into "self-abuse." Religious leaders had successfully turned a natural human activity into a sin for which God would punish them. The Biblical story of Onan, who spilled his seed upon the ground and was struck dead by God, was interpreted as an act of masturbation. However, later scholars reinterpreted the story of Onan and concluded that his crime was disobeying God's order to fulfill his duty by getting his brother's wife with child. Actually, masturbation is never mentioned in any of the old or new testaments of the bible.

In his book, *Solitary Sex: A Cultural History of Masturbation*, Mr. Thomas Laqueur, a professor of history at the University of California at Berkeley, tackles the masturbation taboo by asking, "Why did masturbation, an activity regarded with benign indifference for millennia, provoke such sweeping moral and medical panic around 1700?" He traces it to an anonymous diatribe that appeared in England bearing the ponderous title: *Onania; or, the Heinous Sin of Self-Pollution, and All Its Frightful Consequences, in Both SEXES, Considered, with Spiritual and Physical Advice to Those Who Have Already Injur'd Themselves by This Abominable Practice.* With a ridiculous title like that, you'd think people would question the author's sanity.

This nasty little book was full of bad news. "Willful self-abuse" was epidemic, its author announced, and without the aid of commercially available medical remedies, the prognosis for its victims was dire. Mr. Laqueur speculates the tract was the work of an English quack surgeon named John Marten. Although he was a crude medical huckster, his book spawned many disciples.

During the Age of Reason, masturbation's dangers had become an obsession. Voltaire denounced it as "perverted self-love." Rousseau condemned it as "the equivalent of self-enslavement."

As witchcraft gradually lost its reputation as the major cause of madness, the medical professionals jumped in to take control by establishing masturbation as the next symptom of insanity. Naturally the new priests of medical science had the only remedy. Cruel restraining devices, electrical shocks and alarms, penis cases, sleeping mitts, bed cradles to keep the sheets off the genitals, hobbles to keep girls from spreading their legs, deadly injections, along with male and female circumcision were used to stop children and adults from touching their own genitals for gratification.

In Mr. Laqueur's explanation for this prolonged bout of cultural hysteria over masturbation, he points out that eighteenth-century society was in the throes of drastic change. There was a new commercial economy dedicated to the satisfaction of individual desire. The expanding middle class put a new emphasis on private life including reading novels that took place in solitude giving free rein to the imagination. There was now an alarming new creature whose existence was beyond the reach and control of the church and state. Masturbation was "the sexuality of the modern self" which represented the "dark side" of social transformation.

He is so right on. A massive number of individuals having independent orgasms completely upsets every authoritarian apple cart. What would happen to marital sex and procreation if people started masturbating? A society of self-polluters would destroy the sacred family, motherhood, and what about all the innocent little children? What would become of Christianity if everyone slept late on Sundays with plenty of time to enjoy masturbation? What would happen to all the holidays that bring families together once people discover they'd rather stay home and pet the kitty or spank the monkey? And most importantly, what would happen to a consumer society when people figure out that they can have more fun enjoying cost-free orgasms rather than going out and spending money?

Now here comes a shocking reversal. By the late 1800s, some doctors began performing genital massage to orgasm on "hysterical" women as an ongoing part of their medical practice. Hysteria was seen as a chronic condition in women–the result of sexual deprivation. Since marital sex was solely a penis penetrating a vagina which didn't produce orgasm in most women and masturbation was forbidden, medical authorities were able to justify this clinical practice. Due to a demand from physicians, the first electric vibrator was invented as a medical instrument. These machines reduced the time it took to give a woman an orgasm from around an hour to ten minutes, making doctors' practices more lucrative. Let's hear a round of applause for good old capitalism.

Eventually women were able to buy electric vibrators for home use. They were advertised in women's magazines and sold in catalogs as rejuvenators of youthfulness. But when vibrators showed up in pornographic films in the

1920s, they were no longer available to the general public due to their blatant association with sex. From then on, electric vibrators were sold as massage machines to stimulate men's scalps to keep them from going bald and to soothe sore muscles.

In 1965, my first post marital lover was getting his scalp massaged by his barber with an electric vibrator when he thought, "This would be great for clitoral stimulation!" That same day he went to a barbershop supply store and bought one. The next evening he introduced me to the Oster electric vibrator that looked a bit like a miniature cement mixer. After warming me up manually with massage oil, he calmly strapped the vibrator's rows of metal coils onto the back of his hand. At first I wasn't sure about having a machine in bed with us, but his fingers were doing the vibrating. It was still skin on skin so I figured it was probably okay. The orgasm I had was absolutely amazing and I gradually accepted the vibrator as a sexual toy to be played with from time to time.

In the early seventies, I had the honor of being the first recognized feminist to publicly reintroduce electric vibrators to women solely for their orgasmic benefits. It began with my second one woman exhibition that had a larger than life drawing of a woman using the same Oster vibrator with a finger on either side of her erect clit. I had also drawn a beautiful black man with his head thrown back about to shoot a load as he gripped his stiff eight inch dick. That exhibition ended my relationship with the gallery. Nothing sold and there was a media blackout. Voila, I'd discovered the bottom line of sexual repression.

That's when I became the unofficial spokeswoman for the benefits of masturbation. In my opinion, the acceptance of this sexual activity would be one of the cornerstones of women's sexual liberation. I began writing straightforward articles for magazines on the importance of masturbation for non-orgasmic women and started running workshops to teach women how to harness the energy of these electric pleasure machines.

Many people became concerned that masturbating women would become addicted to vibrators or even worse, we would all become lesbians. While that was definitely true for some, a better term for "vibrator addiction" would be "sexual preference." And instead of all of us becoming lesbian, a more accurate label would be "bisexual" because many of us still liked to fuck with men. We just wanted to have sex on our own terms that included some form of direct clitoral stimulation during intercourse. For those of us who wanted to bring our vibrators to bed for a hot threesome, we needed to find vibrator friendly men.

This next fact belongs in Ripley's *Believe It or Not*–it wasn't until 1972 that the American Medical Association declared masturbation a normal sexual activity. In 1974, I came out publicly as a masturbating heterosexual-bisexual-lesbian in my self-published book *Liberating Masturbation* which later became *Sex for One*. Stringing all those sex labels together was so confusing that no one ever questioned my sexual preference to my face. But behind my back, lesbian-feminists rejected me, many straight women avoided me, and the bisexual community didn't exist at the time. Back then, a bisexual was a person who couldn't make up their mind so we upset both sides of the opposing camps, gay and straight–so much for sexual diversity.

Today, whenever I see the letters GLBT, I think it's great that Gay Pride has finally included bisexual and transgendered people. Sexual diversity among queers has not always existed. There are still pockets of separatism, but for the most part, our community is an example of open-minded acceptance and that's a reason for everyone to celebrate Gay Pride. That includes my postmenopausal women friends who prefer masturbation to partnersex and my Webmaster whose sexual preference is masturbating while looking at pictures of "split beaver."

After more than three decades of teaching women about orgasms, I've learned that most women want some form of clitoral stimulation to continue throughout the entire act of intercourse whether it's a penis attached to a man or it's a strap-on dildo attached to her girlfriend's harness. Freud's idea that the clitoris produces infantile orgasms is a good example of another authoritarian manly man creating more bullshit about what women want. And if a man wants to learn ejaculatory control so he can be a smooth, long-lasting ride worth taking, he's going to do that through the practice of conscious masturbation.

The final level of sexual control comes from peer pressure by our well-meaning friends who warn us not to be too enthusiastic or vocal about enjoying our solitary pleasures. It's best to do it privately and not discuss it openly. So for the most part, we live in a world of closeted masturbators all isolated and alone with our dirty little secret. I agree with Mr. Laqueur when he says that very few people today are willing to publicly defend masturbation as "a morally innocent and socially benign sexual practice." He believes "this solitary pleasure is unlikely to be viewed as an unmitigated social good." In other words, if you do defend masturbation, you will not be taken seriously in academia, or have your book about masturbation reviewed in the *New York Times.*

As a person who dares to speak out about the benefits of self-sexuality and the personal power gained in owning our sexual bodies, I must say it's been a great adventure. While I can't brag about laughing all the way to the bank, I can say that my masturbation book has been in print since 1974. That's thirty years! It's also printed in twelve foreign languages. That means we have the beginning of a global acceptance of J.O. (jacking and jilling off). People in the UK, Mexico, Spain, Italy, Germany, Czech Republic, Denmark, Norway, Greece, Slovenia, Taiwan, Japan and Korea are reading my book at this very moment. One Japanese woman has opened a sex shop for women where she sells my book, vibrators and other sex toys.

There's a lot of satisfaction in knowing that I've helped to make the world a better place with my art, workshops, books, videos, private sessions and

Website devoted to the fine art of masturbation. Two days a week, I freely answer people's questions at <www.bettydodson.com>. Every day I rejoice when I think of all the men and women who have let go of sexual guilt over masturbation and are now enjoying passionate love affairs with themselves as well as their partners.

The following is a statement of purpose on my Website: "I believe masturbation is our first natural sexual activity. Masturbation is the ongoing love affair that each of us has with ourselves throughout our lifetime. Masturbation is an erotic meditation. Masturbation inspires creativity. Masturbation is a way to gain sexual self-knowledge. Cultural denial of masturbation is the basis of sexual repression. Sharing masturbation with a lover enhances sexual intimacy. Taking responsibility for our own orgasm gives us a choice when it comes to partnersex. Selfloving allows us to design a sexlife like an ongoing work of art. Self-sexuality is our daily bread, partnersex is an evening of dining out, and group sex is a grand banquet.

"I propose organizing a sex positive movement with millions of activists joining me on the barricades against sexual ignorance. If you're a friend of sex who would like to take a stand, start today by enjoying your own selfloving sessions without any guilt or apology. Go public by telling a few friends about your favorite masturbation techniques with a description of one of your better orgasms. Finally, sharing masturbation with a friend or lover qualifies you as an activist in the twenty-first century."

As I head into my fourth decade teaching and advocating the advancement of masturbation, way too many Christians, Jews and Muslims are once again on the warpath. So let's celebrate masturbation and sexual diversity with all we've got. Now more than ever, we need an abundance of sexual pleasure to counter all the violence in the world. Let's agree to dedicate an orgasm a week to world peace.

WORKS CITED

Laqueur, Thomas W. *Solitary Sex: A Cultural History of Masturbation.* Zone Books, 2003.

Maines, Rachel P. *The Technology of Orgasm: "Hysteria," The Vibrator and Women's Sexual Satisfaction.* Johns Hopkins University Press, 2001.

Stewart, Michael. "Secrets of Karnak." A&E/BBC Documentary. Lawrence Rees ed. Time Watch, 2001.

[Haworth co-indexing entry note]: "Does Bisexuality Exist?" Clurman, Dan. Co-published simultaneously in *Journal of Bisexuality* (Harrington Park Press, an imprint of The Haworth Press, Inc.) Vol. 4, No. 3/4, 2004, p. 165; and: *Plural Loves: Designs for Bi and Poly Living* (ed: Serena Anderlini-D'Onofrio) Harrington Park Press, an imprint of The Haworth Press, Inc., 2004, p. 165. Single or multiple copies of this article are available for a fee from The Haworth Document Delivery Service [1-800-HAWORTH, 9:00 a.m. - 5:00 p.m. (EST). E-mail address: docdelivery@haworthpress.com].

From Self to Self: Masturbation as the Future of Sex

Eric Francis

http://www.haworthpress.com/web/JB
Digital Object Identifier: 10.1300/J159v04n03_14

[Haworth co-indexing entry note]: "From Self to Self: Masturbation as the Future of Sex." Francis, Eric. Co-published simultaneously in *Journal of Bisexuality* (Harrington Park Press, an imprint of The Haworth Press, Inc.) Vol. 4, No. 3/4, 2004, pp. 167-176; and: *Plural Loves: Designs for Bi and Poly Living* (ed: Serena Anderlini-D'Onofrio) Harrington Park Press, an imprint of The Haworth Press, Inc., 2004, pp. 167-176. Single or multiple copies of this article are available for a fee from The Haworth Document Delivery Service [1-800-HAWORTH, 9:00 a.m. - 5:00 p.m. (EST). E-mail address: docdelivery@haworthpress.com].

SUMMARY. Despite decades of slow progress, masturbation often holds a unique place of shame and derision among sexual experiences. Much of what is hidden most carefully are the fantasies that come with masturbation, which often include imaginary bisexual and polyamorous excursions one would never reveal to one's partners. Opening up the gateways of the heart to our partners and friends, and sharing our feelings about and experience of masturbation, can be truly liberating and life-affirming. Several group masturbation workshops conducted by the author are described. The idea of compersion, which is the full embrace of another person's pleasure, is explained in the context of witnessed masturbation experiences. *[Article copies available for a fee from The Haworth Document Delivery Service: 1-800-HAWORTH. E-mail address: <docdelivery@haworthpress.com> Website: <http://www.HaworthPress.com> © 2004 by The Haworth Press, Inc. All rights reserved.]*

KEYWORDS. Masturbation, sexual fantasy, bisexuality, polyamory, compersion, group solo sex, workshops, solo mirror play

WHAT IS IT ABOUT MASTURBATION? INTRODUCTION AND CONCEPTS

What is it in today's world that makes us shun discussion about self-pleasuring and fear discovery that we like to bring ourselves to orgasm?

In the old days, word got out that masturbation was the vilest of all evils, and that it caused madness and blindness and was tantamount to sodomy. People believed it. In some communities, these pseudo-Biblical and life-denying arguments still carry a lot of weight, and when you mix them with the urgent, burning sexual curiosity that boils out of most adolescents, they produce quite a volatile mix of fear and desire. It's enough to warp one's entire personality, to lead one to question whether their very existence is right. The message of negative sexuality can move through groups of friends and, like that old pamphlet, do significant damage way beyond its intended target.

However, American society also has come a long way in the past three or four decades. The work of pioneers like Betty Dodson, who wrote about masturbation and created all-women weekend masturbation workshops once a month for 25 years, has both helped matters and serves as a barometer of change. Her book *Sex for One* has sold about a million copies, and her Website (BettyDodson.com) is extraordinarily popular. So is Solotouch.com, an all-ages reader-created site where people tell the stories of their masturbation experiences. It is clear that while many contributors feel some apprehension about masturbating, most of them get over it quickly and see nothing wrong with what they feel is a perfectly natural pleasure. It helps to have encouragement, which thousands of other reader stories provide.

A few other things are clear from browsing Solotouch. One is that a lot of boys and men masturbate with their peers, and a lot of girls and women do the same. If they don't do it with one another, many are thinking about and desiring same-sex masturbation experiences even though most consider themselves straight. It would appear that same-sex sharing of masturbation is not just a healthy way to begin one's sexual journey, but also a helpful, pleasurable place for adults to explore themselves and one another.

One of the most common fantasies shared is being seen masturbating, which offers a depth of emotional emancipation and individual expression that is not possible in other forms of sex. I call it *being witnessed* in one's pleasure. It comes very close to one person directly giving another person the right to exist.

It doesn't take a lot of logic to run that backwards: Denying people's right to masturbate, or denying their good feelings about it, is to quite directly deny them the right to be who they are and feel what they feel. And despite the progress that's been made, it still happens a lot. I don't think there's any denying that angst over self-given pleasure is related to the concept of original sin, a sense of shame about life that was brought to Greece by Paul in the first century.

I often experiment with theories of personality that account for the development of people's consciousness in terms of how other people responded to their early sensual and sexual awakening, and how they felt about our masturbation. What were those big people thinking, vibing and saying to us? What did they leave out? What were their apprehensions about masturbation? Can you imagine your parents, or your grandparents, in their self-given moments of surrender? Can you imagine them seeing you? It is usually squeamish territory.

I have a feeling a lot of the apprehension about masturbation hinges on the essentially bisexual nature of the experience, beginning with the fact that sex with oneself is a same-sex experience, hence, a queer experience (though few people think of it that way, it is true, and most sexual feelings are percolating in the unconscious). Queer still comes with a stigma, and there is enormous segregation between the world of straight sex and the queer world; that's what those people do, and this is what I do. Not only does masturbation transgress the queer divide, it also equalizes the erotic marketplace. We all do it, gay, lesbian, straight, bi, old, young–demographically speaking, masturbation crosses every barrier. Masturbation is egalitarian sexuality in a world where sex is one of the biggest (and most petty) power trips.

In one's mind, one can be free. One is not always physically free (or so it seems), but if nowhere else, in the world of the imagination, freedom is possible. With that freedom, we will surely imagine ourselves with anyone we want, doing anything we want. The imagination takes us, for example, outside the strict and rigid boundaries of marriage or monogamy. We can go down on our partner's best friend, or do them both together; we can have the most anonymous, experimental, dominant, submissive or genuinely dark erotic experiences and nobody can control us—much to the contrary of our spoken and unspoken relationships.

In their fantasies and desires, most people are polyamorous: we humans have sexual relationships with people outside our committed partnerships, with people who are unavailable and, for sure, with those of their same sex.

I would propose that the fantasy aspect of masturbation is, in today's world, its most taboo quality. It contradicts the prudish image most of us work so hard to portray to the world, our cool, cultivated nonchalance about pleasure and desire. One can be prim or gentlemanly by day and a raging whore by night (or on lunch breaks, bathroom breaks or in the car, as so often happens). The best way to avoid the discussion of what one thinks about when masturbating is to avoid the whole issue. And that results in a lot of pent-up steam, secrets and hidden desires. Often a kind of high-pressure membrane that exists between intimate partners who don't share that particular aspect of who they are—their innermost desires—and would never dream of doing so. Few would trade the image of good husband or wife for a raging bisexual slut. Yet this denial is dreadfully painful to bear.

One exercise I suggest to partners who want to put a little fire into their sex life is to create a safe space and, going one at a time, masturbate while fantasizing out loud. I suggest that a firm agreement of amnesty be created before the game, that is, that both partners agree to forgive their partner for their desires, no matter what they are. And then just tell the truth. Let it out, free-associating. Learn to encourage one another to desire, to desire whatever, to witness the truth and live with the truth and be fully real in one another's eyes. This creates a closeness that can feel dangerous but is also vivid and satisfying as we go beyond all the emotional mannerisms and choreographed, even crystallized moves of how we present ourselves to our partner.

Usually it's a heck of a lot of fun, if we remember to love. The love that embraces the pleasures and desires of another person is called compersion. Compersion is often described as the opposite of jealousy. I describe it as the place we reach when we get beyond jealousy. It is an affirmation of our partner's love and pleasure rather than an attempt to exercise control over it. It seems clear that jealousy is one thing that gets in the way of most people's attempts to explore unconventional sexuality.

Jealousy goes far beyond what we think it's addressing in sex and relationships; it is a kind of distorted attempt to control the flow of another person's emotions, combined with the fear of a wrenching pain of abandonment. Compersion offers us a way to love that is based on something other than control and conditions. It offers us a way to accept or at least coexist with one another's feelings, which is all we can really do in an honest relationship.

For the past four years at conferences of *Loving More* magazine, I have helped create the communal masturbation experience at what is usually a very intellectually based gathering. In these experiences, adult men and women of all sexual orientations have spent an evening masturbating together, a distinctly sensory, emotional and erotic experience. The process is not about contact sex, but rather, about seeing, hearing, feeling, expressing and showing the erotic.

Loving More is a magazine dedicated to exploring the possibilities of committed, devoted and whole relationships that go beyond the one man, one woman formula given to us as love's mandatory limit. As the years have progressed, I have brought my ideas into the *Loving More* community, carrying with me the understanding that if we can love ourselves shamelessly and fearlessly, it's a lot easier to love and be loved by others.

I would like to use this space to offer my observations from having presented about a dozen masturbation workshops of a variety of shapes and sizes. I would like to offer what I see as a few rich possibilities for the polyamorous and bisexual communities in their truly noble quest for fostering open communication and honesty, redesigning relationship models, understanding sex and teaching compersion.

I am one person who feels that bisexuality implies polyamory, and vice versa. While it is possible to totally segregate relationship experiences, to switch sexual orientations every 10 years, or to hide one's male partner from one's other male partner (and thus avoid same-sex acknowledgement of same-sex desire), when we get honest all that denial is seen for what it is. Bisexual means both genders and both genders means more than one person. Of all the things that have emerged from experiencing men and women masturbating, I've come to appreciate how similar men and women of both orientations are beneath all the window-dressing and cultural rules about sexuality.

A FEW STORIES

Ace of Cups

At a workshop for seven people held in 2000, we played a game which I call Ace of Cups. This is the Tarot card of love itself, the 'fountain that was not made by the hands of men' in the words of Grateful Dead lyricist Robert Hunter. The Ace of Cups is the wellspring of joy and Eros (the Tarot reminds us that these things really do exist).

The setting was a warm, secure, private space, in the country near Seattle, phones unplugged. The group was mixed gender; four women, three men. Two of the women were lesbian.

The group got together the prior night for dinner followed by a kind of self-pleasuring social, an icebreaker where we simply undressed and masturbated together with no particular structure or intention. We then met for about two hours to talk the next morning, debrief the prior evening's experience and plan the events of the coming day. Everyone agreed in advance on the basic scenario, and what our boundaries were (invited touch only, watching and talking to people was okay).

When it was time to begin, we passed the full Tarot deck around and everyone turned over the top card. There was a kind of playful tension in the air. Who could it be? Will it be me? Will it be her? I'd really like to see her. I'd really like to *show* her . . .

Eventually, someone came to the Ace of Cups and got into the middle of the group. They described what kind of experience they wanted, and perhaps stated out loud what he or she was feeling as lying or sitting there naked. This was somewhat personal: coming out with your confessions of desire, like, for example, I want everyone touching me lightly, or holding me, while I make love to myself. Please talk to me. Please hold a mirror to my face, or I want to sit up in front of that big mirror. I want to fuck myself with that nice thing. I want to do it on my belly. Or face to face with a man. I'm a lesbian but I want a man close to me. Or whatever.

The value of this asking alone, just the mere words, has been estimated by government scientists to be worth a large number of therapy sessions.

Then it happens, with six people surrounding you, loving you, witnessing you, and telling you how beautiful you are, and how right it is that you feel this way. This is an experiment in exploring what might be called nourishing communication, the exact opposite of what we have so often experienced when masturbation was an 'issue': secrecy, shame, the fear of disapproval, and the terror of getting caught. These fetters, hung onto masturbation, I believe, lead to much of the sexual crisis that our culture faces. To find our freedom, we need to go back to the erotic source.

In this context, the idea is to feel anything you want, and show your stuff: we're going to love you. We need to love you. You need to love you. You need to be loved. We all gain in the equation.

Ah, sweet compersion.

After the person eases out of his/her experience, there is a short break (snack, water, bathroom), the cards were shuffled and passed around, and somebody else drew the Ace of Cups. This went on for about six hours, at the end of which we all felt like we knew something about one another. For we had all spoken and listened to and experienced the Universal Sexual Language, the inter-gender and inter-orientation tongue that we all know and understand.

Witnessed Solo Mirror Play

At a two-day workshop in California last summer, the first evening's activity (after the get-acquainted go-round, and a great dinner in the warm summer evening) was to watch someone named Tori be with, well, play with, and well, really get down with herself in front of a mirror for about two hours, pretty much nonstop. She went at it. The approximately 12 watchers could talk, observe closely, gaze, stare, listen carefully and move freely about the cabin to try different vantage points.

The effect on all of us is profound. First of all, we are overwhelmed by Tori's honesty, as she opens up and watches herself and studies her face up close and does what really feels good to her. The experience is effortless; no one is required to do anything except feel. There is plenty to feel. Honesty is about feeling, and when we witness it, we want it for ourselves.

When she finally gives herself over to orgasm, we all understand. We are in agreement. We are in one space of beauty. Yet pleasant as this is, there's really a confrontation involved, including being face-to-face with a kind of absolute, that is, an expression of something absolutely and unabashedly human. There is no denying that the person in front of the mirror is an extension of ourselves, or a projection of who we want to be.

To meet this, to encounter this, we must become soft and allowing. This is the inner territory we reach when we no longer need to control the emotions and pleasure of another person. I think this is the easiest way to teach compersion, to immerse oneself in the unconditional approval of another person's pleasure.

We usually seek compersion in the context of our lover being sexual with another person, which can be very beautiful, but equally scary. In the context of witnessed masturbation, the experience is less threatening because it's not about one's lover having sex with someone else, by whom they might be swept away; rather, it's about watching someone one loves have sex with herself or himself. It is usually possible to allow someone we love to be this free without freaking out.

Compersion is the coveted secret elixir of emotions because it promises to turn the pain of jealousy into an ecstatic calm, or ecstatic release. It is the experience of *compassion for another person's pleasure*. There is more to it, but what I am getting to is that a fine way to feel compersion without having to confront jealousy is to just simply watch a person masturbate. For couples who are considering opening their relationships to other adults but scared about the jealousy, this is a fine way to get the feel for things, particularly in a group setting, for example, where three or more people are present.

A Healing Erotic Journey

What I have described are just two possible formats. I have tried lots of others, including a group of 10 people and one mirror and people individually taking a turn before the mirror. A few just watched. These people ranged from about 36 to 80 years old. Then there have been a variety of "traditional" Jack-and Jill-offs, more social types of group masturbation experiences. For group play, there are infinite possibilities once the space is opened and the agreements are made.

Sharing masturbation is good practice negotiating sexual agreements. Very often sex just happens, and we regret it, or go against our better judgment. When we share masturbation many details come out into the open, for open discussion: where do we do this, what are we going to do, who goes first, and so on.

There are more intimate options, too, such as two lovers inviting a friend to masturbate with them. Three-way sex might seem out of the question, water that's a little too deep, but masturbating together might be just delightfully right. Two couples can get together and do the same thing. And it's very nice one-on-one, with a friend or a lover. This is a truly versatile, deeply erotic form of expressing sensuality and sexuality. And it's clear that Lazarus Long never got to experience it in all his five thousand or so years of life, because it's anything but lonely.

Offering a vision of what is possible, I would like to experience a group of people meeting regularly, talking and masturbating together over an extended period of time–say, a year or two. I think that some very unusual, honest and beautiful experiences would emerge.

CONCLUSION: FROM SELF TO SELF

Part of the freedom of these experiences is that we are taking responsibility for our own pleasure. There is no overlay of feelings in the sense that we are usually accustomed to it. One can adore, worship and get off on the beauty of another person, but the experience is ultimately self-given, and it's very difficult to form attachments, or rather, gratefully easy not to. There is a claiming back of our pleasure that happens, and an enhanced state of awareness that *you are you and I am me.* All of our talk about boundaries is necessary precisely because, by whatever phenomenon, in more conventional love experiences we forget who is who. When masturbation is shared, there is no question who is who.

Many of us are looking for ways to more freely express our erotic natures without hurting ourselves or other people. We tend to have two modes of sex, alone, or hot and heavy with someone else. This is a wide middle ground, and a space wherein we can free one another of original sin.

One of my friends, Lindsey, put it this way: "As I read this, it occurred to me that perhaps regular partner sex is dependence, solo masturbation is independence, and masturbating in front of each other is moving towards interdependence . . . a time when you really affirm that the other person is sexually whole unto themselves, and you can be seen by another person as being sexually whole. I think this takes some of the 'neediness' out of the equation . . . it affirms that I am whole, you are whole, we don't *need* each other; instead we're freely choosing to come together to share a moment." If interdependence is the way of the future, then shared masturbation is the future of sex.

As for the future of sex: in our search for a future, there are few places we have not already been. This is one of them, and it's a spacious, luxurious land where we really can be free because we really can be free to feel, and because we can really be individuals. Together.

Part Three: Narratives

Just Like a Hollywood Movie

Taliesin the Bard

http://www.haworthpress.com/web/JB
© 2004 by The Haworth Press, Inc. All rights reserved.
Digital Object Identifier: 10.1300/J159v04n03_15

[Haworth co-indexing entry note]: "Just Like a Hollywood Movie." Taliesin the Bard. Co-published simultaneously in *Journal of Bisexuality* (Harrington Park Press, an imprint of The Haworth Press, Inc.) Vol. 4,
No. 3/4, 2004, pp. 177-198; and: *Plural Loves: Designs for Bi and Poly Living* (ed: Serena Anderlini-
D'Onofrio) Harrington Park Press, an imprint of The Haworth Press, Inc., 2004, pp. 177-198. Single or multiple copies of this article are available for a fee from The Haworth Document Delivery Service
[1-800-HAWORTH, 9:00 a.m. - 5:00 p.m. (EST). E-mail address: docdelivery@haworthpress.com].

SUMMARY. This short story focuses on a bisexual, polyamorous triad formed by Nikki, Levit, and Mike, as they undertake the effort of writing and producing the first major bi and poly movie, entitled *The Compersion Effect*. The narrative focuses on the process of transformation that made their relationship possible, and on how the intimacy and strength of this triadic relationship make the project of the movie not only possible but highly successful. *The Compersion Effect* has become controversial, attracting homophobic attacks the three filmmakers discuss in a press conference. The narrative explores political and personal themes related to polyamory and bisexuality, as well as theories thereof, and the complex balance in a bi and poly triad whose members are part of the Southern California independent film industry. *[Article copies available for a fee from The Haworth Document Delivery Service: 1-800-HAWORTH. E-mail address: <docdelivery@ haworthpress.com> Website: <http://www.HaworthPress.com> © 2004 by The Haworth Press, Inc. All rights reserved.]*

KEYWORDS. Triad, bisexuality, polyamory, monogamy, soft porn, independent filmmaking, Bonobos, press conference, homophobia

PRESS CONFERENCE (JULY 05, 2004)

"Thank you all for coming."

Nikki Norris let go of the hands of the two men standing beside her. She nodded to them and they took a couple of steps back. Setting her hands on the lectern before her, she continued, "And, no, though the number of people who have now seen me naked has jumped to fifteen, maybe twenty, million, that wasn't a sex joke."

The crowd, now several hundred strong, quieted. Somewhat. They had begun gathering more than an hour earlier in West Hollywood, in and around the parking lot of the fire-gutted Rudgley Theater. Anxiousness could be read on their faces, anticipation overheard in their excited chatter. This was a major event in the making, and the polyamorists, gays, lesbians, swingers, and others who had gathered wanted to hear it, wanted to be part of it. Newspaper and televisions reporters had staked out the best spots, closest to the hastily erected rostrum. They, too, wanted to hear what Southern California's newest heroes had to say.

"All of us appreciate that you are here with us tonight." Nikki's husky voice seemed filled, as always, with sexual promise. That voice, as much as her face and body, had allowed her to shine as the star of the erotically charged

Compersion Effect, the first major polyamory-themed movie. The events of the past few weeks, particularly the events of three days before, had brought her, and her companions, international recognition.

Nikki was of medium build, with dark hair and dark eyes, eyes that compelled, persuaded. She had the crowd's complete attention. She looked to be in her thirties; was in her forties. Diet and exercise had kept the aging processes at bay. Standing on the podium behind her were her companions, Mike Stauffers and Leviticus Letch.

"We will take questions, but let me give you . . . Levit will give you an update first. Here he is, Leviticus Letch, the writer and director of our movie."

Levit stepped up to the microphone, removed it from its cradle on the lectern. He stepped to the side of the lectern which had blocked much of his five-foot, two-inch frame. "This place looks like Stonewall after the riots." He beamed bright white teeth at the crowd as he indicated the theater behind him. "And thank you for laughing. That *was* a joke. This is still very hard for us. Let's see . . . Senator Westford is recovering. The doctors have given her a good prognosis. The burns will heal. She's still shaken up, but, despite her injuries, her people have told us that she will be here tonight. She's still rather weak, so we'll answer your questions, and she'll be out here near the end."

"You TV and newspaper folks probably got a lot of that information from the hospital already, about her health and stuff," Nikki said as Levit handed the mike back to her, "but we wanted to let everyone else, everyone who might not have heard, know about that. I can tell you that last we saw her she looked well, considering. And she was in good spirits."

"This isn't the only act of violence associated with the movie," called out one of the reporters, stepping forward, drawing their attention. "There was an incident at the London premiere, wasn't there?"

"A bomb threat had been called in just an hour before the *Compersion Effect* premiere in London two weeks ago. The police checked the theater, found no evidence of a bomb and the movie opened about three hours late. But it did open."

"Is it the same group that was responsible for the London threat, and is that related to this bombing?" The reporter indicated the Rudgley Theater, or what was left of it. Destroyed by fire three days before. A crisscross of yellow police tape was the only touch of color in the gray facade.

"The group in England, the group that called in the bomb scare, were identified by Scotland Yard as a fundamentalist Christian sect, a sect known for their anti-gay agenda. Vocal, but harmless, we've been told. We've been so busy promoting the movie, at Cannes, in Montreal, in New York a few weeks ago. That was the same day as the Pride parade, and there were no incidents.

"We've been all over," Nikki continued, "so we haven't been able to keep up with everything. The police here aren't telling us anything about the bombing. Even Senator Westford's people haven't been told much, I don't think. It was a hell of a deal to get them, get the police, to allow us to hold this press conference outside the theater."

"Do you still feel like you're in danger?"

"Being polyamorous and bisexual in America always makes me feel like I'm in danger," said Nikki. She was not joking.

DADDY, NO! (AUGUST, 1974)

A Saturday afternoon. Fourteen-year-old Nikki Norris is making out with best friend Tammy Rachins behind the circular, above-ground pool in her parents' backyard, near the fence, the spot you can't see from the house, the spot shaded by the big, lovely maple tree.

She hates the hiding, hates lying to her parents. Tammy's parents are more understanding. They don't necessarily approve of the relationship, Nikki knows that, but they let Tammy and Nikki alone, give them privacy in Tammy's room. They'd prefer that Tammy grow up to marry a nice, Jewish doctor, a male doctor, a doctor with a dick. (Tammy and Nikki make a joke of that phrase—a doctor with a dick—laughing hysterically every time either says it, even weeks later.) Most of all, though, Tammy's folks want their daughter to be happy.

Nikki wishes that her folks would want that for her, would want her to be happy. They don't even want her, at fourteen, to date. But on that bright, warm Saturday afternoon, all such thoughts are far from Nikki's mind. All her thoughts are of Tammy; sweet, soft, loving Tammy.

Bikini tops off, lips and fingers are questing, discovering. The two are lost in love and lust.

Tammy's lips and tongue are soft yet insistent against Nikki's own. Sweet, strong, gentle. The sensations are, as always, overpowering and intoxicating, delightfully overpowering, splendidly intoxicating. Nikki's mind swirls and her body tingles from deep inside.

She feels Tammy's body tense, hears a low cry of alarm from her lover as hands suddenly grab her arm and hair, pull her to her feet, pull her from the dreamlike embrace. The hands are rough, strong, hurting. The slaps from those hands across face, breasts, shoulders make any memory of that day a nightmare. Anger rises. She resists. Screams at her father. To no avail. The hands are fists now, pummeling her into submission, into unconsciousness. She hears the words "slut" and "pervert" through the ringing in her ears before everything goes black.

In the hospital when she awakens, she learns that Daddy's fabricated a story for the authorities. Someone broke into the house, assaulted his daughter. Mom goes along with the lie. Tammy's parents go along with the lie. Tammy goes along with the lie, but Nikki can tell she doesn't want to. Nikki goes along with the lie because she does. (She's never known why.) No one seems to notice the smell of liquor on Daddy's breath.

In September, Nikki is sent to a new school. She never sees Tammy again.

PRESS CONFERENCE (CONTINUED)

"And making a movie about it, about polyamory and bisexuality, well, you've seen what happens."

"Are the police really trying to catch the guy, or guys, or whoever did this?" another reporter asked.

Levit stepped up and said, "We have every confidence in the Los Angeles police department."

"That another joke?" Someone from the back of the crowd yelled. "When have those bastards every cared about what happens to us?"

"A state senator was injured in the fire. They care about that, at least. And about the damage to the building. The fire could have spread, destroyed more buildings, taken lives. No, they're taking this seriously."

"Yeah, they care 'cause others were involved, not fags like us."

A rumble from the crowd gave support for this assertion.

"I may have sucked a dick or two in my time," Levit countered, "but I've never been a fag." His eyes searched the crowd trying to lock onto the speaker, but the lights for the TV cameras made that impossible. "Look, I know some of us have tried to reclaim words like 'fag' or 'dyke,' or whatever, and use them to mean what we want them to mean. Use them as our words of power. Sorry, but I don't feel that way. It's okay if you do. It's okay to disagree."

Levit took a moment to consider his next words. "I don't want you to not see the movie because of this, but one of the things we tried to say with the movie is don't use mainstream's words to define ourselves. We get to define ourselves, and the kinds of relationships we want. Polyamory is a word created by polyamorists. Compersion, the same thing. These are words created by our own people."

Encouraged by the rumblings of support for this assertion, Levit pressed on. "Also don't use any labels at all. I can have sex with men and women, but I'm not bisexual by the common definition of that word, which is having sex with men and women. I only fall in love with women. And that's how I define my sexuality, by who I fall in love with not who I have sex with. I love Nikki and I love Mike. But I'm only in love with Nikki. I like flirting with both of them, but I'm never going to fall in love with Mike. That Mike is in love with Nikki and with me is something we have to deal with. The triad in the movie went through some of the same things we have in real life."

"Will the movie open in the U.S. anytime soon?"

"Well, the New York premiere took place in June as we said–gotta pay attention there, Sparky–and without incident. And we've secured another theater for the Los Angeles premiere, which will now happen in two weeks. We've come too far to back down now."

LET'S MAKE A MOVIE (MAY 05, 2003)

"Eight million dollars. That's the budget. I know we've never spent that kind of money on a movie before, guys. But I don't think we can do it for less."

Nikki Norris, Mike Stauffers, and Levit Letch are in Mike's suite of offices at PolyProDucers. From those offices, on occasion, have poured a number of projects and products for the polyamorous lifestyle. The creative output has varied from a "how to" book for poly dating (Table for Three) to poly pride buttons and bumper stickers, to a series of poly-themed porn movies Levit had concocted in the late nineteen nineties. Levit is the showman of the group, considers himself to be the P.T. Barnum of polyamory. Nikki and Mike never have any idea what he might come up with next.

His newest idea, he told them a little over a week earlier, is for a feature film on polyamory and bisexuality. He wants to make it "just like a Hollywood movie."

Compersion Effect, he has said, could be the company's first mainstream production. They have made some moderately successful low-budget erotic movies, but on this one Levit wants to go all out. "The time's right. I know it's right. Think Y Tu Mama Tambien or Romance or Sex and Lucia. Think of the old Emmanuelle movies and what they did for Sylvia Kristel. Made her an international star. We could do something like that. And with a poly and bisex theme it would be even more controversial."

"Controversy equals big bucks," Mike says. He's paying close attention now. "You got it!"

"Let's do it," begins Nikki, taking hold of Levit's hand, "because we want to say something about polyamory or bisexuality. Let's do it because we have something to say about it."

"Of course we do," Levit says. "I've been trying to get to where I could make a statement about polyamory for years, a real statement, something that makes an impact."

The triad can feel the excitement building. This is something they have wanted for a long time. Earlier, their PolyPorn videos had done moderately well. These weren't typical triple-X movies, so it took a while for the porn audience to get used to the addition of the multiple partner relationships (not just multiple partner sex) which were essential to the stories. They proved, however, that movies could be sexually explicit without being vulgar. The triad was not surprised that female porn viewers had a positive response to the videos; however, not enough of the traditional male porn audience connected with their message, and after about a dozen movies produced over a two-year period they had to discontinue the series.

What Levit had proposed was different. They would not be looking to just the porn market for support. They would be reaching out to mainstream audiences, offering them a look into a world they rarely saw.

"Let's make it about us," suggests Nikki. "I've always thought it would be good for people to hear our story, see how we live."

Though Levit agrees, ten days later, when he shows them the plot outline and the budget breakdown, Nikki and Mike discover he's written a science fiction feature. "I simply started writing, and this is what came out of me."

PRESS CONFERENCE (CONTINUED)

"Why make this science fiction?" came the question from another reporter. "That's not exactly the most popular market."

Mike spoke for the first time. He was a stocky man in his fifties. Nikki's husband, as recognized by the state. "Sci-fi has often been used to present relevant issues. Think about the original *Star Trek*, for example." Mike had never cared for the spotlight, preferring to handle the business affairs of the company quietly, behind the scenes. His point made, he simply stopped talking. Levit picked up the microphone, and the thread of the discourse, from him.

"Sci-fi fans have felt as marginalized as anyone," the writer-director elaborated. "So they can relate to the marginalization of others. When do sci-fi movies ever win anything but special effects awards? Great sci-fi acting, great writing in sci-fi novels and short stories often goes unnoticed by the mainstream."

He took a moment to remember.

"The same day I first went to New York to look for writing work, I went to three porn companies and two comic book companies. This was twenty years ago, at least. Over the years, I wound up meeting many of the same people in both mediums. Sci-fi, porn, rock 'n' roll music; these are all on the fringe of mainstream. They're creative outlets for some wonderful and wacky and moving and meaningful ideas. So there's some overlap. Somebody writing a porn script for adults one day might easily write a children's comic book the next. You'd be surprised, you really would."

NEW YORK CITY (MID-MAY 1984)

"Kid, you're nuts."

"Don't you want to do something more with your superheroes than just have them fight bad guys?"

Lawrence Little (the future Leviticus Letch) is in the office of Colorful Comics' Editor-in-Chief.

"Larry—can I call you Larry?—you can write, there's no doubt about that," the editor tells him. "But Colorful Comics just can't take the risk right now. You want to have nudity and four letter words, and weird relationships. You want to make Powerperson, our biggest selling superhero, gay. Gay? No way. And you want to include scenes of three-way sex. You've got to be kidding."

"Not sex. Not just sex. It's a committed adult relationship between three people. Very real. Very moving emotionally. But if you're not interested, what can I do." Lawrence collected his scripts, stuffed them his briefcase.

"*Look, kid, you're good. If you wanna write somethin' for us, we need an inventory issue of* Machine Nun Nelly. *It's already plotted. We just need someone to dialogue it. Her nemesis has trapped her on this island with two dozen mercenaries all out to kill her. She knocks off each one in a different style and escapes. It's really cool.*"

"*You just don't get it. Thanks, but no.*"

LOS ANGELES, CALIFORNIA (FEBRUARY, 1995)

Lawrence has "gone Hollywood," has reinvented himself as Leviticus Letch, has started his own publishing company. He makes sure to be seen around town in the company of beautiful women and handsome men. He knows the hotspots, the "right" people. He's become a celebrity. A minor celebrity, he admits to himself when he must, but a celebrity nonetheless. He has been unable, though, to afford to do more than publish some moderately successful relationship-themed comics. The porn comics are what keep the company afloat. Barely. He needs something to happen. Something big.

Nikki Norris is the new hot porn queen, the rising star of the triple-X screen. Levit knows she is hot. He's pleasured himself to her videos at least a dozen times. He knows also that she's in an open relationship with some guy. They've shared the details of their open relationship on various TV talk shows. Maybe his dream, which seems to be their dream as well, isn't dead. A little checking leads him to Nikki's agent. He arranges for a meeting.

PRESS CONFERENCE (CONTINUED)

There are more questions, and not just from the reporters. Many of those gathered are anxious to find out about the poly trio and their movie. And about Nikki's co-stars.

"Ronnie Royer and Scott McFarland, who were Yolanda and Tom, are also doing promotion for the movie. They're doing an Internet radio talk show tonight, so couldn't be here. But we had a good time working with them. They really challenged me as an actress, and that felt really good, really good."

Though a number of the reporters have seen VHS promo copies of the movie, many of the people gathered know little more than what's been mentioned on the television news.

"Since we weren't able to see the movie, can you tell us the plot?"

FIRST DRAFT (AUGUST 13, 2003)

Levit has worked up a forty-page outline for the movie. He summarizes for Mike and Nikki in Mike's office.

"Archeologists find a six-million-year-old artifact. Touching activates it and a cosmic being is released. He/She/It is a conceptual entity named Compersion. Freed from imprisonment Compersion is now able to set human-ity on its proper course which has been perverted by other conceptual entities led by Jealousy. Fear, Hate, Possessiveness, and Greed, acting as agents of Jealousy, have held sway over humankind for millions of years. Compersion gets help from Trust, Love, Freedom, and Justice. What follows is a cosmic battle for the fate of the Earth."

"No," says Mike.

"Rewrite," says Nikki.

REWRITE (SEPTEMBER 25, 2003)

Levit has been advised to make the story more human, give the audience something to which they can relate. He's getting closer, now has a seventy-five page synopsis. (He's kept the original plot to produce as a comic book, so no loss there.)

"Okay, so here's the plot. Archeologists unearth the most remarkable find of the millennium, the secret of life on Earth! Good, isn't it? C'mon, nod your heads, say it is. It's a really cool idea, yes?"

"Levit, be serious. Just give us the plot. We've got a lot riding on this."

"Okay, Mike, okay. Opening a cave no human has been in for six million years, the archeologists find a strange device. Activating the device causes the Compersion Effect to begin. The meaning of life on Earth is instantly transmit-ted to all humans. All over the world, they suddenly know why they exist and how to exist, peacefully, without war or violence. They will live as humans were intended to live, polyamorously and polysexually."

"That's what happens in seventy-five pages?"

"Oh, no, Nikki. That's just up to page six. Then the story really gets moving. I figured when the Compersion Effect activates we'd go into this James Bond type title sequence, you know, with half-naked women dancing around, but we'd have half-naked men too, then move on with the story."

"I wonder . . ."

"Yes, Nikki?"

"We believe that everyone is poly, that that's the natural state of things, but if we're going to put that forward in a movie, we're going to have to show proof, something that supports our cause."

"In other words the audience isn't to going to buy it unless they think we've done some research into this. I mean, it's one thing to show people behaving openly sexually in a porn movie. That's fantasy. But we want this to be more, I dunno, more credible. More believable."

"Yeah, that's what we're aiming for."

"So make sure we do it right."

FINAL DRAFT (OCTOBER 05, 2003)

"Okay, I nailed it. You're going to like this."

"We'll be the judge of that." Mike laughs and hugs Levit. "But couldn't this wait till morning?"

Mike, Levit, and Nikki are in the master bedroom in their Hollywood Hills home. Mike and Nikki have spent the weekend relaxing. Levit had locked the door of his study Friday afternoon and not ventured out except for food and drink until now. It is late Sunday evening. Mike and Nikki are preparing for bed. Levit's frantic entrance has interrupted this.

The three pile onto the large, circular waterbed and Levit hands copies of the script to each. "This can't wait. You have to read this now."

They begin reading. They are impressed. Levit has 'nailed it.'

The story: Virginia Reynolds, Tom Reynolds, and Yolanda Foster, a poly threesome, are archeologists looking for the origins of early humans in Ethiopia. They discover a cavern in which they find ancient clay tablets with writing on them in an unknown language. It's a remarkable find that sets the scientific community on its end.

While trying to decipher the tablets, Ginny, Tom, and Yolanda have to contend with being openly poly. Yolanda may be fired from her position at Halston University for her poly and gay activism. Tom has to deal with a mother who thinks she's failed as a mother because her son turned out bisexual.

Once deciphered, the tablet leads the three back to Africa where they discover an alien artifact. Activating the artifact they are shown a record of human history unlike any other. The truth of humankind's nature is revealed. Genetically, humans are polyamorous. Scenes set at various times during human history show how religious repression, political power struggles, and basic misunderstanding contribute to humanity's failure at forced monogamy.

The artifact, after activation, has also signaled a group of aliens who have been watching over Earth, awaiting the time when humans would become enlightened enough to enter the peaceful interstellar community that is their true home. On planets in neighboring solar systems, alien people live prosperous, polyamorous lives, each choosing dyad, triad, quad, or single lifestyles. All permutations are permitted.

The arrival of the aliens on Earth ushers in changes in religion, politics, economics, education, lifestyles. The people of Earth, now knowing how the rest of the universe is structured in terms of lifestyle and sexuality, have a solid blueprint for their future. They can, the aliens tell them at the end of the story, choose their own path, and the aliens will be waiting if humans ever choose the path that leads them into the greater interplanetary poly community.

"By Jove, I think he's got it," says Mike. "This is a script we can make."

He takes Levit's face in his hands, kisses him. Levit kisses Nikki, who then kisses Mike.

"Okay now, Mr. Producer, Mr. Director," Nikki says teasingly, running her tongue around her full red lips. "Who do I have to blow to get a part in this movie?" Nikki knows she has the part; she's simply in the mood to play.

"You're already sleeping with the producer and the director, so that won't do it," Mike counters, playing along. "How 'bout doing the dishes sometime. That would be different."

"We have a maid for that."

"Okay," jokes Levit, "how about doing the maid?"

"I think that only works in porn movies."

"Well, you've been in enough of them to know."

"Hey! That's it. Hang on. I wanna be serious for a moment."

"Sure, Nikki. What is it?"

"What if you two were to be in the movie with me? Levit could write a scene for the three of us. My character could have a fling with two guys she meets, or you could be old boyfriends of mine and we reunite. I think playing a sexy or a romantic scene with you would be great."

"I'm in," says Mike. "I'm no actor, but sure. It'll be nice to do that, and finally be in a movie with you. Levit?"

"I'm not sure. I'll do it, but only if you really want me to."

"You can't be shy. Not you."

"It's not that, Mike," says Nikki, laughing lightly. She flops forward, resting her head between Levit's legs, eyeing his crotch. "I think he's worried that if he appears naked in a movie everyone will know he's not really Jewish."

Their lovemaking that night is more passionate than it has been in many months.

PRESS CONFERENCE (CONTINUED)

"Having now described the movie, I hope you all still want to see it," Levit said. "It is different; you must admit that at least."

"Maybe too different," challenged one of the reporters. "And maybe too sexual. I'm bi," the man revealed, "and I've never had group sex, never been to an orgy. I mostly have long-term partners, real relationships that last for years. Did you really need that antigravity orgy?"

"I was not aware," Levit joked, "that seven people constituted an orgy. Where I come from–I think most of you know my porn background–seven people is foreplay. In porn, if all we've got is seven people having sex, we're just warming up."

PRODUCTION PROBLEMS (JANUARY 26, 2004)

"Run that by me again?"

Levit finishes pouring drinks for Mike and himself. It's the end of a particularly tough week of shooting. He hands him one of the glasses, goes to stare out the office window at the dusking sun. He takes a sip of the rich, dark wine, repeats what he has said: "We're at fifteen million now."

He holds up a hand to dissuade any protest. "And we'll probably have to go to sixteen before this is through. Look, this is big, really big. A porn movie is what, what do we usually budget for a feature, sixty thousand or so? We'll make millions more on this movie than we ever made on porn."

"We're betting everything we own." Mike stands beside Levit, puts his arm around the younger man's shoulders. "You know I had to take out a rather substantial bank loan to finance this. And get European investors. It wasn't easy. And all the experts you hired, and all the special effects. And what's with this twenty-seven person orgy in antigravity scheduled for next week?"

"I could cut it to twenty."

"Cut it to seven."

"Oh, all right." Levit looks at Mike, grins. "The special effects guys we've got are great. They're making every shot look spectacular."

"What about the experts, the technical consultants?" Mike moves back to his desk, plucks some papers from amid mounds of clutter. "Have you seen the bills they've submitted for their services?"

"We need a cultural anthropologist and an evolutionary biologist," Levit defends his position. "They're giving the script its credibility."

"I'll greenlight it. But no more cost overruns, you hear."

"Rising costs, production problems, script changes." Levit sighs, shakes his head. Y'know, this really is shaping up just like a Hollywood movie."

BREAKDOWN ON THE SET (FEBRUARY 17, 2004)

"And cut! That was great."

Ronnie Royer rolls off of Nikki, gulps air. She is too tired to cover her naked body, but turns away from the crew to shield herself from their view as best she can. She is not used to working naked. But that is not the problem.

Nikki, who could care less about who sees her body, sits up, greedily gulps water from the bottle Levit hands her.

"You two were great," Levit tells them. "Even our gay gaffer Julio looked like he was turned on. That's saying something."

Ronnie looks past Nikki, looks at Levit. "Shows you what a good actress I am, then, huh?"

"Hey? What's the matter?" Nikki puts a hand on Ronnie's shoulder.

"Don't touch me!" Ronnie explodes.

"What?" Nikki could not be more surprised by this reaction, especially after the passionate love scene they have just completed.

"You're a goddamn whore!" Ronnie glares at Nikki through the tears welling in her eyes. "I'm an actress and nobody who sees this movie is going to know the difference."

"What the hell are talking about?"

"Easy, Nikki. Take it easy." Levit moves over to the other side of the bed. He faces Ronnie. "What's going on? I don't understand."

"I didn't know about you, about her when I took this part. I'm an actress, a serious actress. Your girlfriend or you wife or whatever the hell she is to you, she does porn. And you've directed porn, I hear. I thought this was a legitimate movie, not some raunchy skin flick."

"Hey, I'm famous," Nikki chides, trying to lighten the mood. "I thought everybody knew who I am."

"Somebody should've told me," Ronnie says, "told me before I took this job. I don't want to be playing lesbian lover to some porn slut."

Three days pass before the crew can resume shooting any scenes with Ronnie Royer. Levit and the crew manage to shoot a few other scenes, but not much else during those three days. It is a very happy day for all of them when Ronnie returns to the set and shooting can resume.

"Are you two going to be okay?" asks Levit as Ronnie and Nikki get their hair and makeup done.

"We talked last night," Nikki says. "I think we're good."

"We're good," Ronnie affirms. "We're good. I was just thrown when I found out you had made those movies. I mean, yuck. But if you're okay with it, well, okay."

"I am okay with it," says Nikki. "Levit is too. And Mike. I was surprised when you asked to talk with me last night. I figured you were gone for good."

"Yeah," says Levit. "What made you change your mind?"

"I'm too much a of a professional to walk out like that. I'm an actress. A good actress. And so are you, Nikki."

"You didn't think so three days ago."

"I did, actually. And that's what shook me up. You're almost as good as I am."

"Almost?"

"I'm teasing you," Ronnie went on, "just teasing. You really do know your stuff. You are good. And I guess I got scared because if an actress as good as you did porn, what did that mean for me? Would I do porn if I got desperate, if I couldn't find any other work?"

"I like doing porn. Maybe that's hard to believe, but, really, it's pretty good work most of the time."

"It's the other part of the time I'm worried about."

"Worry about your lines," Levit says, getting back to business. "There's a lot of dialogue in this scene, and–"

"We know the scene. We're ready. We'll be on the set in twenty minutes."

"Ten minutes," says the director as he exits. "Ten."

"I can imagine it's difficult for someone to work for her husband, but you've got two of them. Is it more difficult with two of them?" Ronnie asks Nikki.

"No, I usually get what I want."

"Why's that?"

"There may be two of them, but I've got the pussy."

The two women crack up laughing. It takes five minutes for them to compose themselves enough for the makeup artists to continue. It is more than half an hour before Nikki and Ronnie head for the set.

PRESS CONFERENCE (CONTINUED)

"A number of experts were listed in the credits of the film. Can you tell us what they contributed to the story?"

"If you recall in the scenes showing the evolution of humankind–and if you haven't seen the film, don't worry, I'm not giving away too much, I hope–we needed to accurately show what happened. Humanity started off sharing common ancestry with chimps. We had branched off from gorillas about ten million years ago. Bonobos branched off from us six million years ago, and then common chimps branched off from them. Humans were bonobo-like in their early evolution, and then the more violent chimps branched off from the bonobos after the bonobos branched off from us. Our experts agree that humans are just one variety of the three varieties of chimps. And as bonobos are more than ninety-eight percent genetically similar to humans, we are quite probably naturally as polyamorous and polysexual as they are."

"How do we know this is true?" challenged one of the reporters. "You could be makin' it all up to promote your own agenda."

"Well, we spent a lot of money on experts. Too much, if you ask Mike. But for a few bucks, just go to your local bookshop and get a copy of *The Third Chimpanzee* by a guy named Jared Diamond. There are a number of books on the subject."

"So all this means?"

"That we were peaceful and polyamorous and bisexual as a species from the very start."

"Ha! That is science fiction."

"Not really," Levit countered. "When the first Neanderthal was discovered in 1856, the visible evidence suggested that he was apelike, walking with bent knees. Probably brutal and savage, the scientists of the time asserted. Recently, modern science has shown that this Neanderthal had bent knees due to arthritis. Really. This is true. He actually walked upright like us, and was probably not any more violent than anyone living under the harsh conditions he lived under would be.

"Science is providing new answers every day, resolving old issues, and, most importantly of all, generating new questions that will lead us to newer answers and even more questions. It's a great time to be alive, guys, it really is."

MEETING OF THE SOUL MATES (FEBRUARY 13, 1995)

Levit is meeting Nikki and Mike for the first time. There is an immediate connection between them. He has suggested that they form a business partner-

ship, but that partnership quickly takes second place as their personal relationship rapidly develops. Within two weeks, he has moved in with Nikki and Mike. Two weeks after that, a Pagan priestess performs a bonding ceremony, marrying the three to each other.

"Who'da thought married sex could be so good?" Levit jokes after a particularly passionate bout of lovemaking on the third day of the triad's honeymoon. All three are sprawled across the king-sized bed of a Las Vegas hotel's honeymoon suite. Levit's head is resting on Mike's stomach, his legs are entwined with Nikki's legs.

"Never been married, huh?" Nikki says as she untangles herself from Levit, dashes to the bathroom, sits down to pee.

"Still not. Not legally anyway."

"It's legal as far as I'm concerned," Mike says. "The ceremony maybe wasn't recognized by the state, but it was recognized by us. And that's all that counts."

"I don't think the clerk who checked us in recognized it either. She looked at us kinda funny when we requested the honeymoon suite."

"Requested?" Nikki comes out of the bathroom, rejoins her lovers on the bed. "You were demanding it."

"I was drunk, I think."

"I'm glad that we were able to get it on such short notice," Mike says. "On no notice, actually. I wish, though, we'd have been able to afford to go someplace else besides Vegas. Europe maybe, or Australia."

"You worry too much about money, Mike. I love Las Vegas," Nikki says. "I like high pressure, fast-paced cities. Like Vegas, L.A., New York. That's for me."

"Me too," puts in Levit.

"And," Nikki adds, "I'm happy to be anywhere with the two men I love."

"One day," Mike predicts, "we are going to knock the world on its collective ass."

TESTING, ONE OR THREE (MAY 18, 1997)

"Why won't you? Tell me, why?" Nikki is angry. Angry at Levit. "Mike's agreed. He's going to do it Tuesday. You could go with him."

"I don't see why I should take an HIV test."

"The porn community has started regular testing, every month, for all performers."

"I'm not the performer in the family, you are. You take the test."

"I have been taking the test. Every month for more than a year now. But it's been suggested at the clinic that the spouses and boyfriends and girlfriends of performers get tested too."

"Well, I don't want to do it."

"Don't want to do what?" Mike asks as he enters the kitchen where the argument between Nikki and Levit had begun minutes before. It takes him a few moments to notice that something is wrong. "What's going on?"

"Levit doesn't want to take an HIV test."

"Oh c'mon, it's no big deal, Levit. Not afraid of needles are you?"

"It's not that. No, not that."

"Then, what?"

"You wanna know? You really wanna know?" Levit is screaming now, pacing around the room. "I cheated on you. That's what I did, I cheated on you. Both of you. There, that's it. Now you know."

"Levit, look, we don't exactly hold to the fidelity thing now do we? We've all had other partners from time to time, sometimes all of us together with someone else. It's what we all agreed."

"Yeah. But if not all of us together, we've always told the others about it afterward, or got permission before. This one, I screwed up. I'm so sorry."

Mike takes Levit by the hand, sits him down at the kitchen table. Nikki sits too. "Don't cry. It's okay."

"Anybody we know? It doesn't matter, really. But I still don't see why you're so upset about it."

"A guy in a bar. I'd stopped for a drink after work. That was all I wanted. Just a drink. He and I started talking, had a few drinks, and one thing led to another."

"Okay. Go on."

"Okay." Levit wipes the tears form his eyes. "So I went to the bathroom, after, y'know, and he's sleeping so I'm just looking around and I noticed a loose board in the wall under the medicine cabinet."

"And you had to see what was behind it. I know you."

"Wouldn't you want to know, Mike? Anyway, I find drugs. And needles. And he and I, we didn't use condoms. And I've been freakin' out since."

"Now I'm freaking out," Nikki says. "We had sex just a few nights ago."

"Did you notice the past few weeks that I was avoiding you? Both of you? I mean as far as having sex goes. Making excuses, y'know? I didn't know how to tell you what I'd done."

"And we put pressure on you to have sex, thinking you were drifting away from us. This is not good."

"Okay, I'm not really freaking," Nikki says. "I'm thinking. Not all IV drug users have, y'know, AIDS. It's risky to use needles, but not the end of the world here. If you get tested. I've been getting tested every month. That's the guidelines the adult movie community came up with. And you're going to have to get tested every month too. From now on."

"Okay. I'll go with Mike on Tuesday."

"You put us all at risk," Mike tells Levit, "not by having sex with someone else, but by not telling us about it. Always, keep the lines of communication open. That's what makes for a good marriage. Okay?"

"Okay."

There is much relief when their test results come back negative.

PRESS CONFERENCE (CONTINUED)

"In the movie," says one of the reporters, "you say that monogamy is wrong, that people should be poly. That's going to turn off a lot of people."

Nikki answers this one. "No, we didn't say that. One of the characters says that, believes that. What we say is that people are free to choose the way they want to form relationships. Some people want to form poly relationships, some want to form monogamous same-sex relationships, whatever. And that's the key; whatever you choose should be okay.

"The experts told us that from an evolutionary standpoint monogamy just doesn't make it. Can you imagine a single unit of father, mother, and child or children surviving the hardships of millions of years ago? No way that's going to happen. Humans had to have lived communally, sharing resources. And each other."

Nikki was getting into this. She had greatly enjoyed talking with the movie's science advisors during the shoot. She had always been smart, but rarely did she get to show it.

DOING PORN (JUNE 27, 1993)

"Whatcha readin'?"

"This?" Nikki is on a porn movie set, waiting for the next scene to begin. She holds up a copy of Proposition 31 *by Robert Rimmer, hands it to the actress who has asked about it. "It's a story about legalizing group marriage. Rimmer's quite brilliant."*

"I read a book once," says the actress. "Liked the movie version better."

"Hey, you two ready?" asks the director, coming over to them. "You do your enemas? Remember, you're going to be gangbanged in the ass by ten guys in this scene."

PRESS CONFERENCE (CONTINUED)

"The experts also told us," Nikki went on, "that early humans had no idea of paternity, no concept of basic biological reproduction. Aboriginal cultures existing today often have a similar view of this. They don't ascribe biological paternity. It's quite likely that early humans had sex rather like bonobos do."

"Our ancestors didn't begin to understand human paternity until six thousand or so years ago with the domestication of cattle," Levit added, having become as interested in the science behind polyamory as had Nikki. "They began to see traits passed on from one generation to the next, and wrongly assumed those traits belonged exclusively to the males. They thought sperm was like seed. That is, that all the genetic material, though they didn't call it that, was in the sperm and that the female was like the soil that nurtured the seed and then the plant."

"Right," said Nikki. "And this led to males wanting to ensure the continuation of their genes, their lineage, which in turn led to their control over sex and women. This led to the practice of monogamy and polygamy, a man having many wives; the more wives the more seed spread, the more genes passed on. Since they believed that sperm contained all the traits, women had no value except for the offspring they could produce. That was woman's only contribution, her only value. Everything else was the male's. That's the theory, anyway."

"The problem," Levit stated, "has been that scientists and historians first looked at nature and history through religious filters. Only by transcending any religious or political or social belief can we get to the truth. That's one of the strongest messages of the movie."

LAST DAY OF SHOOTING (MARCH 13, 2004)

"Y'know," says Nikki, "I just realized this is our anniversary. We've been married for nine years. You two didn't plan it this way did you?"

The Compersion Effect *cast and crew are in the Mojave Desert. Scenes in movies are not shot in the order in which they are seen in the finished film. The Mojave has substituted for Ethiopia. The movie's first scenes have been shot last. And now the movie is finished.*

"Who, us?" Levit and Mike grin at each other.

"You guys."

"But," says Mike, "we won't have time to celebrate. Levit has to go straight into editing, and I've got to get the publicity wagon rolling on this thing. It'll be a lot of work but we can be ready for Cannes in May and for the gay pride parade in June."

"So what you're sayin' is that if I want to get laid I'm going to have to go back to making porn?"

"I'm sorry we haven't had much time for each other," Mike tells her. "I truly am. It's been all work for months, for all of us. You've been fabulous as Ginny. You really have. We'll all have some personal time together, soon enough, I know we will."

"But not just yet?"

"But not just yet."

"Besides," Levit teases, "you make over a hundred thousand dollars a year doing porn. You never gave that up. You just took time off to do this movie."

"Our movie," Nikki says. "The movie we always wanted to make."

PRESS CONFERENCE (CONTINUED)

"I've never worked so hard in my life," Nikki told the crowd. "This is what being a real actress is about. The chance to really practice the craft, to really say something meaningful."

"Won't change anything," said a woman from the crowd. "The straights still hate us. They tried to kill you, remember?"

RUDGLEY THEATER (JULY 2, 2004)

"You will let me in! I intend to see this abomination for myself, and, if it's the obscenity I think it is, I intend to shut it down. And you can't stop me."

California State Senator Brenda Westford is shouting at the manager of the Rudgley Theater. The senator is well known to the West Hollywood community for her antihomosexual agenda. She's recently supported a bill against polyamorous relationships. When she turns up at the theater, heads turn.

"You, young woman," Westford addresses the manager, "are promoting filth and perversity."

"We're promoting polyamory," says Nikki as she enters the lobby where this altercation is taking place. "Got a problem with that?"

"Indeed I do. And I intend to see for myself just exactly how bad the problem is." Westford heads for the theater entrance.

"She refused to pay for a ticket." The manager throws her arms up in exasperation. "I dunno what to do. I can't call the owner. He told me yesterday that he was going out of town on business. I dunno where."

"We'll pay for her–"

It is at that moment that the bomb goes off.

Fire, smoke and screams fill the air. Few people remain calm, but fortunately some do. Two older men who are standing near the front doors swing them open, hold them open to let others rush out. The manager begins directing others to a side exit to keep the people moving. The crush of bodies at the front is moving slowly. Too many trying to get through the doors at one time. By the manager's actions, enough of the people are diverted toward the side exit, making it possible for most to quickly escape the rapidly spreading flames. Mike gets on his cell phone, calls 911 to summon firefighters and police. Levit has been in the upstairs projection room chatting with the projectionist. He leads him and others to a fire escape and down to the street.

Nikki rushes after Senator Westford, who had entered the theater just before the bomb exploded. Like many things in her life–falling in love with two men, fighting for gay and poly rights, making porn–Nikki can't say why she does it, she just does. The senator had headed down the central aisle intent upon making a statement to the audience before the movie started. She was close to the bomb when it went off, was knocked off her feet by the force of the

blast. Nikki finds Westford on the floor. The senator is dazed, nearly uncon-
scious. Nikki drags her out an exit.

There are few injuries, mostly minor burns, bruises, some smoke inhala-
tion. Everyone makes it out alive.

PRESS CONFERENCE (CONTINUED)

"Well, some things have changed. Let's bring out Senator Brenda Westford. You've all waited patiently for her; I know she has a lot to say."

Nikki looked around, looked for Levit and Mike. They had gone off to the side where several police officers stood. Along with those officers were the senator's aides, and the senator herself, having arrived only a few minutes before. Her aides had helped her out of her car and into a wheelchair.

Mike pushed the wheelchair up the rostrum ramp, set the senator by the side of the lectern. All through this, the crowd cheered and yelled and applauded.

"All I did," began Westford, "was change my mind. Isn't that a woman's right?" More applause met her words and her smile.

Her position on gay marriage had been reversed in a statement made from the hospital only the night before. Those gathered knew she did not actually support gay or poly rights, but, they also knew, she would no longer oppose them. And for the time being that would have to be enough.

"I may not personally approve of what they, what the gays do in their private lives, but those lives should be just that. Private. They're not hurting anyone. And the madman who set off that bomb, he's the real danger. Religious fanatics are the danger. They don't care who they hurt as long as they make their point. Well, I'm no fanatic. We have laws, and I believe in them." This she had said the night before, when interviewed at the hospital by a local television reporter. She had stated also that she would withdraw her backing for pending legislation that would prevent triad and quad relationships. Without her support, the bill would most likely fail.

Now, at the press conference, she said, "I want to thank you for welcoming me like that. I know some of you still hate me, I know. Don't deny it. I've always been straightforward with what I believed. It's hard to legislate something you don't understand, and I sure don't understand you, or what you do with each other in the bedroom. But I saw what was done to you here three nights ago, and I tell you, again straightforwardly, I am so sorry if I in any way contributed to the attitude of those who would do something like that. Who would try to kill you just because you were different."

Westford paused to take a breath. "I guess that night I got to see you as people, not as perverts. I saw you caring for each other, saw you hurting and bleeding, and I don't want to contribute anymore to your pain. You're not the danger to society, not if you have love and compassion, which you showed me you do. I don't approve of sex outside marriage, or of same sex –"

Suddenly two uniformed police officers and another in plainclothes rushed up to the senator. One held his hand over the microphone, preventing their conversation from being heard. The reporters crowded in, tried to catch snippets of the conversation. Additional police trotted over to hold them, and others in the crowd, back.

After a few moments, the uniforms left. The plainclothes detective remained by Westford's side as she addressed the crowd.

"Well, I was wrong about you gay people, and it seems we were all wrong about what happened here three nights ago." She turned to the detective. "Would you like to tell them or should . . ."

"No, Senator, please continue."

"Thank you. Detective Vosslint has just informed me that they have apprehended the arsonist who–"

Shouts and cheers from the crowd drowned out her next few words. She waited until they had quieted a bit, then continued.

"As I said, we were wrong. This actually had nothing to do with the movie or with the issues of polyamory–polyamory. Am I saying that right?–had nothing to do with polyamory or bisexuality after all. Nor did it have anything to do with my political stance. I read a few newspaper articles that speculated that this might have been your way of getting at me for some bill I sponsored or some such. But that wasn't it."

She took a breath, another. "Sorry, I'm still a little weak. Anyway, the owner of the theater set the fire. It seems this place was losing money and he wanted a way to get out. Torching the place for the insurance money seemed like a good idea to him at the time. Not so now, I'm sure."

She paused again, gathered her strength. "The police tell me that the timer was supposed to go off before, I repeat, *before* anyone was in the theater. Either the owner set it incorrectly or there was some defect in the mechanism. When confronted by the police earlier, he broke down, cried, and confessed. He says he didn't mean for anyone to get hurt. He just wanted the insurance money."

Standing nearby, Levit said to his mates, "So that explains why he was so eager for us to show the movie here. He figured a controversial movie like *Compersion Effect* would be the perfect cover."

"At least it's over."

"So what do we do now?"

"I think we go over to Senator Westford, thank her, thank the people and the press, say our goodbyes and hop on a plane. We leave from LAX at 10:45. We've still got a lot of promoting to do."

"And a lot of work to do to get people to accept that sexuality is different for different people, that sexual orientation is fluid and changing. And that we shouldn't lock ourselves in to one way of thinking."

"Sounds good. Say that in our goodbyes to the people."

"So everything's turned out all right in the end."

"Yep. Just like a Hollywood movie."

The End

Sacred Bi Love:
An Erotic Journey

Serena Anderlini-D'Onofrio

http://www.haworthpress.com/web/JB
Digital Object Identifier: 10.1300/J159v04n03_16

[Haworth co-indexing entry note]: "Sacred Bi Love: An Erotic Journey." Anderlini-D'Onofrio, Serena.
Co-published simultaneously in *Journal of Bisexuality* (Harrington Park Press, an imprint of The Haworth
Press, Inc.) Vol. 4, No. 3/4, 2004, pp. 199-218; and: *Plural Loves: Designs for Bi and Poly Living* (ed: Serena
Anderlini-D'Onofrio) Harrington Park Press, an imprint of The Haworth Press, Inc., 2004, pp. 199-218. Sin-
gle or multiple copies of this article are available for a fee from The Haworth Document Delivery Service
[1-800-HAWORTH, 9:00 a.m. - 5:00 p.m. (EST). E-mail address: docdelivery@haworthpress.com].

SUMMARY. This story is about sacred eroticism in the context of globalization. It is about Gaia and Jean-Luc, a bi and poly woman originally from Italy and a Catholic priest from Africa. They meet in central Italy in the summer 2000, while in Rome the first world gay-pride parade is getting under way. Both are used to navigating world cultures and regions. She has spent her adult life in the United States as a student, teacher, bi activist, sex educator, body worker, and healer. He has left Mozambique in his youth to access higher education through the Catholic ministry, with the ambition of becoming a spiritual leader. A high charge of erotic energy traverses the space between them as they discover their affinities. This energy turns sacred as she teaches him the art of loving and he becomes her eager student. The narrative is part of the author's memoir, forthcoming from Haworth Press. *[Article copies available for a fee from The Haworth Document Delivery Service: 1-800-HAWORTH. E-mail address: <docdelivery@haworthpress.com> Website: <http://www. HaworthPress.com> © 2004 by The Haworth Press, Inc. All rights reserved.]*

KEYWORDS. Bisexuality, polyamory, Catholicism, neo-paganism, gay jubilee, African priests, pivotal point, erotic lessons, female ejaculation

The antique armoire was opposite to the queen-size bed in the large bedroom, next to a marble lavatory. The sunlight came in through the narrow window with the smell of beech trees from the garden below, as the mountain breeze stirred up their branches. On top of the armoire stood a wooden object about four feet long. It looked like a double sledge, with two pairs of arched legs, to which two parallel boards had been nailed. The boards were about one foot apart, blackened from overheating like most of the object itself. I opened my eyes and looked at it. "*Il prete*," I remembered. The building had been around for about three centuries, and in the old days, when central heating did not exist, a little before bedtime people used to place a *prete* between the sheets to warm up their beds. I recalled its bulge under the quilt in grandma's bed, like a person cuddled in sleep, head buried under the blankets from the cold. Equipped with a brazier full of incandescent embers, in about fifteen minutes the *prete* would do its job. Then it would be refilled from the fireplace and passed on to another bed. "How come people call this a *prete*?" I remembered asking my grandmother many years earlier, curious that people would use the Italian word for priest for these quite effective bed-warmers.

Grandma left the answer to my imagination.

* * *

It is the summer of 2000, and the World Gay-Pride Parade takes place in Rome, as a gay jubilee. In June I go to Italy to decide what to do with my property in Fosca, two hours away. Touching a soil that belongs to me brings back my memories. The night I arrive I've nothing to eat at home and I go out. The village is very compact. One can walk anywhere and there's only one restaurant. Tonina, the owner, recognizes me and comes up to my table. We remember the last time I was there about ten years earlier.

"Fosca is now more diverse, we have one black person," she says.

"Who is it?"

"Well, our parish priest from Mozambique, didn't you know?"

"Oh, really! How long has he been around?"

"About a year. He speaks three languages, is very cultured, and people love him. He's nice, and he got us all involved in a council that helps him run the parish. I'm part of it, did you know? Besides, he's not like a typical priest. He doesn't wear a gown, he is social, he likes people, he's got many friends already. I'll introduce him to you. You'll see, he's so amiable."

"Sure, I'd love to meet him."

A couple of days later another female friend, Silvana, hands me a business card. It reads Rev. Jean-Luc Feleon, with phone number and cellular. Silvana is a cousin of Tonina, since in that village everybody is related.

"I told Jean-Luc all about you, that you're back in town after so long, that you live in America and speak many languages, that you've been all over the place. Jean-Luc wants to meet you," she says. "You can call him any time."

I don't do priests, and I'm not even a Catholic. But in this hometown people are so boring I'm thrilled that someone more interesting is around. The same weekend is patron saint's day, San Calisto. I'm told that mass will be celebrated on the church's landing, for the old building has been condemned, typical of the area. I tell myself, "Gaia, you can check him out. You don't even have to get into the church. Just get yourself there before mass is over." And so I do. It is amazing.

On the steep mountain slope past the river and the narrow valley, medium-sized beech trees fill the landscape behind the minister's head. The soft pillow of his well-combed kinky hair forms a black aura around his face. The small medieval church is to his left, with its okra stones and cordoned entrance. The townspeople are gathered in the landing. Most of them're old, and I can recognize the way they are related from their facial traits. The women's faces look like so many saints' portraits, tight pink lips as in prayer, high cheekbones turned red by the brisk mountain air, brown eyes and wavy hair turning gray. Their bodies are trim and sturdy, with bony limbs and bulky chests. The men's sunburnt faces have deep creases and bristly facial hair. Their heavy potbellies protrude above their leaner legs.

There's only three or four main families in this village, and they've inter-married for so long that they all look alike. I'm a hybrid comparatively, since I'm only one-fourth from there. I can see the shape of my grandmother's thin nose on the faces of many women who are for sure her cousins or nieces or some other relation. I look at this group of people, all so provincial, so inbred. "A very narrow gene pool," I think. And then I look at the altar, where their spiritual guide is celebrating the main ritual of their religion, turning bread into human flesh and then offering it to the faithful. The dark of his skin is translucent with deep purple and red. The embroidered garments are white, green, and gold. They look gorgeous against his colors. His hands are raised to receive the universal energy, and the white of his outstretched palms shines against the fine mountain air. The gown itself makes him look feminine, like a transvestite. He is very erotic in a natural way. As he speaks I notice his Italian is perfect, of the kind spoken only by educated foreigners. "He must be a good student," I think to myself. I notice a lot of younger women go to communion these days. They must be excited, it's all so erotic. I feel a contraction in my vaginal walls. Then the singing starts, and the procession begins to flow. I fol-low with others as we chatter away.

I'd never been with a priest, but I remember a movie about a gay priest I saw. I was surprised that seeing a priest as an erotic creature made me uncom-fortable, as if I was in denial of their sexuality. A couple of days later I see Jean-Luc on the low-level wall on the other side of the road from the small church where they have mass on weekdays. It is dusk, and I am walking down the main street, where people socialize everyday. Of course I cannot miss him. He wears a civilian shirt in earth tones, and I notice the colors become him a lot. He is talking to Tonina, the restaurant owner, and Rina, another neighbor. They all look very happy and friendly. I am wearing shorts, which is still con-sidered audacious in the area.

I walk towards them, and say to him, "I'm Gaia, the woman Silvana told you about, the one who lives in America."

He looks out and thinks for a moment. "Oh, Gaia, yes, the woman who speaks English and French, and just returned from America. I'm so glad to meet you, Gaia," and he puts out his hand. Well, we try out our French, then our Spanish. We tell each other a bit about our lives, where we'd lived, and why and so on. The others feel a bit lost.

He says, "My brother is coming," and he points to a car up the road. We walk there, and I am introduced. "Here's another minister from Mozambique. His name is George, and he speaks English as well as Italian and French."

The three of us walk to the *casa parrocchiale*, the parish priest's premises. I look at the books in there, a computer, the office, something very advanced for a town like that. Jean-Luc shows me a book on spiritual trances in Mozambique, and explains it is the doctoral dissertation of one of his friends. Then George asks me what kind of food I prefer.

"Chinese."

"Let's go," he says, and we go out.

We take two cars, for George has to go on to Rome, while I am coming back to Fosca with Jean-Luc. I ride with George. He asks, "What kind of music do you prefer?"

"New Age."

"Really? But, would you mind explaining to me what is this New Age?"

"Of course! It's the movement that brought about a return to a more spontaneous spirituality. New Paganism is my favorite variety. The sacred is in the Earth, and the main deity is feminine. She knows what we are doing to her, and is not happy. Those who understand this love and respect her. All things, animated and not, are sacred, and we, humans, are guests just like everybody else."

"Do you know anything about polyfidelity?"

I think, "What an interesting priest, I didn't know priests were aware of this stuff at all."

"I've been a holistic-health practitioner in North County San Diego, and that's where I've learned to get past monogamy and honor erotic and spiritual impulses in a more cosmic way. I was part of a polyamorous community and loved it for I could love more than one person at a time without cheating. And it's so erotic, with so many people in a love embrace, the energy multiplies, and everything feels so much better."

"I am talking about these things with a Catholic priest," I think briefly as I hear myself continue. "I'm gay, and more specifically bisexual, and I've had these wonderful experiences in Southern California."

"But how do you transfer these things, how do you export them?"

"You don't. For people to feel comfortable with their erotic energy, there has to be a conducive environment, and that can only come gradually with a lot of education."

We eventually get to the Chinese restaurant, and there I am having dinner with two good-looking black priests in civilian clothes, talking about New Age spirituality and other heresies. We all have a terrific time. It feels like family. I'm a foreigner in Italy, for when I go back I always feel so different from those who stayed.

On the way back it is dark. I have never been that close to a priest. I look at Jean-Luc, and notice he doesn't look like any African-Americans or Africans I know. "He looks Italian," I think to myself, "Italian in a way that I don't any more. He looks sweet and sexy, and without intending it–at least, one cannot tell he is posing. He is seductive in a spontaneous way." Sure enough we start talking about celibacy.

"I am aware that the topic is now being debated within the Church," I observe. "Clearly, there is a lack of callings, the church will need to change its rules if it wants to have any priests at all."

He agrees, "I have five parishes. It's a lot of work. Five villages, all under the jurisdiction of only one priest. Lots of masses to celebrate, funerals, baptisms, communions, everything else. And imagine, I'm a graduate student. This is supposed to be a part-time job, I don't even have time to think about my graduate work."

He takes off his eyeglasses for a moment and I can see the thick rim of his lashes around his eyeballs. It looks as if he has some permanent makeup on!

"Not many Italians want to be priests anymore," he continues, "working on Sundays, never being off, no early retirement, no marriage."

"There used to be a time when talented boys from indigent families were recruited into seminary," I reply. "That way they could get an education instead of tending goats. Then some stayed in the church, some got out and became teachers and so on. I know people who've done that. That option was never available to women though, did you know?"

I turn my face and notice his heart-shaped lips, of a light-brown color fading into pink. A hearty smile lightens their pink spot. I imagine how they would feel on mine, both above and below.

"But what do you think," he says, "do you expect a priest to be celibate to respect him, to think he is a good priest?"

I am a bit surprised by the question. "What do I think? Well," I say, "I never went to church because my parents were atheists. I'm not a Catholic, and priests never had charisma for me. I didn't care whether or not they were celibate. But lately I've surprised myself. I read the memoir of a woman who had a relationship with a priest for thirty years, and even had three children by him. It was so passionate, inspiring. The way she described their relationship was so exciting, erotic. I consider myself a very liberated person, and yet, this was new to me. I thought to myself, Gaia, are you being squeamish or curious? I'm still not sure, but, tell me, have I answered your question?"

He smiles, "*Si, certo*," and says, "yes you have, dear, you sure have!"

"Now I have a question," I say. "I get the feeling your sexual desires are very strong. How do you feel about them? Are you comfortable? Where do you stand?"

He looks into the night as the curved road keeps climbing the mountain slope. The off-white collar of his shirt brushes against his ebony jaw. "The celibacy of priests is an issue of ecclesiastic right, not of divine right. It was decided by humans, not by God. I do not see this law as necessary."

The answer surprises me in its clarity and directness. It certainly deserves an A.

At night I keep tossing and turning in bed. I have wet dreams and his body feels almost as real as flesh under the blankets. I have a vision of his heart-shaped lips and black-rimmed eyes on my pillow. I wake up at nine a.m. and call him.

"It's so nice to hear your voice. Did you sleep well?"

"I had dreams of you, as if you were here."

"I can visit you."

"When?"

"This morning?"

"OK, what time?"

"In an hour or so."

"Great! See you then."

He comes to my place and I give him a tour of the house. Then we sit on the sofa, and we kiss. He wears a gray suit and a white shirt. The flat stripe between the two flaps of his collar marks him as clergy. His lips are sweet like honey. He gets up and takes the collar off. It makes me horny. We sit down again. He is embarrassed. I think, "Maybe he hasn't been with a white woman yet. Maybe he is afraid I will blab."

"I am divorced," I explain, "I'm free and I don't want to marry." He seems relieved.

"What kind of sex have you had before?" I ask.

He is a bit shy, reluctant. "It's been about a year, with a gal I met in the library doing research."

"If we like each other and respect each other, and know what we want, we can have a *storia*." *Storia* is the Italian word for a love affair, except that it doesn't have its negative connotations. Like a fling, but deeper.

"Do you think we could really do that?"

"I'm the right person. We're neighbors, but I'm not really one of your parishioners, for I'm not a Catholic and I'm on vacation." We kiss some more and touch all over. We're half undressed and I say, "Let's go to the bedroom. It's better there."

We rush, our pants half down. I explain we only have a half hour to go. We get undressed and into bed. He looks at my body, elongated and dainty, with a soft, padded belly and round breasts. The ash gold of my skin glows against his translucent ebony. He is a fine lover, with a well functioning dick and much control. But I realize I'm gonna have to give him some safer-sex lessons. "Good for you, Gaia," I think to myself.

"I am a safer sex educator," I explain, "I use condoms, and you're gonna have to wear one or I will get pregnant." He stops and lets me lubricate his dick and slide the condom on. I'm proud of exercising my educational skills. We finish off rather quickly, but the chemistry is so good we promise to do this again soon, with more time on our hands.

Next time we get together is for dinner at his home. His brother is back. We speak English, for George and I prefer it. He tags along. "A bit weak in this language," I notice. For some reason we get back on the polyamory conversations.

"Polyamorous people practice safer sex with all partners except one, their primary. My partner Sandra and I, for example, had other lovers, but we exchanged fluids only between ourselves." Before I know it, I feel my face blush up to my earlobes. "I've given myself away," I think, "it's not the fear of losing him, but the shame for not telling him before." I'm not sure they notice my embarrassment, and I keep myself going. After dinner his brother goes home, and here I am, in the parish priest's home, fornicating on the sofa. We eventually move to the bed, which is upstairs, very small.

"I am gay, bisexual. Your brother already knew. I am sorry for not telling earlier," I whisper as we lie down. No response.

We lie down chest against chest. He has cute nipples with no chest hair. I hold one between my fingers. My nipples are perky and he holds one as well. It's like magic. Erotic ecstasy. And we need to do absolutely nothing to keep it going. The energy flows between the aroused nipples and the fingers that hold them. We're on a tantric plateau, and we stay there till about one a.m. We smile and our lips are turgid with joy, our bodies alive and beautiful with erotic energy. We check that the street is clear. I rush out as quietly as possible, and slip myself inside my home. I have the sweetest dreams. I feel elated and happy.

We plan our next meeting as a road trip. The village is small, and I'm sure Tonina noticed that the evening we met, the three of us went to a Chinese restaurant out of town instead of hers. I'm still kind of worried about that, thinking of ways to make it up to her. I'm walking uphill on a paved mountain road towards a nearby village, and he's supposed to pick me up. We drive to a sanctuary, in the nearby town of Cascia. We visit the church. I realize what this means to him. I feel the sacred energy despite Catholicism. More talking.

"I've thought of leaving the ministry many times, marrying, having babies." I see the longing in his eyes.

"In a way, as long as he is in Italy, he is condemned to being a priest bound to his celibacy vows," I think. "He is an *extracomunitario*, namely not a citizen of the European Union. If he left the church he would lose his right to work. If he were not a priest, he'd be just one in a million marginalized people of color who often resort to illegal activities to make ends meet in the rich Italian economy of today." I surprise myself thinking that his dignity depends on the Catholic Church, which brought multiculturalism to Fosca's deep province. "His brother and himself are probably the most cultured and well-read persons in the area. Italy is multiculuralizing at a fast pace, but are Italians ready for what that really means, are they prepared to have these new people protected and integrated?" I remember myself as a graduate student in Southern California, many, many years earlier, looking forward to proving myself in what I thought was a better world. Wanting, at the same time, to become part of it and to learn its secrets and take them back home. "Of course, he could leave the church if I married him," I think to myself. "But then the magic between us would be lost."

We meander through the curvy road halfway up on the mountain slope. I feel grateful for this encounter, this joy. We stop for dinner at a local *trattoria*. He has *primo e secondo*, a first and a second course. I don't. A succulent plate of spaghettis with *Amatriciana* sauce lies before him. He eats it with gusto, properly rolling the noodles on his fork. 'He is more Italian than I am," I think to myself. I quit doing the sequence of double entrees typical of Italian meals a long time ago.

He spends the evening at my place. This time we make love in a more artistic way. I explain that I like to do it well. We have plenty of time, and my bedroom is large and comfortable. I play Loreena McKennitt on the stereo. I turn the electric heater on. I burn some incense. Under the pillow, I prepare my safer-sex toys. A lubricant called For-Play, a nice medium-size vibrator, a large ostrich feather, a pair of Chinese balls. He takes off his glasses, and I notice his rimmed eyes again. He is puzzled about my protests of being gay.

"What do women do together?" he asks.

"Huh," I say, "so you're curious, ha?" He looks at me. "Well, do you want me to show you how you can please a woman if you are a woman yourself?"

"I do," he says. "I've heard about these things, these toys that women use. Do you have them?"

"I do."

"Really?" He is excited. "Can I see them?"

"Of course," I say, and I start fumbling around under the pillow. I unwrap the dildo and hold it out. "See, it's just like a penis, except it always works." I turn it on and move it nearer his face. "It's got a nice buzz, feel that?" He stays interested. "But you've got to know what to do with it," I continue. "o you know how women come, how they feel pleasure?"

"Well, I know some," he says, "I'm sure there's a lot more. Explain!"

"I'll give you the map to a woman's pleasure," I say as I spread my legs. I feel a bit like Annie Sprinkle, and tell myself that I'm doing the day's good work. I point to the entrance of my vagina. "This is the pleasure site you used yesterday," I explain. "It's wonderful, but it's not the only one a woman has. You must be aware of the others as well. There is the clit, and the anus, which you have also." I move my fingers up and show my small labia and the clitoris inside. "A woman feels intense pleasure when she receives clitoral stimulation," I explain. "Can you see that little button between the small labia?" He comes closer and looks more carefully. "Well, my female lover used to spend hours holding it between her lips and pressing it with her tongue."

He looks perplexed. "He probably got more than he bargained for," I reflect. I take the dildo in my hands and turn it on. I press it against my clit. "That's how you use this on a woman's genitals," I demonstrate. "Yesterday, when you penetrated me, I had a vaginal orgasm," I continue, "but you did not stimulate my clit. You can give me a clitoral orgasm with this, or with your fingers. You need to stimulate the entire area, inside the vagina, near the entrance, around the labia, and finally on the clit. The clit is a very delicate object. If properly stimulated, it swells up like a small penis, if not, it hurts." I turn the dildo off.

"Can I put my fingers inside you?" he asks.

"Of course." I show him how to make a small dildo with his three fingers, and guide him inside. My walls tighten up. He looks at me. "See, you're making love to me like a woman now."

He takes the dildo in his hand and turns it on. He starts to play with it as he looks at my genitals. It feels wonderful. I remember the first love lessons I gave to a male lover many years before. He was my student. We started like a game, and then I fell in love. "It might happen again," I think to myself, realizing how deeply, for me, learning and eroticism are related. AI must be a good teacher," I reflect, as Jean-Luc is intensely absorbed in his playing with my genitals. "I love this erotic pedagogy, if only I could teach this to my college students as well!"

He uses the dildo very well, pointing its tip between my clit and the entrance to my vagina. After a while I feel a liquid flowing between my legs, it comes out of the area he is stimulating, it is warm and its ejection gives me an intense pleasure. I am not entirely sure what is happening, though. I touch his hand and gently push it away. I turn around and smell the area of the sheet under my legs. I am afraid I've been incontinent! But no, the liquid has no smell. It occurs to me that I have probably just experienced female ejaculation. I smile at him. He is confused.

"You made me ejaculate! Did you know that nobody has ever done that before? I have never even been able to make a woman ejaculate myself." I point to the wet sheets, and put his fingers on them. "Can you feel that?"

"Yes I can."

"Well, that's a liquid that came out of my genitals. I've never seen it before. I've only heard about it from my bi friends, and I've seen it in soft porn." I am thinking of Annie Sprinkle's *Sluts and Goddesses*. "This is female ejaculation," I repeat, "I can't believe you've done that." I start to doubt the sincerity of his naiveté. "Are you sure you're as new to this as you say?"

He lowers his eyes and there is surprise on his face. Then he looks at me and says, "Gaia, is something wrong? I'm doing as you tell me."

"No, I was just thinking that you beat all of my other lovers in just one lesson. I thought you might have done these things before and pretended you were just learning them."

He doesn't answer.

"Forgive me," I say. "It doesn't really matter."

We resume the play, with more warm ejaculations. Eventually, my clitoral orgasm comes. He keeps watching the results of his work as in an ecstasy. I point to how my anal orifice is now softer and more open. "It's connected to the clit," I explain.

"Can we use it?" he asks.

"Let's leave that for our next lesson," I suggest. Then I show him how to put a condom on, and he penetrates me. I notice the usual control. His dick is slender and a bit curved, its veins pulsating under the thin skin. I look at his shape lying down on the bed, the translucent ebony of his body is smooth like jungle dew and emanates the most aphrodisiac smells. I get on top and ride him until I come, the kundalini energy rising from my sacrum to the back of my head.

Then we turn around and he comes softly, whispering my name. We lie down and he says, "Tonight was better. I saw you come. It was great."

"That's part of having sex that's queer, artsy, a bit gay, if you want. You and your partner take turns. You get to watch the other person and live their pleasure. Then they do the same. Isn't that better than the missionary position?"

"What's the missionary position?" he asks.

"What do you mean, don't you know?"

"I sure don't."

He has proven himself such a great lover that I am embarrassed to explain. "Missionary," I say. "It's called missionary position because Christian missionaries used to teach it to the savages in former colonies, as the only acceptable way to make love." The irony of the situation requires no further comment. "What a great student," I tell myself, "he surpassed the teacher on his first lesson."

I speak a bit about the Fosca I knew from my memories and my family's. "Most people didn't have great sex in this town," I explain, "and that was the fault of the clergy and how they had always scared them that pleasure was bad. The missionary position was very widespread! The climate too, so cold in the winter that people had to always wear long underwear, even in bed. No divorcees, no single people past twenty-five or so, and buildings so packed together that you can hear your neighbors breathe. When push comes to shove," I keep going, "the parish priest was the only wild card in the village, no wonder he was supposed to hop from bed to bed." I point to the *prete* on top of the armoire. "One of those traditional bed warmers full of incandescent embers. It was part of his pastoral mission, in a way," I tease him.

He smiles with his eyes lowered, the pink of his lips lucent with serene joy. "Now that I taught you all these wonderful tricks to give women pleasure, you can be generous. There is at least one beautiful and sensual woman in this town who is, I believe, a good lover, and her bed is cold. Silvana and her late husband Mario were always good lovers, both of them butchers by trade, somewhat familiar with flesh. But now Silvana is alone. I wonder if she's ever been with a woman, even in her imagination. But I won't be here to find out, and you can certainly warm up her bed." He doesn't pick up on this polyamorous note.

As we lie down, he looks at my belly, and touches it with his hands.

"This belly," he says.

"What?"

"Well, you told me I need to use condoms because you have your periods, right?"

"Uh-huh," I say.

"I thought you might have lost it already. That you were menopausal. Aren't you over forty?"

"Yes I am, but my period is actually very regular, which it wasn't before. Maybe it's because I'm healthier, vegetarian and so on."

"You could bake me a couple of kids in that belly," he ventures.

"A couple of kids? I'm way past reproductive age. I just turned forty-five!"

"I don't have any kids."

"You can't," I reply. "It's the life you've chosen."

He looks serious, like the person who feels he is treated unfairly because he does not really belong. "Priests don't have a retirement plan, they often die poor and forgotten. If at least they had children, they could be taken care of," he says. "In Mozambique, Catholic priests from abroad have a couple of women they call wives, and they have children with them. When they retire, they have a place to go."

"Really?"

"Yes."

"But I'm not sure a minister can be also a good parent. Your pastoral mission is loving all people in exactly the same way. How could you give your children the special love they need, and love unconditionally all the children in the world as well?"

He does not answer, and I think he probably believes himself capable of that kind of love. "Does he know that if the Vatican was not as misogynist as a medieval monastery, he probably wouldn't even be here?" I realize how ambitious he is. Coming all the way from Mozambique to the center of the institution he wants to be part of. It occurs to me that, even though I despise the Catholic universities of Rome, for people in the ecclesiastic career, these schools are the top of tops. A bit like Yale for academics in the United States. I imagine raising his child in Fosca, where everybody would know who his father is. People would stare at him, "the priest's child," they'd giggle. In my grandmother's time, there were two ways to call someone a bastard, and one was *"figlio del prete."*

"So, you want to have a child, right?" I say. "What about women who don't even get to be priests at all?"

"Well, I never said women shouldn't be priests. I just want to have a child from you, a child like you."

In my sleep I feel the force of a debt pound against my chest. I call Jean-Luc the next morning. "Can I please see you?" I say. "I have to tell you something important. It is part of your pastoral mission to hear it."

"Come over. I'm home."

I walk to his place, he opens the door and we get into the study. We sit in front of each other and I take his hands into mine. I look at him and say, "You've given me two wonderful gifts, and I want you to know that I am immensely grateful." I pause for breath. "One is that you made me ejaculate, and now I know it's possible and I can give that gift to another person. The other is that you asked to have a child with me. It's a great honor that you gave me, and I have no words to thank you."

"Does this mean we can have a baby then?" he asks.

"No, but it means that I want to thank you for asking me." I put my arm next to his. The sunlight from the window makes our skins glow. "He or she would have a wonderful color," I say, "and would be a wonderful child. Thank you!"

At night Jean-Luc comes for his second lesson. Dinner is ready. As we eat he watches all the antique furniture, the objects, the memories of my whole family that I have there. I show him the chiaroscuro pencil drawing I made of Michelangelo's *Pietà* when I was about twelve. It is framed and hangs from the dining-room wall.

"You guys are not such atheists, then," he observes.

"Well, my grandparents were not. It started with my parents. I think my father's atheism is just a reaction to the tyranny of the Catholic Church. In Italy, there is only one religion. As I got to California, I realized there were many, and they all coexisted. I remember one day wondering, 'Buddha looks Asian, Allah looks Middle-Eastern, and Jesus looks Caucasian. What a coincidence,' I reflect. 'They're all men. How come their religions claim men were made in god's image? To me it looks like it was the reverse.' That's how I started to get past atheism and reach out for a belief system I could call my own."

"How do you feel now about Catholicism?"

"To me, it's a primitive religion," I observe, "it's monotheistic, it's male-oriented, and I mean both in a negative way. I want a world with many deities, and one in which the divine principle is feminine, it's in the Earth."

"Why don't you come to mass sometime, you might feel a spiritual connection even though it's not your belief system, you know?"

"Well, to be honest with you, this is the only town where I ever like to go, because it's so simple and genuine. I'll come if you are sure to understand that for me mass is nothing but a cannibalistic ritual performed by a transvestite."

He lowers his eyes, and smiles peacefully. "I get the cannibalism, but the transvestite?"

"Well, don't you celebrate it in a colorful gown?"

"Oh, OK," he says, and his lips open showing more of the pink inside, "then I'll be waiting for you."

I know that the neighbors are gossiping already. In this town there's no way to keep people from finding out what's going on. I feel, "Well, if I show up those bigoted old ladies will believe he has converted me. That will be a success for him. I owe him that much!" So I show up on Sunday at twelve. It is a great moment. The church is full of men and women of all ages, children and families. He has girls and boys recite some of the prayers. He preaches well, and makes the whole church come alive with his words. I notice he mentions Christ's energetic body, his powerful aura and the healing energy that it emanated. The sacredness of the space comes across to me very strong.

That evening we meet again, this time to make love. "I want to have anal sex with you," I explain, "for it's the strongest orgasm I can have. But it takes me a lot of excitement to get there and really enjoy it. If I'm not ready it's very painful." I'm on all fours, my pussy juicy and swollen with anticipation. I show him how to arouse me and get the anus to open. I lead his hand to the hood and clit. He moves it up and down the labia, spreading the wet juice all the way to the anus. Now the sphincter is opening and his turgid cock slides in like a glove. I feel orgasmic vibrations throughout the area, the kundalini energy going up through the spine to the back of my head. I am happy, for once, to let him come without a condom, since I don't really believe in HIV infection, and practice safer sex for protection against other STDs and pregnancy.

"I want you to feel what I felt, and will penetrate you with a toy," I explain when we're expended. Then I proceed to do just that. He lies down on his belly, and I notice the light on his translucent shoulders, his butt a bit perky, tightened up as if he was afraid of a nurse's shot. I put my finger on his anus, which feels very closed. I realize my dildo is too large, and use my finger instead. I get almost all of it in there. It is the first time for me also. "What do you feel?" I ask.

"It's painful," he says, as the pink of his lips shows. "It's the first time."

"He is willing to stay in the game," I think, as I keep going until he begins to feel the pleasure. I move my finger up and down his ass. I love to see a man's body subject itself to being penetrated. There is a vulnerability that cannot come across in any other way. I feel the flesh inside him quiver around my finger, and remember the first time I penetrated a woman in a similar way. I look at his face pressed against the sheets, his mind feeling his body alive in a new way. I stop as I feel he got a taste of the forbidden pleasure and will want to get more.

"Can I stay for the night?" he asks.

"I prefer to sleep alone."

"Let's meet tomorrow and drive to George's home," he says as he puts his clothes on.

We meet as usual, on the road well outside the town. I have been walking for about an hour under the midday sun, and am kind of tired and worried.

"I always have lots of people to answer and talk to after mass," he says as I get in the car. "Besides, I did not want to rush out and create suspicion." We eat at George's, and I cannot help but notice that his place looks messy, as if he does not have his life in order. "I'm sure that adjusting to the Central Apennines is difficult when you come from Boston," I think to myself. We leave soon after lunch, on my suggestion, and stop the car in a nearby meadow to neck in the bushes. It is my idea, and I realize that he is uncomfortable because we have no viper antidote. I have forgotten, since there are no vipers in North America! We get back to the car. The air is brisk, and the large valley is filled up with the waters of an artificial lake. The hills and plateaus around are covered with green pastures. As we come to the main road, I notice he feels drowsy at the wheel.

"Can I take it?

"Please do, I'm sleepy, it's nap time for me, you know."

I think, "How Italian!"

We get to Fosca, and he goes to bed. He visits again later, and I show him pictures of my family, myself as a kid, my brother, cousins, parents. He is very curious. "You know so much about this town," he says, "you make me see it in a whole different way."

"I want to share all I know with you, so you can use it to your advantage and have an easier time doing your job. I want you to be successful, for I think you are a great blessing here."

"But what about us, are we going to see each other again?"

"You know, my girlfriend Sandra stayed in Southern California when I moved to Puerto Rico. Since then I really haven't had a partner. I love to be single, and don't know what will make me change my mind yet. I've moved so many times, I'm almost afraid to commit to a relationship, since that often means committing to a place as well. I'm an immigrant like you, you know? But this place is different. You're lucky. Every time I come I think I'll sell, then when I see the light come through the window as I've seen it since I can remember, I think if I sold this place I'd be lost. I want to keep it instead. So, if you're here when I come back, we will see each other again, yes. This place is a *punto fermo*, a pivotal point, and that's where I met you. Of course, you might be gone next time, you might get a better parish, and you should take it. But if you don't . . ."

"A pivotal point," he repeats. "I have one at home as well. I'm having a house built on a property in Mozambique, near my relatives, and that's gonna be my *punto fermo* some day. Thanks for reminding me that it's important, that it matters to you as well. The world spins around so fast, and things change, and when you are abroad you always feel expendable, as if there was no firm ground under your feet. I know I wanted to get away, and I'm happy, but sometimes I feel lost, because, like you, I feel the whole world spins without a *punto fermo*. But now that you tell me that for you it is important, I'll be sure to create one for myself as well."

"I wish you the best of luck," I say, thinking that ironically when it is time for me to return to my pivotal point, when I retire that is, it might be time for him to go home.

The next day he drives me to a nearby town to go to the bank. We are entering a tunnel when he says, "But this being gay, is it so necessary? I'm sure one needs to feel compassion for gays, understand them, but wouldn't it be best to help them change?"

"Change?" I answer. "Meaning what?"

"Well, change their ways, move on to the right direction."

I said no word.

"Being gay can't be natural, can it? Besides gays are always made fun of. Why be gay if you don't have to?" His tone is getting pressing, which is a typical way for Italians to debate issues about which they feel very strongly.

"Sleeping with you doesn't make me straight. I'm the one who decides what I am."

"But it doesn't seem right," he insists, somewhat mocking.

"I don't like that tone," I say. "These are not things to make fun of."

"Is that what I'm doing?" he teases.

"I'm not Italian! I'm not Italian!" I yell. "You can't discuss things with me this way. . . . I am speaking Italian with you and it might sound natural to you, but I'm not all that fluent and comfortable, and I don't like to discuss things at a fast pace."

A long silence follows. Then, "I didn't mean to offend you," he says, "I'm sorry."

"I don't like the way things are discussed in this culture. It's irrational and it makes people upset. That's the reason why everybody has heart failure. If you want to know more about what being gay means to me, you can ask me gently, and I'll be happy to tell you."

He has his sweet smile on his face. He is going to tease me for "not being Italian" for quite sometime, but he gets my point. "OK," he says, "tell me all about being gay."

"To you gays might seem just freaks, extravagant types who are fixated with some kind of kinky sex. But if you knew gay cultures from the inside, you would know that to each other gay people are like family. Queer people often don't have a family, because we've been repudiated. Our relatives live thousands of miles away, and they don't want to hear about us for they are ashamed. So queers form communities that are a bit like families. When I was in Southern California I barely had any contact with my relatives. They didn't understand why I was there, and wanted to manipulate me into being 'normal.' The bisexual community of San Diego was my family then. And they were a wonderful family I love very intensely to this day. You are an immigrant, you should know about this stuff already. Immigrant communities are somewhat like gay communities. We help each other, we understand each other, we speak the same language. Don't you have friends from Mozambique here in Italy?"

"Of course," he answers.

"Don't they feel a bit like family to you?"

"They do," he says. "I had my niece come here to study in Rome, and now she's like my local family. My brother is my neighbor as well. We speak our native language, and we cook Mozambican food as well. Honestly, I don't want to spend a lot of my time with them, but I'm sure glad they're around. I hadn't thought about gays that way, thank you!"

He never objects to my being gay after that, which is not quite true of my atheist relatives. "Now I do have evidence that atheists can be more bigoted than priests," I reflect.

"Remember I taught you to love me like a woman, and that a man's orgasm must always be last?"

"I do," he says.

"Well, these are things I learned from my queer friends, so now you are indebted to them. You're part of our community as well, as a student of love and erotic energy!"

The next day I get a call from my dad's girlfriend, Beatrice. "Your father is alone in Rome, would you go and look after him?"

"I'm having terrific sex with an African priest I found in Fosca."

"I believe you! But still," she says. "Here's Dad."

"Gaia, how are you?" my dad says. "I really don't need any help."

"I'll be back in two days, and I'll introduce you to the new parish priest of your hometown. He's very black, from Mozambique."

My dad, Aldo, is an activist in the peace movement. As a retired senator, he became a *terzomondista* as they call them in Italy, one who believes that if poor countries were allowed to do better, we would all be better off.

Jean-Luc is supposed to drive me to Rome. The day before we leave is feverish. Getting things ready, scheduling.

"What should I wear?" Jean-Luc asks me, tentative.

"Dress normal, not as if you are going to meet your future father-in-law, but not as a priest either!"

In the car we talk about the town's gossips, how to take care of them and how to take control.

"Aren't you afraid someone will tell the Bishop you have a lover?" I ask.

"What can the Bishop do?" he replies. "You know, after mass the other day the women in the council asked me about you. It was Tonina and Rina. They advised me, they said, to be careful, that I had been seen visiting you, and some people were gossiping. But the thing is, they're the ones who saw me and gossiped!"

"I know," I say, "they must be envious. How did you respond?"

"It wasn't very difficult," he says, "I've been in that position already. I said, 'But don't you see how lucky you are to have a townsperson so worldly, so educated? She knows more than all of you put together, and look what nasty rumors you are spreading about her!'"

"Is that what you said?" I ask. "I cannot believe his chutzpah. He's so shameless. . . . A good match to you, Gaia," I reflect. "He might get harassed a lot when he does not wear his clergy collar. And maybe he learned about dildos and vibrators in confession–some cute girl describing her sins in minutest details to see how he'd respond," I fantasize.

When we get to my dad's neighborhood I see him lost, afraid. Mostly retired people live there, and they do not see many *extracomunitari*, except for those who do housecleaning and care of the elderly. We have to wait in the courtyard for my father is late. We both miss the brisk mountain air. Finally my dad arrives and looks deceptively healthy. He is very friendly and welcomes Jean-Luc.

"I learned my Latin and math from one of your predecessors," my dad says as we sit to dinner. "When I grew up in Fosca, the priest was the most knowledgeable person."

In the kitchen I'm near the stove and cook some sausage. For once I play good girl. I think maybe Dad imagines we're lovers, and is happy, for he can see this guy is not a girl. It's a bit deceptive of course, but I forgive myself. I hear them talk full of joy and energy. They disagree, but I know my dad loves to talk to ministers who have a sincere faith, and try to convert them to atheism. For the first time in my life, and I am forty-five years old, I feel comfortable with a lover in the same room with me and my dad. "It if had only started earlier," I reflect, "we could have been a happy family."

A few days later I call Jean-Luc from a public phone in Rome. I have just returned from the largest ever gay-pride parade in Rome, on July 8, 2000. More than 200,000 people came. The demonstration was intended as a gay jubilee, affirming the presence of gay Catholics around the world, and the strength of gay communities within Catholic cultures.

"The World Gay Parade was a big success," I say on the phone. "All the papers gave it rave reviews, the news as well."

"I know," he says, "I followed. A major part of myself is invested in this issue now because I love you." I could not have been a happier person.

That week I call him a few times for I am worried. Is the gossip going to spread? Is he going to be transferred away?

"Don't worry," he says. "The church-council women asked me more questions, and this time I put them even better in their place."

"What did you say?" I ask.

"Well, I told them that happy people who aspire to being blessed with serene grace live their lives joyfully, and have no business meddling with the town's gossips."

I cannot believe my ears. "There is something new pagan in his philosophy," I muse to myself. "Why have I always thought that only dumb people enter the clergy?"

The following week I invite Jean-Luc to visit me in Rome. We rent an apartment from an eco-tourist organization. It is next to the clinic where my mother died of cancer more than thirty years earlier. When we drive up to it, I recognize the place and my blood chills up in my veins. It is ominous. "Am I here to learn something or what?" I feel the healing energy of being near a person with a strong spirituality, even though it is based on a belief system I cannot share. We get inside. The apartment is really nice and fully equipped. The bedroom is large, with a queen-size bed in the center, and a twin bed on one side. Ideal for me, since I like to sleep in my own bed. We lie down and start to kiss. He knows he owes me one from the time before, when he forgot to come last and left my clit half turned on. He starts to play with it with his fingers while he looks at my face. The rose becomes all juicy and opened, it makes me think of a host, slippery and wet when it enters your mouth and the saliva moistens it.

I ask him, "Do you like it?"

"Yes," and the rim around his eyes glows. He adds, ironic, "Isn't this saving you from being gay?"

The pleasure of feeling his body next to mine, and feeling him feel my pleasure, fills me with overwhelming joy.

"*Salvami, allora, salvami,*" I whisper, "go ahead and save me then."

Bi Film-Video World

Bi Poly Cinema

Wayne M. Bryant

http://www.haworthpress.com/web/JB

© 2004 by The Haworth Press, Inc. All rights reserved.

Digital Object Identifier: 10.1300/J159v04n03_17

[Haworth co-indexing entry note]: "Bi Poly Cinema." Bryant, Wayne M. Co-published simultaneously in *Journal of Bisexuality* (Harrington Park Press, an imprint of The Haworth Press, Inc.) Vol. 4, No. 3/4, 2004, pp. 219-226; and: *Plural Loves: Designs for Bi and Poly Living* (ed: Serena Anderlini-D'Onofrio) Harrington Park Press, an imprint of The Haworth Press, Inc., 2004, pp. 219-226. Single or multiple copies of this article are available for a fee from The Haworth Document Delivery Service [1-800-HAWORTH, 9:00 a.m. - 5:00 p.m. (EST). E-mail address: docdelivery@haworthpress.com].

SUMMARY. This essay discusses the portrayal of polyamorous bisexuals in film. Hollywood, independent, and foreign movies are cited and contrasted. Films included in this article cover the period from 1968 to the present. *[Article copies available for a fee from The Haworth Document Delivery Service: 1-800-HAWORTH. E-mail address: <docdelivery@haworthpress.com> Website: <http://www.HaworthPress.com> © 2004 by The Haworth Press, Inc. All rights reserved.]*

KEYWORDS. Bisexuality, polyamory, film

BI POLY CINEMA

Polyamory is still a new and poorly understood concept in mainstream America and in the film industry. If the average person on the street has heard the word at all, s/he is likely to have it confused with polygamy, swinging, or simply "cheating on your partner." In general, though, it is not a term that receives much usage among people who are not themselves polyamorous.

A search of the huge Internet Movie Database Web site reveals exactly one instance of the word 'polyamory.' This is in the plot description of a Canadian documentary called *When Two Won't Do*. David Finch and Maureen Marovitch directed this generally well made look at polyamory in North America, which takes the road trip approach to documenting the subject. Along the way, they visit a conference on polyamory in the Catskills, a swingers' convention in Las Vegas, and long-term multipartner families on the west coast.

Much like real polyamorous relationships, the films versions are out there, but can be somewhat difficult to locate. In addition, the relationships we see on film are rarely typical of those we experience in real life.

One of the more intriguing recent films to focus on a polyamorous relationship is *Y Tu Mamá También*, directed by Alfonso Cuarón. The film is set in Mexico, where two teenage boys, Tenoch and Julio, set off on a road trip with an older woman and learn a lot about sex, friendship, life, and each other. The boys are the closest of friends when the film begins, but their attraction for the woman, Ana, severely tests that friendship. It is their attraction to each other, however, that ultimately completes the triangle and pushes their coping skills to the limit and beyond.

Polyamory and bisexuality were, of course, forbidden in U.S. films under the Motion Picture Product Code from the beginning of the sound era to the late 1960s. It was, therefore, left to European filmmakers to break the taboo. One of the first was the gay Italian poet/director, Pier Paolo Pasolini. His 1968 film *Teorema* (Theorem) was a political allegory expressing Pasolini's belief in merging the teachings of Jesus with those of Karl Marx.

Pasolini's angel is played by Terrance Stamp, who later gained fame as the drag queen in *The Adventures of Priscilla, Queen of the Desert*. In this film, made about twenty-five years earlier, he plays a young man who is so gentle, attractive, and . . . angelic that people cannot help falling in love with him. He seems to be completely oblivious to the erotic feelings his presence evokes in people. Indeed, he is the heavenly embodiment of the libido—innocent and ir-resistible.

The movie begins as the family of a wealthy Milan industrialist receives an unexpected telegram announcing the young man's arrival. Shortly thereafter, the angel is seen relaxing in the courtyard where the maid is tidying up. His mere presence arouses her to the point where she propositions him. He seems completely unsurprised and accepts.

Each member of the family seduces the angel in turn. The husband, the wife, their son and daughter each find him irresistible in ways they would not normally feel for a stranger. Each goes mad with longing for the angel when he departs. Despite winning the Grand Prix award at the Venice Film Festival, *Teorema* was banned in Italy and Pasolini was arrested for obscenity.

In 1970, when American filmmakers were freed from the restrictions of The Code, Hal Prince directed *Something for Everyone*, a film about a young man's obsession and his willing to do anything to fulfill it. Ever since he was a child, Conrad has dreamed of living in a real castle. In his travels, he discovers that Castle Ornstein is uninhabited. It is owned by the Countess Ornstein (Angela Lansbury), who lacks the resources to keep it open. The role of Conrad in this dark comedy is played by Michael York, who also plays a bi poly character in *Cabaret*.

Conrad begins his quest by killing the Countess's footman in order to take over his job and become part of the household. He then seduces Annalisa, the daughter of a wealthy couple who want to buy the castle, but then discover that its sale is verbotten. Conrad next easily seduces Helmut, the Countess's gay son.

Conrad arranges the marriage of Helmut and Annalisa. He convinces each separately that, since he will be living in the castle, they can still be lovers. The wedding night is a disaster since Helmut has not the slightest interest in women. When Annalisa catches the two men kissing on the lips, she suddenly understands and prepares to expose the scheme. Conrad fixes that little prob-lem by driving her entire family off a cliff, jumping in time to save himself.

Helmut is now the heir to the wealthy family's money, so there is plenty of cash to reopen the castle. Conrad's scheme is nearing a successful conclusion. He need only seduce the Countess and marry her to become the Count. He meets his match, however, when the daughter reveals that she knows the entire plan. Her demand that Conrad marry her leaves him no alternative. He does so and lives happily with his three lovers in their beautiful castle on the hill.

British director John Schlesinger released *Sunday Bloody Sunday* the following year, featuring a much more realistic poly relationship. A young male artist is in separate relationships with a gay man and a straight woman. Winner of several awards including Best Film in the 1971 British Academy Awards and Best English Language Foreign Film in the 1972 Golden Globe Awards, *Sunday Bloody Sunday* was a breakthrough film of its era.

Heterosexual career woman Alex Greville (Glenda Jackson) and homosexual Jewish doctor Daniel Hirsh are both in love with a young kinetic sculptor named Bob Elkin (Murray Head). While many have read this bisexual character as self-centered, and therefore a negative portrayal of bisexuals in general, he must be viewed in the context of the film as a whole. Bob has made his choice to be sexual with more than one person. In this case, with two people of different sexes. In addition, he has made his art the top priority and that will sometimes interfere with both relationships.

This kind of character had never before been depicted on the screen and certainly not in such a matter-of-fact manner. In a sense, it was just the old "love triangle" story with the twist that one of the relationships was between two people of the same sex. What is unique is that this relationship is not portrayed as anything out of the ordinary. Both of Bob's lovers express frustration and a little jealousy at his choices, but deal with it differently.

Alex is the more troubled of Bob's lovers by his other relationship. She wants Bob all to herself and eventually breaks up with him over the non-monogamy issue (not the fact that he is with a man). In one conversation, her mother tells her, "Darling, you keep throwing your hand in because you haven't got 'the whole thing.' There is no 'whole thing.'" Indeed, that is the theme of this film. The "whole thing" is just a fantasy. Of the three lovers, only Bob has embraced that concept.

Daniel, on the other hand, is resigned to having "half a loaf." In a closing speech, after Bob has left for America, Daniel tells the audience, "They say, 'he never made you happy.' But I *am* happy, apart from missing him. He might throw me a pill or two for my cough. All my life I've been looking for somebody courageous and resourceful. He's not it. But something. We *were* something. And I only came about my cough."

Set in Berlin during the Austrian capitulation of 1938, *The Berlin Affair* (Liliana Cavani, 1985) features a young married couple deep in the heart of Nazi Germany. The word 'affair' in the title is a double entendre referring to the political intrigue in which Louise and Heinz find themselves and to their relationship with Mitsuko, the daughter of the Japanese Ambassador.

Louise and Mitsuko meet at an art class both are attending to relieve their boredom. Before long they are passionately in love. They quarrel, however, when Louise discovers that Mitsuko is also having an affair with the art instructor. Eventually they get back together and Mitsuko becomes lovers with Heinz as well.

The relationship takes a bad turn, however. Mitsuko is drugging the couple, the art teacher is attempting to blackmail them, and they help set up a General who is a social acquaintance, to be purged under the Nazi "Moralization Campaign" for having an affair with a male piano student. Predictably, the scheisse eventually hits the fan–their affair is front page news in the Berlin tabloids and the police descend. In addition to the sad ending for the triad, no one ever seems to take off their clothes during the many sex scenes.

French Canadian Léa Pool directed *A Corps Perdu*, released in English as *Straight to the Heart*. From the start we know that this will not be a typical, boring love story. The film opens with photojournalist Pierre Kurwenal (Matthew Gabich) seated on a crowded bus in Nicaragua. The man next to him, also a foreigner, shows a picture of his family. He asks if Pierre is married. Pierre answers, "I am in love with David . . . and Sarah . . . and Tristan–a man, a woman and a cat."

Pierre's photographs of Contra-instigated violence win him praise at home. Eventually they lead to a Pulitzer Prize and a retrospective of his work. However, he cannot get the images of that violence out of his head. He is haunted particularly by the memory of a woman screaming "assasino" at him, assuming that he was an American, whose Contras killed the child she cradled in her arms.

On returning to Montreal, Pierre discovers that his lovers of ten years have left him to live with each other and that Sarah and David are having a baby. Only Tristan has remained faithful. For the remainder of the film, David attempts to discover what went wrong with his long-term poly relationship. This film was winner of the 1988 Genie Award in Canada.

The 1990s brought a flurry of films with poly bi characters. The decade began with Philip Kaufman's *Henry and June*, a sensuously filmed movie whose characters have all the depth of a Roadrunner cartoon. Set in Paris in 1931, this film is about the love stories of Anaïs Nin (Maria de Medeiros) and Henry Miller (Fred Ward), two excellent and soon-to-be-published writers, and of Anaïs and June.

June (Uma Thurman) is married to Henry but is living in New York while he writes in Paris. Multiple relationships are the norm in Henry and June's marriage. She has both a male and a female lover in New York, he frequents the local houses of prostitution. However, each is jealous of the other's relationship with Nin and this keeps any of the relationships from being happy ones.

Independent director Rose Troche's first film, *Go Fish* (1993) was a refreshing inside look at life in the lesbian community. Its sharp wit and interesting characters made it look almost like a film version of the *Dykes to Watch Out For* comic strip.

Many of the women in the film complain that they aren't getting enough sex. One notable exception is the polyamorous bisexual, Daria (Anastasia Sharp). Each time she gets together with friends Kia and Max, she has a new girlfriend. It is when she sleeps with a man, however, that things get dicey. Many of her lesbian friends insist that she is no longer part of their community and vow never to sleep with her. What is particularly interesting is this scene's juxtaposition with one in which Kia's lover is thrown out of her birth family for sleeping with a woman.

In 1994, Hollywood's version of a poly relationship came with the film *Threesome*, directed by Andrew Fleming. The movie's tagline was, "One girl, two guys, three possibilities." Which just goes to show how limited Hollywood's imagination is.

The premise of the film is that Eddy and Stuart are college students sharing two-thirds of a triple dorm room. Alex, the female with a male-sounding name, is added to their room by mistake. Alex is attracted to Eddy, Stuart is attracted to Alex, and Eddy is attracted to Stuart. It reminds one of the "What a beauty!" postcard that made the rounds in the bi community around the same year. They eventually become close friends and there is lots of sexual tension, but not as much happens as you would hope.

The same year, bisexual actress Sandra Bernhard played the title role in a very obscure Australian film called *Dallas Doll*. In a throwback to *Teorema*, Dallas is an American golf pro with semi-mystical powers who moves in with an Australian family after being bitten by their dog. Excepting the young daughter, every member of the family falls under Dallas's erotic spell. Before long she convinces them to turn the family farm into a golf resort. The truly bizarre ending involves space aliens and cattle.

Featuring soap opera dialog, worse acting and breasts by Dow-Corning, it is not difficult to see why *Friend of the Family* bypassed the theaters and went straight to the discount table at the video store. This is another film about a houseguest who seduces the entire family. The main difference in this film is that the family's lives actually improve because of the visitor.

Linda is having a difficult time with the dysfunctional family she has married into. Her new husband works all the time, his daughter sleeps with every guy in town and goes out of her way to make Linda's life hell, and his son lies about attending law school. Into this chaotic scene arrives Elke, who claims she was robbed in Las Vegas and needs a place to stay. Linda lets her live in the guest house. Over time, Elke seduces each family member. In the process she molds them into a caring, loving family. The biggest transformation occurs with the daughter, who not only becomes nice to people and stops sleeping around, but remarkably loses her valley-girl accent.

The French film *Gazon maudit*, released in English-speaking countries as *French Twist*, is probably the best bi poly comedy available. Director Josiane Balasko plays Marijo, a lesbian plumber whose van breaks down in front of Loli and Laurent's house. Loli (Victoria Abril) is a young housewife who marriage is suffering because Laurent, an arrogant real estate salesman, virtually ignores her while sleeping with several women behind her back. It is only when Laurent learns of Loli's attraction to Marijo that he begins paying attention to her and pulls out all the stops to win her back.

By this time, Loli has invited Majijo to live with them and has made up a schedule of who she will sleep with on which nights. The film takes additional twists when Marijo's old girlfriend arrives on the scene, and when Marijo asks Laurent to father her child.

From the evidence, I believe it is safe to say that filmmakers in general simply do not understand polyamorous relationships. The only realistic long-term poly family we see, in *Straight to the Heart*, is just at its end. Daria in *Go Fish*, Bob in *Sunday Bloody Sunday*, and June and Anaïs in *Henry and June* are fairly genuine polyamorous bisexual characters, but have not established poly family relationships. In almost all cases, the message that viewers receive is that poly relationships are unstable at best, and painful besides. Polyamory has a long road ahead to final acceptance by the mainstream. Acceptance and equality for same-sex relationships is one of the major steps on that road. Existence in Microsoft's spell-checker is another.

Bi Books

"Take Four Pioneering Poly Women": A Review of Three Classical Texts on Polyamory

Maria Pallotta-Chiarolli

http://www.haworthpress.com/web/JB
Digital Object Identifier: 10.1300/J159v04n03_18

[Haworth co-indexing entry note]: "'Take Four Pioneering Poly Women': A Review of Three Classical Texts on Polyamory." Pallotta-Chiarolli, Maria. Co-published simultaneously in *Journal of Bisexuality* (Harrington Park Press, an imprint of The Haworth Press, Inc.) Vol. 4, No. 3/4, 2004, pp. 227-234; and: *Plural Loves: Designs for Bi and Poly Living* (ed: Serena Anderlini-D'Onofrio) Harrington Park Press, an imprint of The Haworth Press, Inc., 2004, pp. 227-234. Single or multiple copies of this article are available for a fee from The Haworth Document Delivery Service [1-800-HAWORTH, 9:00 a.m. - 5:00 p.m. (EST). E-mail address: docdelivery@haworthpress.com].

SUMMARY. This article reviews three classics of polyamory, Anapol's *Love Without Limits: The Quest for Sustainable Intimate Relationships*; Easton and Liszt's *The Ethical Slut*; and Nearing's *Loving More: The Poly- fidelity Primer*. The reviewer defines the authors as pioneering poly women who have mapped the territory for authentic alternatives to compul- sory monogamy in realistic yet visionary ways. *[Article copies available for a fee from The Haworth Document Delivery Service: 1-800-HAWORTH. E-mail ad- dress: <docdelivery@haworthpress.com> Website: <http://www.HaworthPress.com> © 2004 by The Haworth Press, Inc. All rights reserved.]*

KEYWORDS. Polyamory, travel book, ethical slut, polyfidelity, uto- pia, realism, advice, vision, pioneering women, classic

Anapol, Deborah (1992; revised edition, 1997). *Love Without Limits: The Quest for Sustainable Intimate Relationships*. San Rafael, California: Intinet Resource Center.

Easton, Dossie & Lizst, Catherine A. (1997) *The Ethical Slut: A Guide to Infi- nite Sexual Possibilities*. San Francisco: Greenery Press.

Nearing, Ryam (1992). *Loving More: The Polyfidelity Primer*. Hawaii: PEP Publishing.

Take four pioneering polyamorous sexually diverse women crossing terrain they have explored in their own lives and made home.

> Those of us who have chosen this lifestyle like to reach for more. More love, more growth, and more conscious commitment. (Nearing, 1992: 5)

Four women who have written travel guides they wish to share with those who may be thinking of taking similar journeys but don't know where to start nor if starting is possible at all, and doubt that a landscape of multi-partnering may actually exist beneath, beyond, and within the flat desert surface of imposed heteronormative monogamy.

Four women who turned off the monogamist heteronormative highway heading nowhere, and went looking for signposts to guide them through per- sonal emotional jungles, and through the deserts of wider socio-cultural and institutional discrimination and ostracism. They found a few signposts in dusty books, a few buried gems from other cultures and other times. The rest they made up themselves as they went. As Anapol suggests,

> Our culture desperately needs a new set of sexual ethics. We need a middle ground between the free love/do your own thing doctrine of the Sexual Revolution and outmoded lifelong monogamy. We need realistic guidelines that incorporate the highest wisdom from *all* the diverse cultures which comprise today's global village. (Anapol, 1997: viii)

These pioneering women's travel books are for those who wish to explore polyamory. Each book allows for that tourist who wants an experience of polyamory, either as an armchair traveller or as a temporary excursionist, but the one-off packaged tour is not all there is to them. After such journeys, it may be a relief for some to go 'home' to lifelong or serial monogamy, albeit wiser for the journey, ready to scrutinise the taken-for-grantedness of their monogamous relationships, and now see monogamy as a conscious choice rather than as natural and automatic.

> We believe that monogamy will continue to thrive as it always has, a perfectly valid choice for those who truly choose it. We don't think it's much of a choice when you are forbidden to choose anything else. . . . We believe that new forms of families are evolving now, and will continue to evolve, not to supplant the nuclear family but to supplement it with an abundance of additional ideas about how you might choose to structure your family. (Easton & Liszt, 1997: 267)

These are books for lifelong journeys, for those who are setting out to visit many emotional and sexual landscapes and make each a permanent or temporary home, despite a monogamist culture and institutions that appears to prepare us for 'cheating' and 'affairs' beneath the veneer of monogamy:

> Unfortunately, the vast majority of multipartner relationships are neither ethical nor responsible! Lies, deceit, guilt, unilateral decisions and broken commitments are so commonplace in classic American-style non-monogamy [and monogamy!] . . . cheating, unfaithfulness, or adultery . . . We never realize that we can design a lovestyle which is both non-monogamous and responsible. (Anapol, 1997: 3-4)

Immersing oneself into each of these books is to have the strange become familiar, and the taken for granted suddenly up for scrutiny. It is to have words like polyamory and polyfidelity introduced, explored, and become the everyday, while words like monogamy are suddenly exposed for all the silences, erasures, denials that it has disguised. It is to have new labels that would otherwise be seen as oxymoronic such as "ethical slut" and "responsible non-monogamy" seem quite obvious and coherent.

The authors move effortlessly between discussions on *Paradigms*, *Principles and Practicalities*, including

- theoretical overviews of relationship and sexuality *paradigms* and how they (need to) shift; and social, historical and cross-cultural constructions of "normal" and "natural" relationships;
- "let's get real" discussions of the principles of *polyamory*: what it is and what it isn't a cover or cool word for; that it's about sexual adventurousness not sexual recklessness, sexual and emotional negotiations not sexual and emotional exploitations; that it requires dedication and commitment and isn't about "get more love and sex for less effort in relating and communicating";
- clear and concise presentations on the *practicalities* of polyamory: checklists, pointers, advice, "dos and don'ts" on the how, when, where, who and what questions. The basic everyday stuff of raising children and raising money, creating bedroom, kitchen and laundry rosters, courting new lovers and parting from old lovers, as well as working through the "who does what to whom and when and where and how do we work through our feelings on all this?"

For books that would seem to be radical, scandalous, immoral to those who believe they have the power to define morality, there's a lot of fundamental time-honoured values and strategies that get reworked, broadened and applied to diverse sexualities and relationship structures. Words like "ethics," "boundaries," "honesty," "respect," "communication," "agreements" do not sound farcical, trite or condescending in these books. They are suddenly fresh and meaningful again, and applied in realistic inclusive ways. Encountering these books is refreshing, after too many years of "self-help" books on keeping dysfunctional monogamous unions in a death-in-life state, wherein labels like "ethics," "honesty," "agreements" have been used to destroy and coerce two people from daring to be three-dimensional and try something outside the "two as one for life" monogamist model.

But don't get me wrong. These books don't uphold polyamory as the solution to all the woes of love and intimacy. What's also refreshing and realistic about these books is that they deal with the nitty-gritty of daily not dreamy polyamory. Check out Nearing's section on "Whose Dishes Are These?" (1992: 38) and Anapol's chapter "Is Polyamory Right for Me?" (1997: pp23-30). The four writers/travel guides don't say, 'This is for you, this is for everybody." They say, "This could be for you, how about giving it a go? But if you do, here's some things to think about, and by the way, you won't be able to laze your way through this one or use it to have a sex partner every night free of any emotional responsibility." Easton and Liszt's "The Ten Great Lies of Sluthood" include "I never get jealous," "I always tell the complete truth about my outside partners," and "We never compete for the same person." They soon sober up any reader who's exhilarated at the thought of a free-for-all rather than an opportunity to live and love in a way that might require a hefty amount of responsibility but be more realistic and much healthier (1997: 167).

Another groundbreaking facet of these books is that they are highly politi-cised and discuss the impact of the external world on a relationship. In this, they are different from some typical self-help and how-to books that focus on the self rather than on the impact of systemic, socio-cultural and political structures on individuals and relationships. As Easton and Liszt affirm, "From the slut's point of view, the world is sometimes a dangerous place" (1997:205). The social ostracism an ethical slut faces is openly discussed, including discrimination and legislative barriers in the workplace, in children's schools, and in accessing housing and health services. Echoing these concerns, Nearing comments, "Big Brother [is] in Your Bed" (1992: 40). Yet, while each book addresses controversial issues, each also provides strategies of empower-ment and agency. For instance, Anapol likens current poly issues to GLBT peo-ple 'coming out' issues, providing sound advice and questions to work through, reflecting on the merits of staying in the closet against those of 'coming out,' and asking how, when, and who to 'come out' to (1997: pp79-84).

Thus, the writers deal with the external dilemmas that will confront pio-neering polyamorists. They don't ignore what can go wrong, nor the fact that polyamorists are faced with the trappings of a dominant culture which is offi-cially monogamist, and is propped up by health, legal, political, educational and religious institutions (or else it would be even more exposed for the falsity that it is!). Anapol's, Nearing's, and Easton and Liszt's books deal with poten-tial individual and interpersonal issues, including jealousy, gendered power relations, exploitation and coercion, as well as the basic question "Are there other polys out there and how do I find them?" While being realistic, the works do not implode into what Anapol describes as "an atmosphere of pessimism, stuckness and scarcity" (1997: 86). Their vision inspires hope, agency, com-munity, possibilities, and future.

Finally, these pioneering authors are very clear that they did not set out to write the ultimate travel guide, or become colonial territorialists owning the terrain they're mapping out. They're aware of inheriting and honouring cross-cultural and cross-temporal examples. As Easton and Liszt comment,

> A slut living in mainstream, monogamy-centrist culture . . . can learn a great deal from studying other cultures, other places, and other times: you're *not* the only one who has ever tried this, it *can* work. (Easton & Liszt: 1997: 45)

The authors are also aware that their experiences are not universal–that they do not speak for all. They are aware of varying laws, of cross-cultural, eco-nomic, religious and political perspectives outside their own realms of knowl-edge and experience, some of which have been addressed by Lano and Parry (1995). They believe in working with allies and collaborating with many groups, and indeed have been the mentors and inspiration for other women to embark upon their own textual journeys, including Munson and Stelboum

(1999), Pallotta-Chiarolli (2002), and West (1996). Each book also provides a substantial resource list of organisations, books, films, and other groups that the reader can access and continue the journey according to their own needs and contexts.

In conclusion, I believe these so-called 'controversial' texts are what future generations will come to identify as classics. Read them now and pass them on to show your descendants you were there from the beginning, inspired by four women who chose the supposed chaotic and unchartered landscape of poly-amory; retrieved what had been lost from the past; lived the immediacy; and provided landmarks that will take us into a future of sustainability. Indeed, each book's conclusion situates polyamory within broader and urgent goals for the evolution of humanity. In her last chapter entitled "On a Mission," Nearing talks about "living evolution" and "saving the humans":

> [by] creating a more loving world complete with individual freedom, personal responsibility, and social tolerance for human diversity . . . [w]e can develop new and better ways to live together. Biological and chosen families, intentional clusters and ecologically balanced approaches. Polyfidelity is one part of the answer . . . In the interest of human poten-tial and on-going evolution, let the strength of social diversity of which we are a part, prevail. (1992: 86-87)

Anapol links interpersonal constructions of control and ownership, and insular nuclear families only looking out for themselves, to the larger world where is-sues of ownership and property keep throwing us into further and further dev-astating international and internal conflicts. As she comments,

> polyamory can help create a world of peace and abundance where all of humanity recognizes itself as one family. Idealistic? Yes. Realistic? Also yes! Our exclusively monogamous culture enshrines jealousy and possessiveness . . . Polyamory breaks down cultural patterns of control, as well as ownership and property rights between persons, and by replac-ing them with a family milieu of unconditional love, trust and respect, provides an avenue to the creation of a more just and peaceful world. (1997: 152)

Easton and Liszt complete this visionary framework by calling for a "slut uto-pia." As they affirm,

> We want to create a world where everyone has plenty of what they need: of community, of connection, of touch and sex and love. We want our children to be raised in an expanded family . . . We want a world where the sick and aging are cared for by people who love them, where re-sources are shared by people who care for each other . . . We dream of a

world where nobody gets to vote on your life choices, or who you choose to love, or how you choose to express that love, except yourself and your lovers. (1997: 268-269)

So, in the words of Nearing, "It's your move" (1992: 87).

AUTHOR NOTE

I would like to thank Ryam Nearing and Deborah Anapol and to say what a privilege and inspiration it was to meet you both in 2001. You're right up there in my list of women who have signposted my life.

REFERENCES

Lano, Kevin and Parry, Clare (EDS) (1995) *Breaking The Barriers of Desire: New Approaches To Multiple Relationships*, London: Five Leaves Publication.

Munson, Marcia and Stelboum, Judith P. (EDS) (1999) *The Lesbian Polyamory Reader: Open Relationships, Non-Monogamy, and Casual Sex*, New York: Harrington Park Press.

Pallotta-Chiarolli, Maria (2002) "Polyparents Having Children, Raising Children, Schooling Children," *Loving More* 31: 8-12.

West, Celeste (1996). *Lesbian Polyfidelity*, San Francisco: Booklegger Publishing.

Index

BOOK ORDER FORM!

Order a copy of this book with this form or online at:
http://www.haworthpress.com/store/product.asp?sku=5353

Plural Loves
Designs for Bi and Poly Living

_____ in softbound at $29.95 (ISBN: 1-56023-293-5)
_____ in hardbound at $49.95 (ISBN: 1-56023-292-7)

COST OF BOOKS _____	❑BILL ME LATER:
	Bill-me option is good on US/Canada/
POSTAGE & HANDLING _____	Mexico orders only; not good to jobbers,
US: $4.00 for first book & $1.50	wholesalers, or subscription agencies.
for each additional book	
Outside US: $5.00 for first book	❑ **Signature** _____
& $2.00 for each additional book.	
	❑ **Payment Enclosed: $** _____
SUBTOTAL _____	
	❑ **PLEASE CHARGE TO MY CREDIT CARD:**
In Canada: add 7% GST. _____	
	❑ Visa ❑ MasterCard ❑ AmEx ❑ Discover
STATE TAX _____	❑ Diner's Club ❑ Eurocard ❑ JCB
CA, IL, IN, MN, NJ, NY, OH & SD residents	
please add appropriate local sales tax.	**Account #** _____
FINAL TOTAL _____	**Exp Date** _____
If paying in Canadian funds, convert	
using the current exchange rate.	**Signature** _____
UNESCO coupons welcome.	_(Prices in US dollars and subject to change without notice.)_

PLEASE PRINT ALL INFORMATION OR ATTACH YOUR BUSINESS CARD

Name

Address

City   State/Province   Zip/Postal Code

Country

Tel   Fax

E-Mail

May we use your e-mail address for confirmations and other types of information? ❑Yes ❑No We appreciate receiving your e-mail address. Haworth would like to e-mail special discount offers to you, as a preferred customer.
We will never share, rent, or exchange your e-mail address. We regard such actions as an invasion of your privacy.

Order From Your **Local Bookstore** or Directly From
The Haworth Press, Inc. 10 Alice Street, Binghamton, New York 13904-1580 • USA
Call Our toll-free number (1-800-429-6784) / Outside US/Canada: (607) 722-5857
Fax: 1-800-895-0582 / Outside US/Canada: (607) 771-0012
E-mail your order to us: orders@haworthpress.com

For orders outside US and Canada, you may wish to order through your local
sales representative, distributor, or bookseller.
For information, see http://haworthpress.com/distributors

(Discounts are available for individual orders in US and Canada only, not booksellers/distributors.)

Please photocopy this form for your personal use.
www.HaworthPress.com

BOF04